Praise for
Identification Revolution:
Can Digital ID Be Harnessed for Development?

"Alan Gelb and Anna Diofasi Metz have done a remarkable job of studying recent advances in the sophistication of ID systems across the globe. They offer a unique lens on what is possible, what has been done, and more importantly, why it was done. This kind of a critical look at the design choices of an ID system is illuminating especially since they capture the context in which those decisions were taken. Legal identity to all is a development target in the SDGs, and many other SDG goals will depend on it. Hence, the developing world will need experts who understand the power and innovation capability of identity systems. With this book, Alan and Anna have shown their deep understanding of ID systems at a global level."

> Nandan Nilekani
> *Co-founder and Non-Executive* ... *n,*
> *Unique Identification Authority*
> *Co-founder and Chairman, EkSt*

"It is no exaggeration that there is an Identification Revolution and it is important and moving rapidly. [This book's] masterful presentation brings the reader up to date, analyzing the potential benefits and pitfalls of biometric ID. This is a must-read for all those interested in economic development and the potential that the ID Revolution offers."

> Anne O. Krueger
> *Senior Research Professor, Johns Hopkins School of Advanced International Studies; Senior Fellow, Stanford Center for International Development*

"Digital ID is fast becoming an essential tool for twenty-first century development. This book spells out in fascinating detail the opportunities and challenges, the perils and pitfalls of this digital ID revolution."

> Ngozi Okonjo-Iweala
> *Board Chair, GAVI; former Finance Minister, Nigeria; former Managing Director, World Bank*

"This is a must-have manual for anyone interested in the important topic of identification systems as drivers of social and economic development. The book is written with exceptional depth and clarity compatible with the exceptional status of its authors as individuals who have followed and have contributed first hand to the advancement of our knowledge about the impact of identity systems on society. The book not only presents the positive consequences of identity schemes, but does a great job explaining some of their risks. The authors outline ways for how to address these risks and for how to channel identity systems within responsible frameworks that respect human rights, enhance gender equality, fight against discrimination, and protect privacy in various contexts.

I found the book sober, thoughtful, and pragmatic in its recommendations and thus [it] should be of great utility to practitioners from development agencies as well as government identity authorities and policymakers.

It is a pleasure to finally see a comprehensive and timely account that has staying power—one that I expect will remain a top reference in this field for many years to come."

Joseph Atick
Executive Chairman, ID4Africa; Executive
Chairman, Identity Counsel International

"Anyone interested in the current transformation of identification and registration systems underway internationally—students, researchers, policymakers or implementers—should begin with this book."

Keith Breckenridge
Professor and Deputy Director, Wits Institute
for Social and Economic Research

"Methods for identification have been fundamental for human groups and for the scale of their political and economic activities throughout history. It is no accident that the first industrial nation, England, innovated the first nationwide identity registration system nearly 500 years ago. But ID systems can also be abused, resulting in terrible consequences. Digital ID in the age of the internet offers a transformative opportunity for citizens of the poorest states at last to acquire their rights to recognition, but it is equally vital that they be protected against potential abuses or exploitation of their economic vulnerabilities. Alan Gelb and Anna Diofasi Metz are to be thanked for their timely intervention in providing an authoritative review of this fast-changing field and its current best practices in, for instance, Estonia and Peru. This excellent book affords invaluable practical guidance for states and governments hoping to reap development gains while avoiding the serious pitfalls in engaging with this most important governance revolution of the third millennium CE."

Simon Szreter
Professor of History and Public Policy, University of Cambridge

IDENTIFICATION REVOLUTION

IDENTIFICATION REVOLUTION

Can Digital ID Be Harnessed for Development?

ALAN GELB *and*
ANNA DIOFASI METZ

CENTER FOR GLOBAL DEVELOPMENT
Washington, D.C.

Library of Congress Cataloging-in-Publication data are available.
Names: Gelb, Alan H., author. | Diofasi Metz, Anna, author.
Title: Identification revolution : can digital ID be harnessed for development? / Alan Gelb, Anna Diofasi Metz.
Description: Washington DC : Center for Global Development, [2018] | Includes bibliographical references and index.
Identifiers: LCCN 2017035951 (print) | LCCN 2017054551 (ebook) | ISBN 9781944691042 | ISBN 9781944691035 (pbk. : alk. paper)
Subjects: LCSH: Biometric identification—Economic aspects. | Sustainable development.
Classification: LCC HD9999.P3952 (ebook) | LCC HD9999.P3952 G45 2018 (print) | DDC 338.9—dc23
LC record available at https://lccn.loc.gov/2017035951

9 8 7 6 5 4 3 2 1

Contents

THREE

Identification as an Enabler of Sustainable Development   59

FOUR

Identification Systems: Innovations in Technology and ID Provision   91

FIVE

Confronting the Risks   125

Preface

Digital identification programs are being rolled out at a dizzying pace across the developing world. Within the last fifteen years, over sixty low- and middle-income countries have launched foundational national identification (ID) programs. In addition, many public and private entities have rolled out their own functional ID programs to serve a number of specific purposes, whether for registering voters, delivering social transfers, or enabling financial institutions to satisfy enhanced regulatory requirements. Advances in digital technology, notably multimodal digital biometrics and mobile technology, have greatly enhanced the capabilities of these systems and expanded their reach across a more mobile, digitally connected world.

Identification is, of course, only one manifestation of the explosive spread of digital technology, with all of its implications. It is, however, an important one: the identification revolution foreshadows a major change in the relationship between citizens and states. With the rollout of modern digital ID systems, citizens are becoming better equipped to exercise their rights and to prove with unprecedented certainty who they are, in both the physical and the virtual realms. ID systems offer the opportunity to regularize the situation of over a billion people—often the poorest and most vulnerable members of their community—who today lack any effective proof of their identity. As for states, they can utilize their digital ID programs to deliver services and transfers with greater effectiveness, precision, and transparency than ever before.

In this book, Alan Gelb and Anna Diofasi Metz address the question of how to maximize the development impact of this identification revolution. Ensuring "legal identity for all, including birth registration" by 2030 has been recognized as Target 16.9 of the Sustainable Development Goals, but there is no consensus on exactly how to define legal identity in the development context and how to reach the target. As the book demonstrates, effective and inclusive identification systems can facilitate the achievement of this and many other SDG targets; they can widen access to real and financial assets, support gender equality, and reduce corruption. But much depends on how the new systems are designed, rolled out, and used. Any system set up to *include* can also *exclude*—some are not able to use the new systems and technologies, while others face an enhanced risk of statelessness. Personal data can be stolen and be (mis)used in ways that harm people rather than benefit them; many developing countries lack data privacy laws or the capacity to enforce them. Investments in identification systems and technology can generate high economic and social returns, but many countries have been wasting large sums on poorly conceived and implemented systems.

In setting out a baseline study of this new area, Gelb and Diofasi Metz recognize that there is no single ideal model for a perfect identification system. Developing countries are at different stages of identity management, implying different sets of priorities and readiness to make use of the latest identification technologies. There are also major differences in the acceptability of certain system features, such as the use of a common identifier across various programs, even among the OECD countries. There are, however, a number of common principles that any good ID system should follow—it should be inclusive, robust, and effective, and be governed in a way that builds and sustains trust. In the last chapter, the authors lay out some practical recommendations on how to ensure that new ID programs live up to these principles, drawing on the many cases presented in the book.

The book turns a spotlight on some leading examples, including those in Peru and Estonia, and the remarkable Aadhaar program in India. These centrally managed systems all have important lessons for other countries; the newest of these, in India, has set many innovation benchmarks and is underpinning the largest reforms in social transfers, subsidies, and other schemes in the world, as well as serving as a platform for services. Recognizing the relentless rise of digital societies and economies, Gelb and Diofasi Metz also cover recent developments in "federated" ID and identification through "e-village" social networks. These approaches are not substitutes for centrally managed, foundational identity, but their capabilities are growing as the cloud of digital data around each of us increases.

How does the identification revolution relate to development policy and to the programs of development institutions? Donors and partners have been quite extensively involved in supporting a large number of diverse identification initiatives across many countries. These ID programs have, however, been viewed as mechanisms to support relatively narrow objectives, for example, to identify beneficiaries for a health or social transfer program, rather than in the context of a coherent identification strategy for the country or region. This is beginning to change, with more organizations adopting a strategic view. A first step has been taken with the sign-on to the ten Principles on Identification for Sustainable Development by almost all of the significant development players in the area. But—as explained in the book—much more needs to be done before the identification revolution delivers on its promise.

Though far more monitoring and far more rigorous research are needed to fully understand the implications of the identification revolution and its impact, this is the right time to take stock of this rapidly evolving area since ongoing policy decisions in many countries promise to map out ID trajectories for years into the future. It is our hope that this book, and CGD's ongoing technology and development research program, will contribute to furthering that understanding and lead to better policies and outcomes for people in developing countries.

Masood Ahmed
PRESIDENT
CENTER FOR GLOBAL DEVELOPMENT

Acknowledgments

This book draws on studies conducted over a number of years and on academic and operational interactions, including discussions with participants at many conferences and workshops. We are grateful to Nancy Birdsall for urging us to write it and to the many experts from whom we have learned so much over the years. CGD colleagues, including Masood Ahmed, Charles Kenny, Todd Moss, Anit Mukherjee, and Emily Schabacker, have provided helpful comments; Julia Clark and Caroline Decker, formerly at the Center, contributed to the work program at earlier stages. We owe large debts to colleagues outside of CGD, including Robert Palacios, Joseph Atick, Keith Breckenridge, Simon Szreter, Jacqueline Bhabha, Himanshu Nagpal, Shahid Yusuf, and Vasumathi Anadan, who provided very thoughtful comments on the manuscript; several of these have also been instrumental in the development of the ideas in this book. We also want to recognize, with thanks, the time that many other industry experts, government officials, and academics have been willing to share with us.

Especially in a relatively new area, meetings and conferences are essential for exchanging information. Among the many, we must single out the annual ID4Africa meetings in Dar es Salaam, Kigali, and Windhoek. These have provided a unique forum to improve our understanding of the evolving ID situation in Africa, as well as in other regions. The meetings of the Digital Identity Forum in The Hague and Johannesburg have also been formative, and we have greatly appreciated the many insights from the Bhalisa Forum and from

Jaap van der Straaten of CRC4D. We would also like to acknowledge productive interactions with colleagues at the ID4D initiative at the World Bank, including joint work and collaboration on the Principles on Identification which, to date, have been endorsed by twenty-one organizations.

The initial research that led up to this product was supported by the UK Department for International Development as part of its programmatic support to the Center. We are also grateful to the Omidyar Network and to the Bill & Melinda Gates Foundation for their generous support at various stages of preparation.

None of those mentioned above bears any responsibility for errors and shortcomings; these would doubtless have been far more serious without their support and advice. Needless to say, the views expressed are those of the authors and should not necessarily be attributed to any of the individuals or organizations noted above.

CGD is grateful for contributions from the Bill & Melinda Gates Foundation, the Omidyar Network, and the UK Department for International Development in support of this work.

IDENTIFICATION REVOLUTION

ONE

Introduction

In India, proving your identity is only a fingerprint scan away. In less than seven years, more than 1.1 billion residents have enrolled in what must be the most innovative identification system in the developing world. Each resident can now authenticate themselves at banks, government offices, shops, and a host of other point-of-service facilities across the country by providing only their unique Aadhaar ID number and either a fingerprint or iris scan. Using the number and a scan, they can satisfy Know-Your-Customer (KYC) requirements to open bank accounts, with no need to laboriously assemble and copy documents. Beneficiaries of the country's public distribution system are increasingly authenticated through fingerprint scans when they receive their subsidized food allocations through Fair Price Shops. In Andhra Pradesh's Krishna District, where reforms are most advanced, the supply chain for the public distribution system has been totally revamped. Deliveries are checked on electronic scales and must be signed off jointly by the transport operator delivering the goods and the Fair Price Shop proprietor, each certifying by registering their ID number and fingerprint.

The same identification system can be used in an unlimited range of transactions and interactions: to receive pensions and administer scholarship programs, to monitor the attendance records of public officials, or to administer energy or fertilizer subsidy programs. India's Aadhaar-enabled reforms of liquefied petroleum gas marketing have shifted household price subsidies to direct transfers into bank accounts; they are already among the world's largest

1

reforms in the energy sector. Measures are now under way to extend the use of the system to an ever-widening range of applications, such as registering property, filing taxes, and identifying children for school meal programs. Digital payment is now possible from any Aadhaar-linked bank account to any other account simply with the payee's Aadhaar number.

More advanced digital services are also in progress. Indian residents will soon be able to sign documents electronically and to store key credentials, such as digitally certified copies of birth or school examination certificates, in a secure digital locker opened by a biometric scan. Documents can be shared as desired with potential employers or other entities linked to the country's digital ecosystem. The process even distinguishes between copies of certificates uploaded by the applicant and those directly issued and certified by the relevant authority.

Such a sophisticated system has become possible only recently. Before it demonstrated its capabilities, there was considerable doubt over whether biometric technology would be precise enough to successfully distinguish among individuals in so large a population. Comparing every one of India's people against each of the others to ensure that identities are unique involves a huge number of pairwise comparisons and requires extremely high accuracy. This accuracy appears to have been achieved—proof-of-concept tests conducted in 2012 suggest an error rate in deduplication of less than 7 in one trillion (Gelb and Clark 2013b).

India's system offers capabilities far ahead of those available to residents of other countries, even those in the Organization for Economic Cooperation and Development (OECD). It also appears to be the lowest-cost digital identification system on a per-head basis, by a considerable margin. But it is only one of many transformative identification programs being implemented today, in some cases with significant technology and institutional innovations. National ID programs intended to provide "foundational" identification for multiple purposes are being rolled out across the developing world at an unprecedented pace. "Functional" identification programs, designed to support a particular purpose or service such as access to healthcare, a pensions program, or voting, have also mushroomed in the past decade and a half. Virtually all of these programs incorporate digital technology, including biometrics.

The right to a recognized identity has long been an element in the human rights agenda. The 1948 International Declaration of Human Rights, for instance, contains the right to recognition before the law and the right to a nationality. Yet it was only in 2015, with the adoption of the Sustainable Development Goals (SDGs), that the global community recognized identification as a development priority. SDG target 16.9 sets out to "provide legal identity to all, including through birth registration, by 2030" (UN 2015). It is not entirely clear how to interpret this target, or whether a simple enumeration of those with and without legal identity is a sufficient metric. The only quantitative indicator attached to SDG target 16.9 refers to birth registration: the percentage of children under age 5 whose births have been registered with a civil authority, disaggregated by age. However, ensuring that all members of society—no matter how poor or isolated they may be—have their existence officially recognized is only a start.

Robust identification systems designed and implemented with the SDG aspirations in mind can be a catalyst for achieving many other development goals and targets, from gender equality to environmentally sustainable energy systems. For these ambitions to become a reality, formal identification systems must open doors rather than lock in hardship, and be used to expand freedoms and capabilities rather than enable exclusion or coercion.

Although the "legal identity" target is new, donors and partners have supported many identification programs in developing countries over the past two decades. However, with only a few notable exceptions, engagement has been fragmented and driven by individual applications. Identification has been considered as a mechanism for a particular purpose, such as improving the accuracy of a voter roll for a particular election or implementing a social transfer or health insurance program more effectively. This has encouraged the emergence of multiple ID programs, often disconnected and with little or no synergies between them—an inefficient and wasteful approach, considering that programs to register people and provide identification services are inherently multiple-use investments. The stakes are raised as they include higher levels of technology that boost their capabilities but also increase their costs and threaten the sustainability of fragmented systems.

What are the implications of the rapidly changing identification capabilities and new aspirations for development policies and programs? How should countries and their development partners respond to the identification revolution? Any effort to address these questions has to recognize that knowledge gaps are large; these are still early days in the identification revolution. Far more evidence, and far more rigorous evidence, is needed to understand the longer-term impact of the new systems and their underlying technologies. Only a limited number have been analyzed in any detail, and even in those cases the systems and their uses are still evolving. Nevertheless, this is a good time to take stock of ID programs and policies, especially as the development discourse around them needs to respond to the SDG target for establishing "legal identity" for all.

This book aims to provide an overview of the rapidly changing area of identification, including evidence on positive effects, good practices, and innovative solutions, and at the same time pinpoint the need to address crucial risks. It should be of interest to policymakers and development partners that invest in and implement ID programs, or are planning to do so; development practitioners, including the staff of international financial institutions (IFIs), multilateral organizations, and donors that want to learn more about systems and technologies that can accelerate the achievement of the SDGs; and researchers, academics, and others who would like to gain a better understanding of how new ID technologies can be and are being used.

Robust and inclusive identification systems can be an important pillar of sustainable development, particularly when leveraged by new technologies that greatly increase their accessibility, precision, and usefulness. The emerging evidence suggests that, at their best, they can be a tool to recognize and realize individual rights and expand economic opportunities, including for the poorest segments of society. They also can help build state capacity to deliver public services and social protection programs more effectively, to manage public spending, and to make public institutions more accountable. With the adoption of the legal identity SDG target 16.9, policymakers and practitioners alike are seeing the appeal of a more strategic approach to the role of identification in countries' development strategies. Such an approach requires a stronger focus on multipurpose country systems, including both civil registration and identification, rather than simply seeing each possible use-case as a separate venture.

Yet success is not guaranteed. Achieving positive development outcomes depends on many factors, including the design of the systems and how effectively they are implemented on the ground. At their worst, they can exacerbate existing problems and introduce new ones. The formalization of identification processes and requirements can exclude poor and vulnerable groups and support institutionalized discrimination; ID systems can also facilitate state and commercial surveillance. Even in less unfavorable contexts, they can waste valuable resources on costly programs of little value, especially as more expensive technologies are employed. Not surprisingly, views differ on the contribution that such systems can make to development and the possible ways to balance potential gains and risks.

This book will not delve deeply into all details of the current systems, as these details are evolving, in some cases rapidly. Nor will it produce a manual for digital identification systems or advocate for any particular system as a model for all countries; doing so would be neither realistic nor appropriate. However, even from the emerging evidence to date, it is possible to outline sensible guidelines and approaches that will enable the identification revolution to help achieve many of the wide-ranging development outcomes articulated by the SDGs. The authors' more modest objective is to contribute to this process.

Why Does Identification Matter for Development?

All communities—families, bands, tribes, nations—require mechanisms to establish and manage the identities of their members. "Identity" can have many interpretations. In this discussion, identity comprises the range of attributes that go into defining a person as a distinct and unique individual.[1] Some attributes may relate to appearance, others to behavior, still others to ethnicity, friendships and family connections, or the details of a person's birth—date, location, and parentage. Within any community, individual identity is linked to rights, entitlements, and responsibilities, including the critical question of whether or not an individual is recognized as a member of that community. The ability to distinguish between people is essential to administer community affairs, including security, as well as to establish and enforce private contracts.

Establishing an identity—one that exists and is unique—can pose a challenge even in the richest countries. Alecia Faith Pennington, the "girl who does not exist," was born in Texas to conservative religious parents. Her birth was purposefully not recorded, this being seen by her parents as a way of making her "sovereign" and independent from the wider, more secular, society. She lived on a farm, was homeschooled, and her medical treatment was provided in ways that left no medical records. Her plight became apparent in September 2014 when she left home at the age of 19, only to find that she was unable to provide sufficient documentary proof of her actual existence to obtain a birth certificate. Without some proof of existence, she could not function in society or the U.S. economy. She could not apply for a Social Security number to work

---

1   The definition of "identity" in the Merriam-Webster dictionary includes: "sameness in all that constitutes the objective reality of a thing" or "oneness" and "the distinguishing character or personality of an individual" or individuality. This definition does not mean, of course, that an individual might not be distinguished by different attributes in different contexts, but it points to the combination of features that renders the individual unique.

or a license to drive; nor could she hold a bank account. She was not covered by existing provisions for aliens or refugees; they came from "somewhere," but she came from "nowhere." Her situation was only resolved by the passage of a special bill, HB 2794, which was signed into law in Texas in June 2015.[2]

Validating oneself against a known identity can also be a challenge. One celebrated case is the still-debated story of Martin Guerre, a French peasant who disappeared from his village and his wife, Bertrande, in 1548, only to apparently reappear in 1556. The arrival looked similar to the man who had vanished and could support his claim to be Martin with detailed knowledge of his previous life. He was accepted as Martin by Bertrande and lived with her for three years, and he also claimed the inheritance of Guerre's deceased father. He was, however, not accepted as Martin by other members of Guerre's family, who continued to search for the "true Martin." The case was finally resolved after the appearance of another man with a wooden leg who claimed to be Martin Guerre, although he was apparently less able to recall previous details of his life with Bertrande than the first arrival. After a series of legal proceedings, the second arrival was accepted as the true Martin by Bertrande and other members of the family. The imposter confessed and was hanged.[3]

There are millions—by some estimates, over 1.1 billion—Alecias and Martins living today: people who do not have an officially recognized identity or are not able to provide necessary proof of who they are. They live mostly in poor countries and are usually among the poorest and most marginalized members of their societies.[4] The global identification and identity verification gap limit the freedoms and capabilities of the individuals directly affected, and can have system-wide effects that hamper the development of effective and capable institutions and constrain sustainable development and economic growth.

Globally, it has been estimated that some 2 billion children and adults have not been issued with birth certificates. In some countries, schools may turn away children who do not have an official birth record. If these children are

---

2   See, for example, Ohlheiser (2015), or the 2016 Radiolab podcast "The Girl Who Doesn't Exist," www.radiolab.org/story/invisible-girl/.

3   Martin Guerre's story is described in detail in Natalie Zemon Davis' 1983 book *The Return of Martin Guerre*. It has also been adapted to a film ("Le Retour de Martin Guerre") and was the subject of several musicals.

4   The contemporary problem of proving identity is not confined to poor countries, however. Bradley (2017) paints a jarring picture of the difficulties faced by homeless and other poor people in Washington, D.C., who have lost identity documents even though they have been registered.

permitted to enroll, they may not receive scholarships, grants, or other support to ensure their continued attendance or to help improve learning outcomes. Without adequate identification, they may not be allowed to sit certifying examinations; after all, what use is a test if there is no way to assert the identity of the person who claims to have taken it? Without recognized identification, they may not be able to enroll in higher education, or to get a job in the formal sector.

More fundamentally, an official proof of identity, one that is recognized for official purposes, lies at the heart of the social contract. Who gets to vote, who gets to receive a social grant or pension payment, who gets to be seen by a doctor, who gets to open a bank account or even register a mobile phone number is increasingly a function of who has a recognized identity—an official record of their existence as a unique person—and can validate themselves against their claimed identity. With the consolidation of communities into nation states and the formalization of rules to define membership, as well as the duties and privileges associated with it, identification processes have similarly become more formal. People without an officially recognized identity face myriad barriers to full economic and political participation. Because of KYC requirements, they cannot place their savings in a bank account or receive cash payments electronically. Tighter identity requirements mean that they increasingly are not even able to purchase a prepaid SIM card to operate a mobile phone.[5] Lack of officially recognized identification or identity credentials[6] is also a severe barrier for international travel and migration and for the economic opportunities they afford.

Lack of strong and verifiable identification poses considerable difficulties not only for individuals but also for the broader communities and states where they reside. Government agencies will struggle to administer programs effectively—for example, to ensure that social transfers or pensions are not received multiple times by the same beneficiary, or to eliminate ghost workers or pensioners. Private companies and banks will find it harder to operate profitably in settings where they cannot reliably verify the identities of their em-

---

5   GSMA (2016) discusses the increasing prevalence of SIM registration and how different countries are managing this.

6   The terms *identification credential* or *ID credential* include any widely accepted proof of identity, generally issued by or on behalf of a state. Common examples include a national identification card, a driver's license, or a passport, but many other types of identification documentation could fall into this category, including the combination of identification number and biometrics in systems that do not rely on cards.

ployees, clients, or business partners, or where they need to develop their own customized and costly systems. The absence of any single consistent identifier makes it difficult for credit bureaus to operate and for banks to offer credit to all but the wealthiest, most well-established, and best-known customers. The use of many different and unrelated identification systems greatly complicates tax administration because it is difficult to combine data on different income sources and assets by an individual taxpayer.

The difficulties in bridging the global identification and identity verification gaps are manifold. In some cases, no official identity may have been established at all. In others, identity credentials may be lost; in still others, credentials may be produced but be of low quality or not easy to verify. Many countries still rely on decentralized paper-based local registries rather than digital databases. Although there is a continuing role for physical records, if these are destroyed by conflict, a natural disaster, or another calamity and have not been backed up—not an uncommon situation in poor countries—those registered have no way of proving that their claimed identities are valid. Without an underlying registry, whether paper or digital, an ID credential may not provide the level of assurance needed to access public services or for some private sector transactions, particularly when the document is easy to alter or falsify. Those whose identification claim is unverifiable or whose credentials are weak may thus face much the same barriers as someone with no established identity at all.

Verification challenges are becoming more complex as populations turn increasingly mobile, both within and between countries. The global migrant total has reached 1 billion, about one in every seven people. About three-quarters are internal migrants; India alone has some 400 million internal migrants who live and work outside their traditional communities. Records in paper-based registries as well as offline digital ones may be difficult to consult and verify remotely even within the same country, while cross-border identity verification can run into even greater obstacles.

Refugees—now at a post–World War II high of 21 million within the total of 65 million people displaced by natural disasters and conflicts—pose another huge identification challenge. Even if they had well-recognized ID credentials in their countries of origin, a paper copy of a birth certificate or other identifying document (even one with recognized security features) may not be adequate to persuade officials in other countries that they are who they claim to be, because these officials may not be able to check the document against a registry and may lack confidence in the issuing process.

How Is the Identification Landscape
Changing in the Digital Age?

Of course, the need for identification and the challenges in providing it are not new. The registration of births and deaths goes back centuries in many countries, as do the precursors to many modern national identification systems. China has had an elaborate system of identifying its people for many hundreds of years. The precursor to Japan's civil registry dates from around 1670 and listed the name, age, and sex of each individual in each village by household. Impressively, it was updated annually. Large-scale civil registration in France started in 1792, at the behest of the revolutionary government, while church records of vital events go back far longer. Many of the needs and challenges documented in the outstanding historical compilation by Breckenridge and Szreter (2012) have an eerily familiar ring today.

From the earliest times, identification systems have relied on some subset of the many different attributes that together distinguish each of us as a distinct person. They may be bundled into three main factors and combined in different ways to form the basis for identification:

- **Something you are:** A biometric such as physical appearance, a distinctive voice, or a smell or behavioral pattern. This is surely the oldest form of recognition, as well as the most recent. In modern digital times, it can encompass digital biometrics such as fingerprint, iris or finger-vein-patterns, voice patterns, DNA, dynamic signature, or, on a computer, keystroke rhythms or mouse movement patterns.

- **Something you have:** A birth certificate; an ID card; or a mobile ID, token, or other physical credential. Something you have could also be a person, such as a well-respected and credible individual ready to vouch for you. The best identifier for an infant is still probably its mother.

- **Something you know:** A personal identification number (PIN) or password, or the ability to provide personal information that is unlikely to be known by others.

Modern identification systems often combine all three factors: are, have, and know. Estonia's pioneering digital ID system, which is supported by comprehensive civil registration, is one such case study considered in this book. At the age of 15, fingerprints are taken on registration for the national ID system (who you are: to prevent multiple identities). An ID card is issued (what you have); it includes digital certificates to enable the holder to both authenticate his identity and to sign documents electronically. For these purposes, the holder authenticates himself against the card by providing two user-selected and private PINs (what you know), one to authenticate himself and the other to sign. Multifactor authentication offers extra security relative to the use of only one factor. But, as in the case of Martin Guerre, even multiple factors—his appearance (are), testimony from Bertrande (have), and the ability to provide personal information about his life with her (know)—cannot fully eliminate the possibility of identity fraud or error.

Phases of Identification: Village, Central, and the "e-Village"

Identity management systems are evolving over time and with advancing technology and economic development. Although they can differ in many ways, it is useful to think of them in three phases (figure 1-1).

- In the initial "village" phase, most social and economic interaction is local, as is identification. Identities are established and verified based on personal connections—who you know and who knows you—sometimes supplemented by local documentary evidence.

- As societies become more mobile and fluid and wider market-based transactions replace local trade and subsistence economies, countries usually transition to the second phase of centralized national identification and other centrally administered systems. These have traditionally been paper based but are increasingly supported by digital technology and provide identity management services to support a widening range of virtual interaction and transactions. This is the current frontier for identification in the development context.

- However, centralized systems may not be the last word. The shift toward digital societies and economies has created the possibility of a third phase, of "federated" or "e-village" approaches to identification and authentication. In this phase, evidence to support the existence of an identity and to authenticate a claimant is drawn from a wide range of sources that can include databases held by private service providers, such as banks, as well as by membership and active participation in online communities, in addition to official identifying data and ID credentials such as passports.

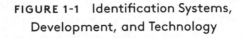

FIGURE 1-1   Identification Systems,
Development, and Technology

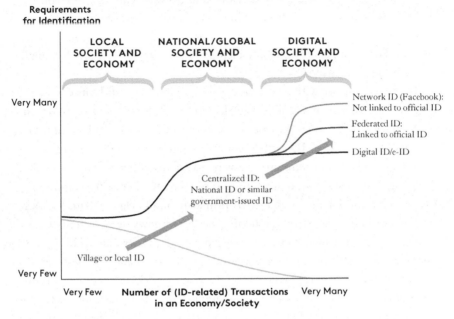

The first stage. "Village" identification remains important in many countries despite the rapid adoption of new systems and technologies. One example of "village" identification would be the family card systems in some Asian countries, which predate other forms of identity management such as civil registries or centralized national ID cards. A number of Asian countries, including Cambodia, China, Indonesia, Laos, and Vietnam, have long operated some version of the household registration (hukou) system, with details of all family members included in a family book held by the designated head of the family. These systems have often been driven by a desire to control movement between regions and particularly migration to cities.[7] As another example, Ethiopia's *kebele* ID system is administered by some 16,000 administrative units that each typically includes around 8,000 people.[8] The initial identity is certified and validated by a system of subadministrative units and groups within the kebele

---

7   For the example of Vietnam, see World Bank and Vietnam Academy of Social Science (2016).

8   See World Bank (2017b, 2017c) for more information on Ethiopia's identification system.

down to the level of ten or so households—a very local form of identification. Each kebele issues its own ID card or booklet to adult residents in Amharic or the local language or both, and the cards and booklets can vary in color and design. In the absence of a functioning civil registration system or a conventional national ID system, the kebele card provides full legal identity to adult citizens. For example, it is the only identity documentation required to apply for an Ethiopian passport.

In other countries with no nationwide system in place, affidavits from local government officials may still be considered to provide the most reliable form of identification. This was the case, for example, in Tanzania, at least until the rollout of the 2015 voter ID card. In countries with weak civil registration systems, local officials and committees may be asked to confirm that an individual enrolling into an identification program is really a member of the community. Identification in Somalia is still based primarily on the clan system. Verification can include exhaustive questioning on clan knowledge and tests of genealogical history extending back many generations (Rader 2016). This process raises severe hurdles for those with unusual or uncertain ancestral histories.

Decentralized "village" systems can work adequately in conditions of limited mobility, but face a number of limitations. One problem is how to ensure the integrity and quality of the processes carried out at local levels and the ID credentials issued by local governments. Usually these will be on paper and vulnerable to alteration or forgery. Poorly maintained local records pose another problem, especially in low-income and rural settings. Most seriously, local systems require tight administrative controls to prevent multiple identities, and begin to break down as people move more frequently, migrating to cities or moving between communities. In Vietnam, at least 5.5 million people lacked permanent ID documents in their place of actual residence (World Bank and Vietnam Academy of Social Sciences 2016).

Centralized identity management. As societies and economies become more complex, geographically fluid, and market based, the demand for portable identity services increases because of the rising frequency with which individuals need to prove their identity in situations where they are not known personally. Transactions become more impersonal and local systems come under pressure. The systems transition to the second phase of centralized identification, usually managed at the national level. Records are standardized and digitized, with personal identifying information consolidated into one or several databases, depending on the country's choice of identification architecture.

Authentication is then against a centrally issued ID card or other credentials, or directly against the database. Locally administered or issued identification continues to support some transactions, but an increasing number rely on centrally issued proof of identity. Kenya and Malaysia are two of the many examples of countries that have built centralized systems issuing ID cards that are used for virtually all identification purposes.

The essential features of such systems are shown schematically in figure 1-2 for the case in which the country operates a civil registry and a national identification program. Individuals can be registered at two points in life, at birth in the civil registry and at a later age, generally ages 15 to 18, for the national ID. In countries with a strong civil registry, this system can provide a flow of information into the population register that underpins the national ID program; it can also validate a birth certificate and other information presented at registration. Where civil registration is weak and many people lack birth certificates, the national ID will need a separate process to assemble other evidence of identity at the point of enrollment. This could include school or baptism certificates, letters from local authorities, and oral testimony.

The system also checks to ensure that the person is not already registered under the same or another identity; each new enrollee must be compared with all those who have already enrolled. This can include both biographic and biometric deduplication. An ID card with a unique number, or just the number, is issued and the number is then seeded into the databases for various functions, services, and programs. As people engage with these programs the process generates new information so that the central identity data can be updated. Some OECD countries with strong civil registration processes have chosen not to implement a centralized national identification program; they rely on civil registration and other documentary evidence to issue functional ID credentials, such as driver's licenses or passports, for various purposes.

The quality and integrity of centralized identification depend on the features of the system and how it is managed. As depicted by the arrow in figure 1-1 and also in figure 1-2, especially in the many developing countries with weak civil registration systems, centrally managed identification programs still need to rely on local processes to confirm the identities of adults at the point of enrollment. One example is the "introducer" option for enrollment in India's Aadhaar program, whereby a known and respected community figure, such as a local official or a schoolteacher, can vouch for a person's identity. This provision was put in place to enable people with no documentary evidence of

FIGURE 1-2   Centralized Identity Management System

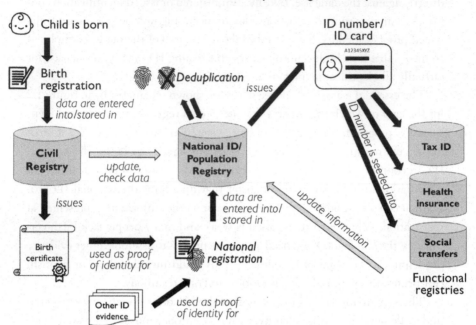

identity to enroll. In the case of Kenya's national identification program, local vetting committees review candidates, particularly in border regions, to ensure that they are who they claim to be. Local systems thus provide the basis for the "official" identification recognized by government agencies, which is used more frequently as countries become richer and the frequency of remote and digital interactions increases.

Decentralized identification and the potential of the e-village. With increasing connectivity and the rise of digital societies and economies, providing identity services remotely has become the new frontier for identification systems. With about 5 billion subscribers, mobile communication is becoming ubiquitous across the globe, and the number of mobile phones in circulation has risen to about 7 billion—close to the population of the planet. Broadband access has become quasi-universal in most developed countries, and though it lags somewhat behind in poorer ones, even there, connectivity is rapidly expanding.[9]

9   In 2016 it was estimated that mobile operators covered 95 percent of the global population with 2G connectivity and 84 percent with 3G mobile signal (ITU 2016).

The growth of the digital society and the digital economy opens up new possibilities for providing services more efficiently. According to the 2016 United Nations (UN) E-Government survey, 148 countries provided at least one form of online transactional service, a substantial increase from previous years (UN 2016). The shift toward digital societies and economies throws up new challenges for providing identification services, in particular how to identify participants for remote transactions. To meet this challenge, a growing number of centralized systems, including those in Estonia and India, offer full remote digital identification. However, the growing "digital cloud" of data, drawn from increased participation in online communities and the rising number of digital transactions, offers a new decentralized approach to managing identities. They can again be established and verified on the basis of "who knows you?" as in the "village" phase of identity management but through the use of digital technology and virtual communities. As before, the level of identity assurance rests on the credibility of the entity that conducts due diligence and the range of evidence considered.

Figure 1-1 distinguishes two different types of third-stage identity management that could allow for remote verification of individuals for online transactions based on digital information. Federated identity providers or assurers, such as those authorized by the British GOV.UK Verify program, are vetted and authorized by the government. They can draw on official databases such as passports, driver's licenses, or gun permits, and can tap into other sources of information, such as financial data or payment records, to verify identities to higher levels of assurance. Banks and mobile companies are perhaps best placed to offer such identification services as they require their own customers to provide official identification for KYC purposes. The strength of this type of system is that it can be "double-blind"—the identity assurer does not know the purpose for which identification is requested, and the requiring entity does not know the range of evidence considered.

A second type of "e-village" identification is that provided by social networks, such as Facebook. These systems do not necessarily require government-issued credentials from those seeking to become members. The identities of their users could be verified, however, based on testimonies from other members and their interactions across the network, as well as pictures and location information that they have shared with the virtual community. The algorithmic processes of social networks may not provide an acceptable level of identity assurance for all purposes, but their power is increasing and other businesses increasingly are using them as references for identification and verification.

This third stage of identity management may not be the first priority for poor countries seeking to endow their citizens with basic identification. It does not provide "foundational identity" in the same sense as the previous stages, and there are still questions about the strength of the business case for private entities to provide high-quality identity assurance services. However, systems of this type have made some important contributions to thinking about identity management. They are bound to become more precise and more important as the volume of digital data continues to grow at the staggering rate of 42 percent per year, as projected by market studies (Rizzatti 2016).

The Explosion in Identity Management Systems

The proliferation of registration and identification systems, the improvements in the precision and affordability of the technologies they rely on, and the growth in the number and scope of government programs and private sector companies that depend on accurate identification have been nothing short of revolutionary. Figure 1-3 offers a broad global picture of the spread of birth registration systems and national-level identification programs[10] based on evolving data from the World Bank's Identification for Development (ID4D) Program, distinguishing high-income countries (HICs) from middle- and low-income countries. In considering the figure, it should be recalled that the number of widely recognized sovereign states has increased over the period: 149 in the 1960s, 171 in the 1970s, 193 in the 2000s, and 195 in 2017.[11]

From figure 1-3, even as far back as 1960, the vast majority of countries maintained a birth registry. The number has increased steadily in subsequent decades to the point where almost all countries have such a system in place today, even if its coverage may be incomplete. In contrast, very few countries, particularly those in the low- and middle-income categories, had a national identification program five decades ago. It was only after 1990, and especially after 2000, that such systems began to be deployed rapidly across the devel-

---

10 The term "national-level" allows for the inclusion of programs administered at the national level that are not conventional national identification programs, such as India's Aadhaar program.

11 Note also that the income categorization of countries over these five decades has also changed considerably. High-income country (HIC) categorizations refer to countries' status as of 2016. For more detailed information, see the World Bank ID4D initiative's 2016 ID4D Global Dataset at http://data.worldbank.org/data-catalog/id4d-dataset.

oping world. As of 2016, World Bank data indicate that all but 12 low- and middle-income countries have established or initiated a national-level identification program. Almost half of existing national ID programs in developing countries—a total of 63—have been launched within the past 15 years. Every country in sub-Saharan Africa, for example, has now implemented or committed to a "foundational" national ID program, with the objective of providing a multipurpose proof of unique identity, although some are still at a preliminary stage.

These multipurpose programs are only part of the picture. Many "functional" ID programs have been launched for particular purposes, such as registering voters, identifying beneficiaries for social transfer programs, or performing due diligence on clients for financial services. Some countries now have multiple large-scale programs—Mexico has at least seven, and Nigeria

FIGURE 1-3 Identification Programs in High-Income Countries (HICs) and Others

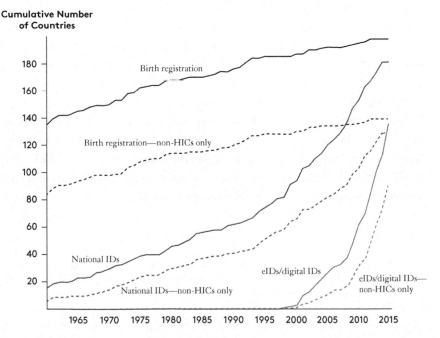

Source: World Bank ID4D dataset; January 2016 edition.

has at least a dozen.[12] There are also many smaller programs, such as that launched by the West Africa Examinations Council, to register students biometrically to reduce the incidence of examination fraud.

The rapid proliferation of identification systems reflects several factors integral to the functioning of the modern state. Developing countries are creating ID systems in response to growing perceived needs, whether to strengthen national security in the face of an increase in perceived threats, improve the credibility of elections, or implement large-scale economic or social programs. In some cases, providing national identification services to the population is seen as an integral component of state-building. How have various developments contributed to the explosion of ID systems over the past two decades?

Security. One critical driver has been an increase in perceived security threats. The rise of international terrorism, conflicts in border areas, and growing refugee flows have made knowing who is who a priority for many governments concerned with protecting their citizens. Regulatory authorities have needed to respond to growing international pressure for higher standards. In the aftermath of the events of 9/11, concerns over money laundering and the financing of terrorism have led to more stringent regulatory recommendations from the Financial Action Task Force (FATF). In response, national KYC regulations and processes have become more stringent. A verifiable identity is now a prerequisite for engaging in almost any formal financial transaction. Customers who lack credentials are unable to open financial accounts; likewise, financial institutions that are unable to comply with identity verification requirements risk being cut off from correspondent banking relationships. "Derisking" threatens not only poor countries that have inadequate identification systems but also customers of money transfer organizations that traditionally have relied on less rigorous customer information than that required by banks (CGD 2015).[13] Enhanced security requirements for global travel also have intensified demands for accurate identification, including more secure travel documents.

---

12 Such a proliferation of identification programs was also characteristic of 18th-century England and Holland, where a strong state and commercial economy was associated with a profusion of registration systems promoted in civil society (Breckenridge and Szreter 2012).

13 Pressure for stronger KYC processes since 9/11, including for poor customers, may seem ironic in the light of the leak of over 11.5 million confidential documents in the Panama Papers scandal of April 2016. These files showed how the rich and powerful continue to be able to conceal their beneficial ownership in offshore tax havens.

Elections. Following the end of the Cold War, the average number of multiparty elections has jumped from one per year to around seven in sub-Saharan Africa alone. Registering voters has become a priority to support the consolidation of democratic processes and state-building, and often has been generously supported by international donors. The mixed record of biometric voter registration, and the less frequent attempts to authenticate voters biometrically at the polls, suggests that these costly programs carry significant risks (see chapter 2, and Gelb and Diofasi 2016a). The use of high-technology identification systems has not been consistently successful, and despite their considerable expense, voter registration drives often have not left much behind in terms of more permanent identity management assets. Nevertheless, elections have certainly been a powerful driver of spending on identity management systems.

Expanding public administration and government transfers. By 2014 over a billion people were receiving government transfers and other payments, with the average developing country operating about 20 different social safety net programs at an annual cost of 1.6 percent of its gross domestic product (GDP) (World Bank 2015). Ensuring that social transfers reach their intended beneficiaries and improving the targeting of social safety net programs—as well as unifying the beneficiary rolls for the programs to reduce overlap—are part of the global identification challenge. So is the need to prevent fraud and diversion in other public payments, including subsidies, government payrolls, and pensions. A general rise in literacy, the spread of communication technologies, and increased data availability probably also have played a role in placing countries' public administration systems and the effectiveness of their public spending under greater scrutiny, and encouraging the use of robust identification systems capable of ensuring that identities are unique.

Digital technology. Technology has also been a driver of the new systems, in both positive and negative ways. On the positive side, the new systems bring new capabilities to support the more effective administration of public programs and service delivery. Digital identification is also a valuable resource for the private sector, whether in banking, health insurance, or other applications. Its adoption is a necessary step toward satisfying the growing private and public service demand for e-identification for remote transactions and for the world's 3.5 billion (and counting) internet users. On the negative side, some programs may have been driven by the opportunities for side payments afforded by less-than-transparent high-value technology procurements. A number of countries have opted to purchase state-of-the-art biometric equipment and introduce high-tech multipurpose smartcards with advanced identity verification capabilities even where the authentication and service delivery infrastructure to effectively use these features had not been put in place. By requiring more demanding identification and raising the prices of passports, driver's licenses, and other credentials to excessive levels, governments can also compel those needing identification to foot the bill at the expense of inclusion.

Transformative Identification Technologies: Catchup and Lags

Whatever the motivation in particular cases, as shown in figure 1-3, the proliferation of national identification systems has gone hand in hand with the adoption of digital technology, especially over the period since 2000, which has seen a sharp uptick in the deployment of digital ID systems (or e-IDs).[14] Virtually all new programs, as well as upgrades to older paper-based ones, use digital technology in some way. Digital biometric identifiers, usually fingerprints (and increasingly face and iris), are used in the vast majority of the new systems. In the first instance, biometrics are taken to limit the possibility of multiple registrations—to ensure that each registrant can only enroll once and thus that each recorded identity is unique, if not absolutely then at least in a statistical sense.[15] At present this is the only known approach to deduplicate enrollments, so as to ensure statistically unique identification in large populations. Their second function is to authenticate people against their claimed identities—but this is not, of course, the only digital approach toward authentication. Other options such as PINs and one-time passwords are widely used and will continue to be so, possibly in combination with biometrics to provide multifactor authentication. Biometric technology has also opened the door to new ways of sequencing identification programs by reducing reliance on detailed biographical information.

Table 1-1 summarizes available information on the diffusion of this technology across countries at different levels of development.[16] At 75 percent, the

---

14 Digital identity systems or e-IDs refer to identity systems that use digital technology in several ways: electronic databases to store and manage records; electronic credentials to serve mobile, online, and offline applications, including PKI (public key) infrastructure; and digital biometrics to identify and authenticate individuals.

15 The term "statistically unique" refers here to systems where the probability that any individual has multiple identities is very small. No system is able to guarantee absolutely unique identity. See chapter 4.

16 There are still substantial data gaps in these areas; table 1-1 draws on information available as of January 2016. For more detail on the state of indentification systems in Africa, see World Bank (2017b, 2017c).

nology, but some of the gains are more superficial than real. Many will need substantial investments in digital infrastructure to complete the transition. They face formidable implementation challenges to build up their digital identification systems and the underlying databases and processes, as well as to put in place authentication ecosystems that are able to take full advantage of the capabilities offered by the new technologies.

From Identification to Development: Challenges and Risks

Despite their development potential and proliferation, identification programs are still controversial. Although countries may be converging toward a broadly similar model, there is no standard system for how identities should be managed or what an "ideal" identification system would look like. Some of the new systems represent a radical departure from traditional approaches to managing identity, in terms of their institutional arrangements as well as the technologies deployed to register and authenticate individuals and to coordinate the sharing of identity data for administrative purposes. There is considerable uncertainty about how these features will affect the development impact of a given system. Even those designed with user needs and development objectives in mind will likely need continuous adjustment as unintended consequences or limitations of the system come to light. Identification programs are also associated with a number of risks, including the erosion of privacy and the possible exclusion of those who are unable to satisfy tightening registration requirements. Wasteful spending on ID systems is also a problem—too often, expensive investments in high-tech identification infrastructure generate no returns as programs languish at low levels of coverage and provide few real opportunities for use.

There Is No Single Formula for Change . . .

Across countries, there are astonishing differences in how people are identified and how they can authenticate their identities, whether for real or virtual transactions. Some countries have strong foundational identification systems whose use is required for virtually all transactions. Others have multiple systems of varying quality serving different purposes. Still others have little in the way of identification infrastructure and issue only low-quality credentials, if at all. ID credentials are also extremely varied; the only common global standard is for machine-readable travel documents issued by the International Civil Aviation Organization (ICAO).[17]

These differences reflect a host of initial conditions including administrative and technological capacity, past civil registration and identity management efforts, and the institutional and bureaucratic arrangements in place to provide identity services. They also reflect differences in social and political views. National identification systems accepted as normal and useful in some countries are political anathema in others. Some see a centralized, multiuse ID system as empowering, whereas others perceive it as a mechanism to reinforce the control of oppressive regimes. Indeed, many identification systems, even those now accepted as contributing positively to society, had their origins in repressive systems of control and surveillance. Breckenridge (2005) provides the example of South Africa's national population register, which was established to help control movement under the apartheid regime but now supports the administration of a comprehensive system of social grants. Spain offers another example. Its early forms of identification responded to the desire to exclude descendants of Moors and Jews from the Americas. The roots of the current ID system, initiated in 1951, lie in the institutionalized repression of Francoism (Clavell and Ouziel 2014). Today the system is accepted as a matter of course.

All OECD countries have well-established and comprehensive civil registries with birth registration rates at or close to 100 percent, but their arrangements for providing identification services vary. At one extreme is Estonia, which, as already noted, has probably the world's leading e-ID system with a vast array of public and private services provided via remote online access. It is built upon the central national population register and provides a unique ID number used by virtually all public and private service providers. Citizens and residents can use card-based or SIM-based mobile ID to access online services that include voting, submitting and checking tax returns, and starting a business; they can also sign documents digitally with the full legal authority of a handwritten signature. Access to many digital services has been extended to nonresidents through Estonia's e-Residency program, the first "global identification" system in the world.

One of several OECD countries at the other end of the identity management spectrum is the United States. It has no national identification system

---

17 For more information on the ICAO's Traveller Identification Programme, see the ICAO website at www.icao.int/Security/FAL/TRIP/Pages/default.aspx.

Somaliland, covers only between one and two million voters—a fraction of the estimated Somali population of 11.3 million.

In Asia, Malaysia contrasts with the Philippines. The former stands out as the first country to implement a comprehensive digital multiple-application national identification card; the MYKAD card can be used as a driving license, a library card, or a health records repository. Children above the age of 12 are issued a MYKID card as their own official identification document. In the Philippines, efforts to establish the national ID system as the basis for identification have stalled. People need to carry several credentials and permits (out of as many as 28 possibilities), and there are few rigorous cross-checks on the consistency of information. India's distinctive Aadhaar program has already been mentioned.

With such diverse starting points, there is no simple formula for strengthening identity management across all countries. Even though there are many common areas for action and certain universally applicable principles that should be followed, country needs and priorities differ. Some countries can build on a strong base; others need to consolidate diverse systems; still others are almost at the point of needing to start from scratch. The diversity of experience makes it even more important to draw lessons across systems to help shape individual country strategies, to strengthen the systems themselves, and also to understand how the systems can be used to support sustainable development.

... And Risks Must Be Recognized

There is widespread consensus on the relevance of civil registration and vital statistics systems and their essential features. In addition to providing a basis for identification, they provide essential statistical demographic and health information. Like statistical systems more generally, they often have not been adequately supported by national governments or their development partners, but this is not because the systems themselves are contentious. Their features have been codified by the UN Statistics Division in the form of handbooks and training manuals (UNSTATS 1998; UNSTATS 2002). Yet some details, such as the target age for birth registration or the role of paper records in an increasingly digital age, are debated.

There is much more debate around identification systems, especially those that facilitate the tracking of transactions and interactions. National population registers and government-issued national ID cards are common in the civil law countries of continental Europe, but have been rejected in many common and issues no national credential. The best that most people can count on is a number issued by the Social Security Administration together with a simple paper card (no photo) and/or a state-issued driving permit. Only about 38 percent of citizens hold a passport. About 10 percent of citizens (and 25 percent of African Americans) do not hold any federal or state government-issued photo ID card (Gaskins 2011). The consequences include substantial losses from continuing identity theft and fraud, as well as partisan struggles over state-level efforts to impose photo ID requirements for voting, which are invariably challenged in the courts. In the United Kingdom, even though most of the population holds a driver's license (to drive, not as an identification document) or a passport (to travel), there is no specific credential that establishes or confirms a citizen's identity. Hospitality New Zealand's 18+ photo card is reputedly held not as a general proof of identity but for the specific purpose of proving that the holder is old enough to be allowed to consume alcohol.[18]

The differences in identity management systems are equally stark across less-developed countries. Some have comprehensive systems. During the past 20 years, Peru has created a multipurpose national registration and identification system with almost universal registration of adults and children. In opinion polls, RENIEC, its civil registration and identification agency, is among the most trusted institutions in the country (Reuben and Carbonari 2017). Pakistan has also created a comprehensive central system that is used for all identification purposes, including voting and the administration of social transfers to poor households. In Africa, Kenya has a well-developed though less technically advanced national ID system with origins that date back as far as 1920. Other African countries with long-established systems include Botswana, South Africa, and Zimbabwe. Rwanda and Uganda also have systems with high coverage, but have rolled out their current systems relatively recently. Some other countries, like Ghana, Nigeria, and Tanzania, have been attempting to roll out national ID systems for a number of years, but progress has been fitful, with slow gains in enrollment. Somalia and the Democratic Republic of Congo are examples of countries with still less-developed systems. The identification ecosystem in Somalia is fragmented and undeveloped. Very few births are registered, and there is no consistent countrywide system to establish and verify the identity of citizens. The most advanced system, for voter registration in

---

18 New Zealanders do, of course, virtually all have birth certificates and could present these to establish their age, but since they do not include a current photograph they do not alone provide credible proof of identity.

law countries like Australia, the United Kingdom, and the United States. Opponents of these national ID systems stress the risk of eroding privacy, arguing that the use of a single national identifying number for all transactions can help to merge individual records across many databases, potentially increasing the ease of surveillance (Hosein and Nyst 2013). Citing examples as diverse as Korea, Israel, and also highly publicized security breaches in the United States and other countries, critics also argue that large centralized identity databases create an irresistible honeypot for hackers. Another concern in some OECD countries is that the costs of such systems will outweigh the benefits of introducing them, especially in contexts where established systems are widely felt to work "well enough" for most people and most purposes. Some of the countries with strong opposition to a national ID system are at the forefront of efforts to create alternative modes of establishing and verifying identities that do not rely on a centralized identity database.

For developing countries, the rapid implementation of sophisticated ID programs raises even more pointed questions about benefits, risks, and costs. On one hand, as an increasing number of cases show (see chapter 3), the potential gains in terms of both individual inclusion and administrative efficiency are probably larger in lower-capacity developing countries than in rich ones. On the other hand, in settings with weak rule of law and limited independent oversight over government programs, identification systems will be more prone to misuse and less likely to offer high returns on what are often substantial investments of public funds. Although these risks must be recognized, there is little prospect of realizing the SDGs if countries are not able to strengthen their capacity to implement policies and programs and deliver services effectively. Neither will the SDGs be achieved if poor and vulnerable people are not able to participate in political, social, and economic life because they lack the recognized identity to do so.

The most relevant risks to the development-enhancing implementation of identification programs fall into three categories:

Exclusion. Vulnerable individuals and groups could be excluded if new ID systems are deployed and linked to various applications without considering their needs and limitations. The new systems may be too costly or difficult to access—for example, if registration involves high fees or lengthy travel to a registration office. Where remote authentication is required to access essential subsidies or services, beneficiaries could be seriously inconvenienced and even excluded if the quality of connectivity is too low to use the system reliably. Manual workers who are unable to provide high-quality fingerprints for authentication could also be marginalized if no alternatives are made available. If the formalization of identity is associated with the formalization of national status, an unknown but considerable number of people face the prospect of statelessness.

Misuse. Many countries lack the legal and regulatory underpinnings to ensure that ID systems manage data securely and do not pose a threat to privacy. Only around half of all developing countries have data privacy protection laws that conform to global standards for fair information practices. Though the number is rising, those that do not have such a framework—or lack the capacity to implement its provisions—are mostly lower-income countries. The implementation of digital ID systems may pose particularly serious risks in countries where the rule of law is weak and there is little prospect for holding individuals, the government, or private entities accountable when personal data are accessed or used unlawfully. No system is completely proof against misuse, including identity theft, even if some appear to be more robust than others.

Ineffective investments. A further concern is the balance of benefits versus costs. ID systems require substantial investments as well as an ongoing operations budget. For a medium-size developing country, the costs of setting up the system and the initial enrollment phase alone can easily run into the hundreds of millions of dollars. The rapid expansion of technically sophisticated systems has not always taken place using the most suitable or cost-effective identification solutions. High-value technology procurements offer lucrative opportunities to both vendors and officials in client governments. Combined with weak oversight by national authorities as well as donors, this has helped to reinforce the natural bureaucratic tendency to work in silos. The consequence has often been costly and sometimes overengineered programs that are not interoperable with each other. Donor support for individual functional ID programs in the context of a specific operation may have reinforced fragmentation. Programs have sometimes been implemented under undue time pressure, increasing their cost. Voter registration programs are one such example; their expense (often around US$20 per voter per election) suggests that without generous continued donor support or a change in the model, elections will not be financially sustainable for some poor countries.

Nonetheless, in addition to supporting many SDGs and targets, effective and well-used ID programs should be high-return public investments for developing country governments. Not many ID applications have been fully assessed, but several appear to have generated a high rate of financial return. However, many countries have been wasting large sums in this area because of redundant programs, slow implementation, excessive costs, or simply because they have not used their ID programs to strengthen capacity and deliver services. Although to date there have not been any comprehensive assessments of the financial and economic benefits and costs of ID programs, these cases almost certainly would show negative rates of financial return to their investments, and probably also negative economic rates of return.

What Does the Identification Revolution Mean for Development Organizations?

Development partners have supported a wide range of identification programs. In a survey of 160 biometric ID programs of many different types, Gelb and Clark (2013a) found that at least half had been supported by development partners and donors. However, foundational identification, or the provision of multipurpose identification services, typically has not been supported as an end in itself. This may not be surprising in light of the Millennium Development Goals (MDGs), the precursor to the SDGs, which do not signify identity management as a broader strategic goal or legal identity as a development target. With the notable exception of the Inter-American Development Bank, which has a long record of support for civil registration and identification in Central and South America and the Caribbean, both IFIs and bilateral donors have viewed identification programs merely as a mechanism to help implement individual projects, depending on the donor's mandate.

In spite of their limitations, these fragmented projects have provided some useful experience. They have supported experimentation and innovation and have also provided "proof of concept" for the use of technically advanced approaches in low-income, fragile contexts. For example, as early as 2006, iris recognition was successfully used to help deliver demobilization payments to 110,000 ex-combatants in the Democratic Republic of Congo (Gelb and Decker 2011). Such an unsystematic and diverse engagement is perhaps inevitable in the early stages of work on a new area and with rapidly evolving technology, but it is now an opportune time to build on this experience to develop a more integrated, forward-looking approach to managing identity in the context of development.

Development partners are beginning to establish such a strategic approach, and some other important initiatives are under way, such as the ID4Africa movement.[19] This is a promising start, but these initiatives are at an early stage and there is still a long way to go to develop a coordinated approach. The first step must be to work toward a common understanding of the ways in which identification systems should contribute to development. As discussed in more detail in chapter 7, some 21 organizations have endorsed a set of principles for the application of identification to development (Principles 2017). The 10 principles for the coverage, design, and governance of ID systems can serve as a valuable starting point for planning and implementing inclusive, robust, and trusted systems, as well as a benchmark for evaluating them (see box 1-1).

Considering the uncertainties, the fast-evolving identity management landscape, the close association of many programs with law enforcement and security, and the repressive origins of many identification systems, it would not be surprising if some development partners felt that the area poses too many risks to be involved in it. But this perspective sidesteps the challenge. By their nature, ID programs are multiple-use systems and multiple factors are propelling them forward. The practical question is not *whether* they should be implemented, but rather *how*, and how they should move forward in a way that maximizes their positive impact on sustainable development.

Summary Overview

As already emphasized, this is a fast-moving area and one with many large information gaps. It is still not possible to come to a definitive view on the impact of many new identification systems. Far more data collection and analysis is needed to understand their implications for the exercise of rights, for strengthening state capacity, for the functioning of markets and creation of new opportunities, and for sustainable development in general, as defined by the SDGs. Implementation and impact are high priorities, requiring careful

---

19 ID4Africa is now in its fourth year. Its 2017 meeting in Namibia followed annual conferences in 2015 and 2016 in Tanzania and Rwanda, respectively. The 2018 conference will take place in Abuja, Nigeria. For more information, see the program's website at www .id4africa.com/.

**BOX 1-1   Principles on Identification
for Sustainable Development**

Inclusion: Universal Coverage and Accessibility
1. Ensuring universal coverage for individuals from birth to death, free from discrimination.
2. Removing barriers to access and usage and disparities in the availability of information and technology.

Design: Robust, Secure, Responsive, and Sustainable
3. Establishing a robust—unique, secure, and accurate—identity.
4. Creating a platform that is interoperable and responsive to the needs of various users.
5. Using open standards and ensuring vendor and technology neutrality.
6. Protecting user privacy and control through system design.
7. Planning for financial and operational sustainability without compromising accessibility.

Governance: Building Trust by Protecting Privacy and User Rights
8. Safeguarding data privacy, security, and user rights through a comprehensive legal and regulatory framework.
9. Establishing clear institutional mandates and accountability.
10. Enforcing legal and trust frameworks through independent oversight and adjudication of grievances.

Source: Principles (2017).

monitoring and research as the frontier shifts from creating the new digital systems toward integrating them into a wide range of programs. This book could look quite different if it were written 10 years in the future. With these strong caveats, it nonetheless provides a concise picture of the evolving situation and sets out some of the choices that developing countries and their partners might consider.

also have valuable lessons to offer.) The first three cases offer interesting lessons for centralized ID systems. Starting from a civil registration and ID system greatly damaged by the Shining Path insurgency, Peru set out to identify its people as a priority for national reconstruction. It has created one of the strongest and most integrated ID systems in the world with an institutional and financial model that can be relevant to many countries. Estonia has been the world's leader in e-ID. Proving that digital identity knows no boundaries, it has also extended its service to nonresidents through the e-Residency program to provide the world's first global service. As mentioned earlier, India's unique identification or Aadhaar program is truly unique in multiple dimensions and offers lessons for many other countries. The other two cases, GOV.UK Verify and social networks, are more speculative but offer some intriguing prospects. Neither provides "foundational" legal identity or can be considered as the "first stage" option for poor countries seeking to establish an identity baseline and mechanisms to authenticate against it. Indeed, they demonstrate the difficulty of managing identities without some such foundational system, even if it is not a fully integrated one. However, they raise the important point that identity assurance need not always be "gold plated," but can be calibrated to the needs of the particular application at hand.

Chapter 7 concludes with the implications for designing and implementing identification systems that can work as effective tools for achieving the SDGs, while ensuring that risks are mitigated. Countries and development partners are evolving toward a more strategic approach on this front, but it is still early days. The first step is to reach agreement on a set of common principles, which this chapter presents by drawing on the previously discussed cases and examples. It also considers some further necessary steps and the need for more research on the functioning, use, and impact of the rapidly evolving systems of identification, particularly in developing countries.

TWO

How Big Is the Global Identification Gap? Can We Measure It?

In a first attempt to estimate the global number of people without a "legal identity," the World Bank suggests that over 1.1 billion people, about 15 percent of the world's population, lack official recognition (World Bank 2017a).[1] The largest concentrations of unregistered people are in South Asia and sub-Saharan Africa, and in lower middle-income countries, although, at 36 percent, the share of the unregistered population is highest in poor countries (figures 2-1 and 2-2). Gender differences are modest overall, but they can be greater at the country level.

These estimates draw on several types of identification. For those under the age of 15, they are based on the number of children who have not been registered at birth, generally by the age of 5. For 162 out of the 198 countries included in the analysis, the registration rates for adults are based on voter registration data, which often are more readily available than the coverage data for national identification systems. In many low-income countries, voter registration rates are also higher than those of national IDs; therefore, depending on the type of identification considered, the estimates of the registered population may be on the higher side, at least for poor countries. These are imperfect measures of official recognition, and the 1.1 billion estimate should only be viewed as a rough

1 This figure is still evolving, but reflects the ID4D database in June 2017. The estimate excludes 11 countries without a national ID but with comprehensive civil registration systems.

FIGURE 2-1   The Identification Gap by Region

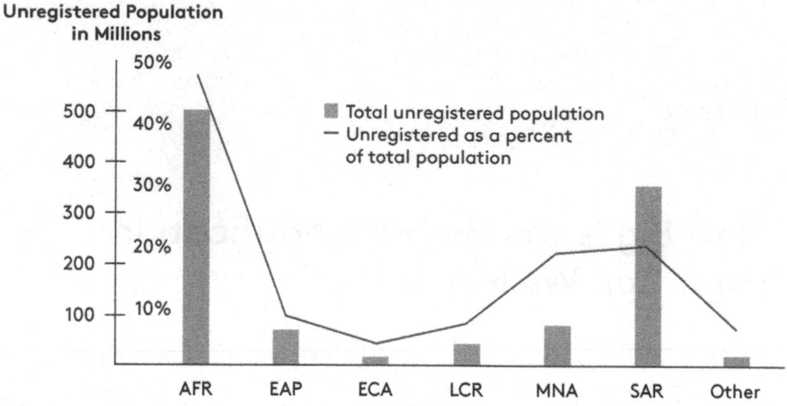

AFR = Sub-Saharan Africa I EAP = East Asia and Pacific I ECA = Europe and Central Asia I LCR = Latin America and the Caribbean I MNA = Middle East and North Africa I SAR = South Asia

Source: World Bank ID4D dataset, June 2017 edition.

quantitative assessment of the global identity gap. It does offer some indication of the scaling-up needed to provide all with core identification credentials, but the size and nature of the "identification gap" is not a simple question.

The challenge of measuring the global identification gap in the sustainable development context begins with defining "legal identity"—the term used in Sustainable Development Goal target 16.9. As mentioned earlier, the SDGs do not provide a clear definition of "legal identity," nor do they provide guidance through a quantitative indicator other than for under-5 birth registration. This limited framework does not stem from a lack of discussion or efforts to develop further measures, but rather because there is no simple answer to the measurement question.

Another complicating factor is the diversity of identification systems and credentials. In addition to birth certificates, national ID cards, and voter cards, people hold a bewildering range of credentials—ration, pension, health, or medical insurance cards; passports; and other IDs that satisfy particular purposes. On the surface, it may seem like a good thing to have so many options, but these alternatives can depress the demand for a national ID credential and hamper the development of an effective nationwide identity management system capable of ensuring that identities are unique. The quality of the systems underlying these varied credentials is often low; their data may be incon-

FIGURE 2-2   The Identification Gap by Income Level

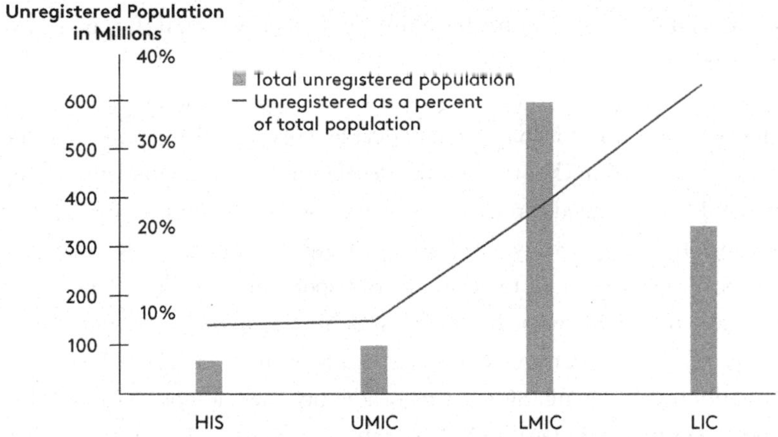

**Unregistered Population
in Millions**

Source: World Bank ID4D dataset, June 2017 edition.

sistent, and they may fail to ensure unique identity either within individual registers (because they fail to deduplicate enrollments) or across them (because people are not consistently identified by the different systems). In these cases, the challenge of identity management may be less about including those with no identification and more about improving the coherence and effectiveness of overall identity management.

A further complication is that the same credential—a birth certificate, voter card, or passport—may not open the same opportunities to its holder in different countries. In that sense, it will not provide a uniform level of legal identity. Passports, for example, are not identical in quality even if they conform to a common technical specification. Fortunate holders of Swiss or German passports enjoy visa-free travel to almost all countries. Less fortunate holders of Afghan or Somali passports do not, and in addition are subjected to heightened scrutiny when crossing borders. Credentials can be revalued and devalued depending on perceptions of their quality, which is closely linked to the (perceived) trustworthiness of the issuing entity.[2]

2   For example, in 2009 the United Kingdom introduced visa requirements for South African passport holders, following concern over the integrity of the passports being issued by the South African Department of Home Affairs (Harper 2012).

A third question is whether the SDG concept of legal identity should include recognition as a national of some country. Do people who are stateless, or
whose national status is in limbo, have full legal identity even if they may have
documents?

These difficult questions complicate the numerical estimation of the identification gap, but in fact it may not be possible to express the gap in quantitative terms. As argued in chapter 3, in the development context an identification
system should be evaluated through its contribution to outcomes. To what extent
does having an official identity enable an individual to transact easily, to access a
wide range of public services, to benefit from opportunities in the private sector,
and to travel freely? To what extent does identity management strengthen a
state's capacity to deliver on the SDGs? Is identity management actually useful?
Such metrics involve qualitative aspects of identity that cannot be captured in
any single quantitative indicator. A thorough assessment of the quality of identity would need to consider a broad set of features, including how easy it is to
acquire and use it, how widely it is accepted, whether it is robust against errors
and fraud, and how strong its data and privacy protection protocols are.

Bearing in mind these difficulties, this chapter examines how to define
"legal identity" from the perspective of the SDGs, with a special emphasis on
the nationality question. To better understand the various aspects of the identification gap, it presents summarized estimates of children and adults whose
births have not been registered; looks at national identification programs and
the problems in assessing their coverage, especially in countries with weak
death registration; examines the coverage of voter rolls; and considers other
"functional" forms of ID. The data gaps are large, and all of these estimates
are subject to considerable error, but they offer at least an initial perspective on
some coverage indicators.

How to Interpret "Legal Identity" in the
Context of Sustainable Development

Legal identity has been defined in various ways. The most succinct definition,
perhaps, comes from Hannah Arendt (1951), to the effect that that legal identity is "the right to have rights." In Arendt's view, being a recognized member
of a community (or, in the modern world, a state) is fundamental to the practical realization of human rights, even if these rights are considered in principle
to apply universally to all humanity. Looking at "identity" in a holistic way, as

a concept embodying the wide range of attributes that together define a unique person—appearance, behavior, family relationships, friends, and experiences, as well as a number of associated entitlements and rights—it is evident that having legal identity in Arendt's sense of "the right to have rights" can be taken as a shorthand for having a particular bundle of rights, with a heavy emphasis on those associated with recognized nationality or citizenship.

To date, this bundle of rights has not been a major focus for development in general, or for policy discussions between development agencies and their sovereign clients. Development policy discussions seldom, if ever, focus on the legal rules governing citizenship and the practical implementation of these rules. At the same time, exclusion related to (the lack of) national status can affect the living conditions of groups and communities in many countries and limit the opportunities available to large numbers of people.[3]

Among the multilateral development banks, the Inter-American Development Bank has been most active in having an integrated program to support civil registration and identification. One of the bank's most influential publications defined legal identity as "[l]egal civil status obtained through birth registration and civil identification that recognizes the individual as a subject of law and protection of the state" (Harbitz and Molina 2010). This definition is helpful, but limited in the sense that it does not directly refer to the developmental dimensions of identification. The Asian Development Bank has presented the relationship between identification and development in a more flexible and operational way:

> Broadly speaking, "legal identity" refers to a human being's legal (as opposed to physical) personality. Legal identity allows persons to enjoy the legal system's protection and to enforce their rights or demand redress for violations by accessing state institutions such as courts and law enforcement agencies. Proof of legal identity consists of official, government-issued and recognized identity documents—documents that include basic information attesting to the holder's identity and age, status, and/or legal relationships. . . .
>
> Generally, birth certificates, administered through a civil registra-

---

3   See, for example, Crunden (2016) as a comment on the muted U.S. policy response to Myanmar's treatment of the Rohingya people. Another example, out of the many documented by Manby (2016), is the situation of the Nubian community in Kenya, which for many years has been a focus for human rights activists but has not been elevated into a major issue in development dialogue.

tion system, are favored as the preferred standard in establishing legal identity. This is primarily because birth certificates have the advantage of documenting age, place of birth, and familial relationships from the very beginning of life. However, the study shows that in a number of instances, other identity documents, such as citizenship certificates or family and lodging books, proved to be more important than birth certificates in so far as access to benefits and opportunities are concerned. (Vandenabeele and Lao 2007, p. vii).

This definition places greater emphasis on the different functions that identity management can play in everyday life and the reality that not all of the multiple attributes or layers of identity are needed for every purpose. Some development programs may need to know only whether a person is entitled to perform a particular transaction or receive a service. It may not even be necessary to provide a name. A health center that needs to track a patient through a series of treatments for HIV/AIDS or tuberculosis or an infant through a series of immunizations will only need to know—perhaps through an iris scan—that the individual at hand is the person identified in the facility database as having already had two, three, or four treatments and is therefore prepared for the next one. For other purposes, evidence of name and address may be required but proof of nationality or even legal residence status may not be considered relevant. In the United States, for example, an undocumented migrant can open a bank account by providing a Tax Identification Number, which can be obtained from the Internal Revenue Service without requiring evidence of legal status. Access to food stamp benefits, by contrast, does require proof of legal permanent residency or citizenship.

The type of credential required to enroll in social protection programs differs across developing countries and programs. In Kenya, inclusion in the unified beneficiary register for the integrated National Safety Net Program, which provides cash transfers to poor and at-risk populations, requires a national ID number, even though the program issues its own card to enable beneficiaries to be identified using two-factor authentication (card and fingerprint). In addition, all payments are disbursed through bank or mobile money accounts, and these also require holders to be registered for Know-Your-Customer purposes using the national ID card and number. The large social protection programs in Tanzania (Tanzania Social Action Fund, or TASAF) and Ethiopia (Productive Safety Net Programme, or PSNP) follow a different process: they issue their own ID credentials without requiring other official identification. Documentation is simple—cards with pictures—and the programs rely on local community-based processes to guard against multiple enrollments by the same individual. In India, Aadhaar can be used to identify program beneficiaries without requiring additional nationality or legal residence tests, although program beneficiaries may need to prove that they are state or district residents. This is the case, for example, to acquire a family Bamashah card in Rajasthan, which has unified the administration of most benefit programs into a single system.

Shifting from multiple functional program-specific identification systems toward the use of a single nationwide foundational system has many advantages. However, one of the risks is that poor people could be excluded from programs and benefits if a nationality or legal residence test is required for enrollment in the nationwide system. This has been a concern in some cases and will continue to be so as national ID systems continue to supplant program-specific systems.[4]

These examples suggest that from the perspective of development, "legal identity" need not necessarily revolve around a single all-purpose identification credential or system. For this reason, in looking across a large number of programs Gelb and Clark (2013a) introduced the term "official identity" defined to include the various forms of identification that individuals can use to interact with formal institutions, such as government agencies and programs, formal employers, or banks, or to access benefits and take advantage of opportunities, a definition more in line with the approach of Vandenabeele and Lao (2007). In the last resort, "adequate" identification is identification that is needed and accepted for a particular purpose by the responsible entity. Viewing identity as a set of attributes or layers is more relevant than ever for development, since digital technology is making it easier to segment identity attributes in ways that were not previously practical.

---

4   Kenya's National Safety Net Programme (NSNP) aims to ensure that the design and implementation of transfer programs are coordinated and that delivery is cost-effective. The multiple programs covered by the NSNP include about 500,000 recipients, and it is planned to scale this up to 1 million. Although the coverage of the national ID system is estimated at between 80 percent and 90 percent, it is lower in border areas. Beneficiary registrations conducted by the Hunger Safety Net Programme in four poor northern Kenyan counties found that around 20 percent of target households did not have one or more adults with an ID card (World Bank 2016a).

The Question of Citizenship

This foundation still presents the difficult question of to what extent the dimension of national status, or citizenship, is relevant for a definition of legal identity from the perspective of sustainable development. Should the development community insist on nationality as an element of legal identity, or count people who are "identified" as having full legal identity even though their credentials might not provide proof of citizenship—or even of legal residence—in any country?

From the examples above and the many cases to follow, legal or official identity, seen in the broader sense of facilitating inclusion and improving the implementation of development policies and programs, need not be related to national status. Indeed, for many purposes it would not be desirable to distinguish between residents of a country based on their ability to prove that they are citizens. This would create immense difficulties, and would discriminate against many long-time residents who either lack the documentary proof needed to prove their citizenship or cannot readily satisfy complex citizenship laws and processes (chapter 5).

Delinking indentification from national status has many advantages. However, as Gelb and Manby (2016) argue, the dimension of citizenship cannot be ignored in the development context, especially in the light of the inclusive framing of the SDGs that aim to "leave no one behind." This framing represents a vast elevation of the level of development ambition and also a major shift toward the perspective of human rights. In contrast to the earlier Millennium Development Goals, which emphasized targets for progress, the SDGs are universal in multiple areas in the sense of aspiring to extend the benefits of development progress to *all*, without exceptions. Though the SDGs and their targets are expressed not as rights or entitlements but as aspirations, there is a fine line between asserting something as a right and setting out as an objective that everyone should have it.

This framing of the SDGs also brings in the citizenship dimension because the formalization of legal identity, through the adoption of more rigorous identification systems and processes, risks leaving members of marginalized communities and those with insufficient prior documentation effectively stateless. As discussed in chapter 5, where exclusion associated with statelessness is addressed as one of the risks of stronger identity management, this has already occurred as deliberate policy in at least three cases: the Dominican Republic, Mauritania, and the Gulf States. In other countries that are rolling out national ID systems,

**BOX 2-1   What Individual and Socioeconomic
Factors Matter for Birth Registration?**

In countries with incomplete birth registration, lack of registration tends to be more prevalent among some groups and some households than others. As the UNICEF data also show, children born in the poorest 20 percent of households are less likely to have their births registered. Two recent studies, one from South Africa (Garenne and others 2016) and one from Indonesia (Duff, Kusumaningrum, and Stark 2016), shed further light on the individual and household factors that influence birth registration.

The South African study examines trends in a rural community not far from the Mozambican border with 110,000 inhabitants. The rise in birth registration is remarkable: it grew from only 6 percent in 1993 to over 89 percent in 2014. Yet there are significant and persistent gaps based on individual and household characteristics. The mother's age plays a role: young mothers under age 17 are considerably less likely to register a birth than their middle-aged (22–36) counterparts. Being a (Mozambican) refugee is also associated with lower probability of registering a birth. The household head's education matters, too: those with a high school diploma were found to be 43 percent more likely to register the birth of a child in a timely manner than those with a primary or lower level of education. The South African study also found evidence for wealth-based divergence in birth registration: children living in the richest 20 percent of households were over 80 percent more likely to be registered than those living in the poorest 20 percent.

The Indonesian study, which surveyed 1,024 heads of households in three of Indonesia's most impoverished jurisdictions, echoed these findings on the "wealth gap." Those in the two richest quartiles of the population were 80 percent more likely to have a birth certificate than those in the poorest quartile (bottom 25 percent). Interestingly, neither study found any difference in birth registration rates based on the sex of the child.

to access sometimes distant registration offices—possibly at least twice, once to report the birth and another to pick up a certificate, assuming that the certificate is available and that more visits will not be needed. Fees can be another deterrent. Initial registration is free in many countries within a statutory period, but some authorities charge for a certificate. Late registration often incurs additional charges and penalties. These are intended to encourage prompt registration as well as generate some revenue, but they can deter later registrations that might otherwise have taken place. In Cameroon, registering a birth after six months requires the petitioner to appear before a court, and costs range from US$20 to $2,000 due to fees and bribes; in the Democratic Republic of Congo, the penalty for late registration can be as high as US$1,000 (World Bank 2017b).

Mobile technology is starting to be used to reduce the logistical barriers to registration, or at least to reporting births as they take place. The MOVE-IT program in Kenya seeks to report real-time birth data by district and display comparative results on a dashboard to encourage local officials to take a more active role in registration. Combining technology and stronger collaboration with health ministries could boost registration since most infants will have been visited by health workers. Vaccination rates are higher than birth registration rates in many countries. According to the World Health Organization (WHO; 2016), about 86 percent (116 million) of infants worldwide received three doses of diphtheria-tetanus-pertussis (DTP3) vaccine in 2015 and coverage in 126 countries reached at least 90 percent. Incentive payments to health workers combined with some level of devolved responsibility for registration could ease the constraints on access to birth registration and strengthen the supply side.

However, low registration rates can also reflect weakness on the demand side. Especially for poor, rural populations, there may be a view that birth registration brings little or no short-term, tangible benefits to the parents or the child. This is more likely to be the case in low-income countries where few services are provided or in countries where other, competing forms of identification, such as family books or school IDs, are widespread. Demand can be incentivized by making registration easier and requiring a birth certificate to access benefits. South Africa expanded under-5 registrations from 21 percent to 84 percent between 1992 and 2012, partly because the receipt of a generous child grant was linked to possession of a birth certificate (Statistics South Africa 2015). However, the process of linking benefits to registration needs to be managed carefully to avoid registration from becoming another hurdle. This can happen even if there are provisions for exceptions for poor families, if these provisions are not communicated clearly to social workers, local officials, and the families concerned.

Low registration can also reflect socially or culturally insensitive legal requirements for fully documenting a birth that depress demand. In Indonesia, birth certificates could only recognize an infant's paternity if the parents were in a legally registered marriage (Sumner 2015). Unmarried mothers, and the large numbers of couples who had had religious marriages but had not civilly registered them, were reluctant to stigmatize their children as not having a recognized father and so chose not to register the birth. A multivariate analysis found that children of parents with a marriage certificate were 90 percent more likely to have a birth certificate than those without. This was a similar difference in the probability of registration as that between the richest two quartiles and the poorest quartile of the population (Duff, Kusumaningrum, and Stark 2016).

In such cases, legal reforms can help to reduce impediments to registration. In a notably progressive ruling, the Constitutional Court of Indonesia has determined that evidence of a legal marriage is not needed to establish paternity, and that refusal to recognize the wide range of potential available evidence (including voluntary acknowledgment of paternity as well as scientific evidence) violates constitutional provisions against discrimination, in this case against innocent children (Sumner 2015). Though the implementation of the court's recommendations remains incomplete, the paternity recognition requirement has been relaxed to some extent.

Birth Registration as Legal Identity

Although birth registration may constitute the initial building block for legal identity, it may not always be sufficient to provide a strong and easily verifiable identity in later life. Registries are in poor condition in many countries. Many are yet to be digitized—a task that can involve scanning entries in hundreds or thousands of volumes and transcribing the information into a database. The cost can be high, especially if the information is decentralized and held in many local registries.[6] It can be difficult to locate an entry without knowing the associated birth number; this can prompt duplicate registrations as people find it

---

6   For Morocco, it is estimated to cost US$0.90 to digitize each existing entry, in addition to the costs of shifting new entries from paper-based to digital format (J. Atick, presentation to Connect:ID, Washington DC, September 2015).

easier to create a new entry than to locate the original one. Identification is also weakened when conflict or natural disasters destroy birth records—as is the case in Cambodia, Peru, and other countries. The lack of a register for verification undermines the value of any paper-based credentials that may have been issued. In addition, birth on national territory does not automatically confer nationality, except in a limited number of countries.

Being registered at birth may facilitate access to services or transactions later in life, but does not guarantee them. For example, there is only a 4 percentage point difference in birth registration between male and female children in Nepal, but a 13 percentage point difference between men (87 percent) and women (74 percent) in possession of a citizenship certificate. This latter credential is needed to receive social welfare payments, to register land and property ownership, or to open a bank account (FLWD 2014). The gender gap in official identification and in users' ability to access services and exercise their rights based on the same ID credential may be greater than appears on the basis of birth registration.

Conversely, the absence of a birth certificate also does not necessarily mean that a child is not officially known to exist. In Indonesia and a number of other Asian countries, children may not be registered at birth but may be recorded in family books that list the name, address, and date and place of birth for the head of the household and all family members. This includes much the same data as would be shown on a birth certificate. In Indonesia, the information is entered in the SIAK (Sistem Informasi Administrasi Kependudukan; Population Administration Information System) database that forms the basis for the national digital ID card, the e-KTP. However, these are considered administrative data and do not confer full legal identity. A birth certificate, or a passport that requires one, is the only legally recognized evidence of citizenship. It is needed to attend school (although this requirement is not always enforced), to be eligible for government employment, and for other purposes (Gelb 2015; Sumner 2015). Children who do not have a birth certificate remain vulnerable to the discretion of local officials; when faced with space or other constraints on enrollment, those that have not been registered are more likely to be excluded.

Achieving the SDG target of universal under-5 birth registration would be a huge achievement, but it would not be sufficient to close the identification gap. It would not address the problem of children and adults who are alive today without a recognized official identity. Neither would it provide full legal identity, including a recognized citizenship, for the millions of people currently unable to fulfill citizenship requirements in the country of their birth or in any other country, given that only 30 out of 194 countries grant citizenship automatically based on birth on national territory.

National Identification and Similar Programs

As shown in chapter 1, the number of national identification and similar programs has grown exponentially during the past two decades, to the point where almost all developing countries have at least one such program under implementation. A few cases are difficult to classify. India's Aadhaar is a nationwide foundational identification program but not a traditional national ID program, since enrollment does not relate to or confer national status or even legal residence. Ethiopia's kebele ID program is another conundrum. This highly decentralized program provides identification services similar to those offered by a national ID program and has high adult coverage across the entire country. However, it is locally administered and relies on simple paper-based cards, and the quality of recordkeeping varies considerably across kebeles. These features, as well as the possibility that individuals could register in more than one locality, limit the kebele ID program's robustness and usefulness for mobile populations.

Among the many low-income countries that have begun to roll out a national identification program in the past decade and a half, progress has been varied. At least 15 programs are at an early stage of implementation; several others languish at low levels of coverage. A review undertaken at Washington University (Anderson and others 2015) covered 36 national ID programs and 12 other initiatives in 43 developing countries, drawing on information from a variety of reports and sources. Of the 48 programs examined, 3 were still in the planning phase and 3 were currently enrolling but not yet operational. The data collected indicate that 35 programs were in use, with 10 programs still actively increasing enrollments. Three of the national ID programs were deemed to have stalled due to political instability, technical challenges, or disputes.

Turning to coverage, the number and vintage of programs provide little guide to how many people are enrolled. Although a number of lower-income countries like Kenya have had national identification programs for decades (in that case, as far back as 1920 for African males over the age of 15) and others like Tanzania, Nigeria, and Ghana have made slow progress in rolling out their programs, some countries have moved astonishingly quickly to register and identify their population. In Rwanda, as discussed by Atick (2016) and in chapter 4, more than 9 million people were registered over a long weekend, although processing the data and issuing cards of course took longer.

It is difficult to determine live coverage for programs outside of a short period of mass registration, particularly in countries where only a fraction of deaths is registered. Even where good-quality data are available on the number of cards issued, in the absence of accurate death records one can only arrive at rough estimates regarding the live identification gap. In Kenya, for example, ID cards are mandatory and are issued to citizens, resident aliens, and refugees above the age of 18. Kenya registers 1.2 million new adults each year and has issued some 24 million ID cards to date. This is close to the country's estimated adult population, but the number of active holders cannot be easily determined. Only 46 percent of deaths are registered, so that some IDs issued in previous years may not have been deactivated. Survey data reported in table 2-3 suggest that live coverage of the national ID card is about 81 percent, but some of those surveyed might not have satisfied Kenya's stringent citizenship laws or have been declared a legal resident or a refugee, and so they might not have been covered by the ID because they were not entitled to a card. An estimate based on the number of deaths since the last mass registration in 1995 and the percentage of these that might have held ID cards but not had them deactivated comes out a little higher, at 88 percent (World Bank 2016a).

Estimating live ID program coverage is not only a challenge in Kenya. Death registration data are incomplete for many low-income countries. The most recent figures cited may go back two decades and be reported within a wide and not very meaningful range, such as "under 90 percent." The UN provides point estimates for death registration in only 11 low-income countries and 33 lower-middle-income countries (UNSD 2014), and the median death registration rate among these low-income economies is only 14 percent, ranging from 2 percent in Niger to 51 percent in Rwanda. The median death registration rate for lower-middle-income states is a more encouraging 68 percent, ranging from 5 percent in Sudan to close to complete coverage (over 95 percent) in post-Soviet states such as Armenia, Kyrgyzstan, and Ukraine. Registration rates also vary greatly between sources and years: India's death registration is reported at 48 percent by the UN as of 1994—the most recent report from that source—but at only 8 percent by the WHO in 2012. Still other sources indicate that India's death registration rate was as high as 71 percent in 2013 (Debroy 2016).

Again, the reasons for low rates of death registration include both supply-side factors such as distance and inconvenience, and lack of demand. For South

Africa, Garenne and others (2016) note that the relatively high rate of death registration is because death certificates are required for burials in cemeteries and to access pensions for widows or widowers, part of the country's extensive system of social grants. These data gaps will make it difficult for national identification authorities and statistical bodies to estimate live national ID coverage without the use of sample surveys for many years in the future.

Surveys can provide a picture of the country's identification landscape and the number of residents with a recognized proof of identity. Not many detailed surveys of the possession of ID documents are available, but Intermedia's Financial Inclusion Insights Program has surveyed the ownership of ID credentials for eight developing countries. At the dates of their surveys (generally 2014/2015), the percentage holding a national ID card ranged from 2 percent in Bangladesh and Uganda to 94 percent in Indonesia (table 2-3).[7] The surveys showed that most respondents held some other identification even when they did not hold a national ID, and that in five out of the eight countries the voter card was the most widely held credential. The reported differences in ID card ownership by gender were very small in Bangladesh, India, Indonesia and Kenya, within one or 2 percentage points, while the other four countries showed larger disparities. Uganda had the largest gender gap in identification, a 10 percentage point difference between men (72 percent) and women (62 percent). These numbers would look different today, particularly after Uganda's rollout of its national ID program; its National Identification and Registration Authority (NIRA) claims to have issued over 16 million ID cards (*The Observer* 2016).

Data on live coverage are helpful to be able to confirm whether an identification program is inclusive, but depending on how people are authenticated, this information may not be essential for the system to be used to improve the effectiveness of service delivery. In cases like India's Aadhaar, where identification relies on biometric authentication at the point of service rather than on cards, the identity numbers of deceased participants can simply be placed on inactive status and retired after the identity fails to be authenticated over a long period. They never need to be formally extinguished and will never be reissued.

---

7   The authors are grateful to Leora Klapper for access to the Intermedia data.

TABLE 2-3 Identification Survey Results in
Eight Countries: ID Ownership

Country	% of respondents who have some form of ID[a]	% of respondents who have the national ID	Most frequently held ID
Bangladesh	93	2	voter card
India	98	68	voter card
Indonesia	100	94	national ID
Pakistan	92	87	national ID
Kenya	94	81	national ID
Nigeria	89	36	voter card
Tanzania	68	4	voter card
Uganda	67	2	voter card

Source: Intermedia Financial Inclusion Insights Program.

a. Including national ID (government-issued ID), passport, driver's license, school-issued ID, voter card, ration card, employee ID, military ID, and birth certificate.

Voter Cards and Other Functional Forms of Official Identification

Although biometrics have a checkered record in ensuring free and fair elections, electoral competition can be a great spur to registration, as it galvanizes political parties and movements to sign up as many potential voters as they can. Nigeria offers one of many examples, with some 70 percent voter registration for its 2015 elections—a notable contrast with several different identification initiatives that have failed to enroll many Nigerians. Propelled by competition and often with only light due diligence to verify identities at the point of enrollment, voter registration has often been far faster, as well as more complete, than registration for the national ID. In 2015 Tanzania registered some 23 million voters—virtually the entire adult population—in four months. In contrast, the national ID project managed to issue only 2.5 million cards over a four-year period.

Reported voter registration rates are surprisingly high (figure 2-3). In poor countries, reported voter registration is often far higher than the rate of birth registration—the opposite of the pattern in high-income countries, where almost all births are registered but not all potential voters. In low-income coun-tries, registration estimates varied from around 50 percent of the voting-age population in Burkina Faso to close to full coverage (above 90 percent) in the Democratic Republic of Congo, Sierra Leone, and Tanzania (IDEA 2015). In fact, 20 low-income countries reported voter registration rates above 90 percent, with registration rates in 6 countries, including Afghanistan, Nepal, and Zim-babwe, above 100 percent. Very high coverage is not unique to poorer coun-tries—8 high-income countries, including Chile, Finland, and Greece, also had more than complete voter registration.

To what extent can we trust these figures? One reason why voter registra-tion estimates can show coverage greater than 100 percent is that the estimates of a country's voting-age population may rely on baseline census data collected a decade or even longer ago. These can underestimate the size of the voting-age population to which voter registration numbers are compared. The accuracy of the population data in censuses is sometimes debated as officials may seek to manipulate numbers to increase the political influence of a given region or city (Africa Check 2014). Voter registration rates beyond 100 percent can also reflect the existence of large national diaspora abroad, increasing the number of registered voters relative to the estimated size of the voting-age population within the country's borders.

Although these possibilities offer some "legitimate" reasons for high re-ported voter registration rates, the quality of the voter roll is of course also an important factor. When Pakistan cleaned its voter roll for the 2013 elec-tion, authorities found that 45 percent of the existing roll consisted of "zombie" voters—deceased voters, duplicate voters, or voters with no valid ID (Malik 2014). In this case, the number of people deleted from the roll during the clean-ing process was offset by the number of new voters registered, so that the overall size of the roll changed little, but this gives some idea of the possible magnitude of inaccuracies. Because of the large numbers enrolled relative to the popula-tion, Ghana's 2012 voter roll was suspected of being heavily padded with false entries. Some voter registration exercises, even where supported by biometric technology, may not have fully deduplicated the roll as they have claimed to do.[8] The true coverage of some of the voter programs could therefore be lower

---

8 Full deduplication of a voter roll poses a formidable logistical challenge, especially in countries with dispersed populations and limited connectivity. In such situations, some voter registration exercises have limited themselves to local deduplication (Gelb and Clark 2013a). Rader (2016) provides the example of Somaliland's 2008 voter registration, where failure to deduplicate fingerprints led to people registering several times.

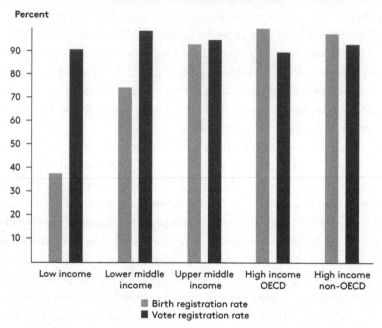

FIGURE 2-3   Birth and Voter Registration
Rates in Selected Countries

Source: IDEA (2015); UNICEF (2014).

than indicated by the data. Nevertheless, given the low coverage of many national identification programs and lagging civil registration in a large number of developing countries, voter cards continue to be the most widely held and most readily accessible proof of identity in many states.

Do voter cards provide legal identity? Because they are often the most widely held identification in low-income countries, and also some middle-income countries such as Mexico, service providers may accept them for validation purposes, especially when few better alternatives are available. The situation, however, differs across countries. Logically, voter cards should also provide recognized proof of citizenship, but often this is not the case because they are issued without requiring enrollees to provide birth certificates or comply with the demanding standards mandated by complex nationality laws and processes (see box 2-2 on Togo). Special provisions may be enacted to ensure that those who lack official identification are not disenfranchised. Electoral officials often accept witness testimonies about an individual's identity and eligibility to vote from village leaders or relatives (Carter Center 2012). In Liberia, where less than 5 percent of the population had been registered at birth, the sworn testimony of two other registered voters or a confirmation by a traditional leader was accepted as proof of identity for registering to vote. In Indonesia, although the widely held e-KTP or electronic ID card is accepted as a credential for voting, as noted earlier the Constitutional Court has ruled that only a birth certificate or passport provides evidence of status as a citizen.

In other cases, voter registration may be a key part of the process of nation-building, including the determination of nationality. Rader (2016) describes the rigorous (and even discriminatory) verification processes applied in Somaliland's 2016 voter registration drive. In the absence of alternative identifying information, registrants had to prove their eligibility through tests of accent,

BOX 2-2   The Complexity of Nationality in Togo

A review of Togo's electoral roll ahead of its 2015 elections revealed that the identity of over 75 percent of its 3.5 million registered voters had been verified exclusively through testimonies of village chiefs without any "official" (state-issued) proof of identity or nationality (CENI 2015). Although voter registration represents de facto recognition of Togolese nationality, those who seek to hold a Togolese national ID card in addition to their voter ID first need to obtain an official certificate of nationality. This, in turn, is conditional on the applicant holding a birth certificate or being able to present the birth certificate of a close relative (La Cour d'Appel de Lomé 2015)—a condition that many Togolese cannot fulfill. UNICEF estimates that about 22 percent of births of children under the age of 5 have not been registered, while the share of adults without a birth certificate is considerably higher. Deficient birth registration coupled with the combined cost of $16.50 for the certificate of nationality and the ID card prevents most Togolese from obtaining these credentials, as the country's median daily income in 2011 was $1.25. In contrast, voter cards are free and cover almost all of Togo's adult population.

appearance, and knowledge of genealogy, to show that they were members of one of Somaliland's original clans. Applicants with unconventional ancestry or those who were not able to produce members of their families to vouch for them faced higher burdens of proof. Rader notes that the functions of the voter cards go well beyond that of electoral identification. They are taken as authentication tokens for Somaliland nationality and a building block for the (not internationally recognized) Somaliland state itself.

Toward Bridging the Identification Gap

Where does this leave us as far as SDG target 16.9? Even though the exact size of the identification gap may not be clear, the available data provide at least an order of magnitude for a quantitative estimate that can be refined over time. They also indicate the populations and groups that are most likely to lack legal identity. Poor, rural populations are most at risk, and sometimes women, but other vulnerable groups including religious or ethnic minorities or refugees are also susceptible to exclusion. As will be discussed in more detail in chapter 5, in order to fully close the legal identity gap and ensure that no one is left behind, it will be particularly important to address the identification needs of groups and individuals with uncertain national status.

Moving toward universal birth registration, the indicator for SDG target 16.9, will be a major step in the right direction but is not sufficient to close the identification gap. Additional steps are needed to include children over the age of 5 and adults who have not been registered. As shown by successful voter registration drives, as well as by the remarkable rollout of the Aadhaar program, mass registration can be completed rapidly and inclusively if there is political will and incentive to do so, and provided that the enrollment process does not require documentation or other evidence that is difficult or time-consuming to provide.

Mass registration, on its own, does not create a sustainable system. There is still the challenge of ensuring that data remain current through continuous registration and updating. Peru's case, discussed in chapter 6, offers an example of how a lagging civil registration system can be invigorated and linked to the population register underlying the national identification system, while the case of Pakistan shows how continuous use of the ID for a wide range of programs can help ensure that information is updated (chapter 4). But from the development perspective, closing the quantitative identification gap is only a start. It is equally important to focus on the use of the system.

THREE

Identification as an Enabler of Sustainable Development

In addition to being its own Sustainable Development Goal target, the provision of legal identity to all is also instrumental to achieving many other sustainable development aspirations. Indeed, meaningful progress toward identification as a development target cannot be measured solely based on the number of persons registered or ID credentials issued. It needs to include how the identity management system contributes to individual well-being and overall development progress—namely, what it enables individuals and societies to accomplish. Does more inclusive and reliable identification help people to assert their rights and access the programs and services to which they are entitled? Will it strengthen state capacity by enabling more effective and accountable public administration that is able to deliver a wide range of services and programs more effectively? Can it help create opportunities by reducing transaction costs, including for the private sector, and so stimulate inclusion, innovation, and growth?

The SDGs set out 17 goals and 169 associated targets to provide the development community with a comprehensive agenda for the next 15 years. Robust identification is important in order to achieve several of these goals and targets. Dahan and Gelb (2015) found that it was an enabler—if not a prerequisite—for progress toward at least 10 targets, in addition to the legal identity target in 16.9 itself. Extending this analysis, this chapter identifies where the successful achievement of a development goal appears to be most closely related to effective identity management (figure 3-1). Identification can be a vehicle for more inclusive and more effective development policies and programs through its role as an "enabler" for at least 8 of the SDGs and 19 associated targets. Robust identification systems can not only support the exercise of individual rights and access to development-relevant programs and services but also promote labor market opportunities and strengthen state capacity and the effectiveness and accountability of public institutions.

This assessment is not intended as a bean-counting exercise, or as advocacy to promote investments in identification systems. More important is the point, stressed in chapter 1, that large expenditures on ID systems will be wasted unless the systems are used for economically or socially productive purposes. If they are not applied to high-priority areas and recognized to be useful, it is also unlikely that they will be maintained and sustained. The SDGs and targets therefore provide a helpful checklist to assess proposals for investments in these systems. If there is not a clear plan to build on their capabilities to improve performance in at least some of the SDG priority areas, the proposed systems are unlikely to be good investments. The demand side for identity management services is as important as the supply side.

For any particular SDG target, the importance of a proof of unique identity varies. For some targets, like being able to access financial services and secure land rights (target 1.4), such forms of official identification are essential. (These cases are marked with a star in figure 3-1 for easier orientation.) In other cases, such as combating AIDS, tuberculosis (TB), and other communicable diseases (target 3.3), unique, robust identification will be helpful but not a prerequisite for success. To achieve the SDGs, it also may not be necessary to make use of the most high-tech authentication solutions an identification system can offer. For social transfers, a deduplicated beneficiary registry can help to strengthen the administration of programs, but it may be less essential to fingerprint beneficiaries at every point of service, especially if community-based or other mechanisms can help to validate recipients.

Similarly, not all the applications described in this chapter necessarily require a single "foundational" system such as a multipurpose national ID number. For many purposes, a single system and number are essential, such as for strengthening tax administration by making it possible to integrate a wide range of data on wage, self-employment, property and investment incomes and assets, and spending patterns on an individual taxpayer basis. Many countries are attempting to rationalize excessively large numbers of often over-

FIGURE 3-1 Identification-Enabled SDGs and Targets

ACCESS TO FINANCE
- Prove ownership over property ▶ **Goal 1 and Target 1.4** ☆
- Satisfy KYC requirements for banking ▶ **Goal 1 and Target 1.4** ☆
- Unique ID for credit registries ▶ **Target 8.3 and Target 1.4** ☆
- Reduce remittance costs ▶ **Target 10c**

GENDER EQUALITY AND EMPOWERMENT
- Full participation in economic and social life ▶ **Goal 5**
- Closing the gender gap in access to finance ▶ **Target 5a**

ACCESS TO BASIC SERVICES
- Registration and school exams ▶ **Goal 4**
- Higher childhood vaccination rates ▶ **Goal 3 and Target 3.3**
- Unique ID for health insurance ▶ **Target 3.8** ☆
- Biometric tracking of TB and HIV/AIDS treatment ▶ **Target 3.3**
- Civil registration health data: reduce infant and child deaths ▶ **Target 3.2**

CHILD PROTECTION
- Proof of age: help eliminate child labor ▶ **Target 8.7**
- Proof of age: help end child marriage ▶ **Target 5.3**

LABOR MARKET OPPORTUNITIES
- Reduce transaction costs in hiring ▶ **Goal 8 and Target 8.5**
- Facilitate orderly and safe migration ▶ **Goal 10 and Target 10.7** ☆

SOCIAL PROTECTION: GRANTS AND SUBSIDIES
- Improve targeting, timeliness, cost-effectiveness of payments ▶ **Goal 1 and Target 1.3**
- Unique ID to improve transparency and reduce leakages ▶ **Target 1.3** ☆
- Facilitate fast and efficient delivery of emergency aid ▶ **Target 1.5**
- Energy subsidy reform: price subsidies to cash payments ▶ **Target 12c** ☆

MANAGING PUBLIC PAYROLLS ☆
- Remove ghost workers and generate public savings ▶ **Goal 16 and Target 16.5**

TAX COLLECTION
- Common identifier can bolster tax collection ▶ **Target 17.1** ☆

CLEAN ELECTIONS
- Unique ID to clean the voter registry ▶ **Target 16.7** ☆

Source: Icons by Freepik from www.flaticon.com.

lapping transfer and subsidy programs; these efforts also benefit from at least a common "social security" identifier, but a dedicated system could be used to track patients through a course of health treatment.

Even if one single system is not essential for all purposes, the cost, inconvenience, and limitations of relying on multiple unrelated systems for various purposes—systems that often will not be sustainable without continued donor support—require careful consideration. Nevertheless, the architecture of country systems and their degree of integration, considered in chapter 4, should be recognized as a social choice.

Despite their demonstrated potential, there is no guarantee that robust identification systems will contribute to achieving the SDGs and their associated targets. Identification policies can be exclusionary as well as inclusive; features relating to design or pricing may raise barriers for members of certain vulnerable groups, like women, ethnic or religious minorities, or the poorest members of society. As multipurpose systems, ID systems can be used for purposes unrelated to the SDGs. They can create further obstacles or, once constructed, be used for very little at all. Even if a country implements a robust ID system with good intentions, elites or officials further down the decision chain may resist using it for purposes that threaten their privileges and limit their discretion. Chapter 5 considers some of these risks together with possible policies to mitigate them.

Finally, many of the examples below have not been rigorously evaluated. The number of development applications is growing, but far more monitoring and research is needed to establish the impact of robust identification—how particular approaches affect the performance of programs and the convenience and satisfaction of beneficiaries, and how the overall gains (if any) compare with the costs of creating and maintaining the identification system. This is a serious limitation on the analysis, but in many instances there is at least indicative information on the relationship between identification and the SDGs.

Access to Finance and Economic Resources

In many countries, having an official proof of identity is a basic condition for full participation in social and economic life, making it vital for SDG 1—"to end poverty in all its forms everywhere"—and target 1.4 in particular, which sets out to provide all with "equal rights to economic resources, as well as access to basic services, ownership and control over land and other forms of property, inheritance . . . and financial services."

Equal Rights to Economic Resources

Access to a range of economic resources is often contingent on having official ID credentials. Without a verifiable identity, it can be difficult to buy or sell land, a house, or other valuable property; to prove ownership of the same asset; or to assert one's right to an inheritance. Moreover, robust identification systems help ensure that those participating in a transaction are entitled to do so and underpin the creation of accurate ownership records over time. As with many other SDGs, there is also a gender element here: women, along with other vulnerable groups, tend to be at the greatest risk of not having their property rights recognized as a result of not having an official proof of identity and due to the lack of centralized and/or digital registries (Niasse 2012).

An officially recognized proof of identity is also necessary to formally register a business—as promoted by target 8.3—and to take advantage of the benefits that formalization can provide, such as access to financial services, including credit, at lower costs.

Equitable Access to Financial Services

With increasing customer due diligence requirements for bank clients in response to global efforts to tighten Know-Your-Customer regulations, all countries require an officially recognized proof of identity to open and operate a bank account, whether for payments, saving, or credit. A robust and verifiable identification system can thus significantly boost financial inclusion by reducing the transaction costs of opening accounts, particularly for poorer customers. Digital authentication via e-KYC using India's Aadhaar program is estimated to have reduced the cost of onboarding a customer from around $5 for commercial banks to only $0.07 for the new payments banks being set up to increase financial inclusion and move toward digital transfers of benefits. Some 290 million Aadhaar-linked bank accounts have been created. Total deposits in the accounts were close to $5.5 billion by the end of April 2016 and will likely multiply as a growing share of social transfers is channeled through the financial system (Srivas 2016). It remains to be seen how rapidly the holders of these "transfer accounts" will move on from cashing out their payments to access a wider range of financial services such as digital payments, now facilitated by the India Stack and Aadhaar-Enabled Payments System (see chapter 6). The progression may have been encouraged, at least temporarily, by the demonetization exercise initiated in November 2016. But even if the use of cash recovers, from a longer-term perspective, the program is a huge first step toward financial inclusion.

In countries with less-than-adequate identification systems, banks have sometimes taken on the task of identifying their customers by using custom biometric systems to support KYC due diligence and also to reduce opportunities for fraud. In 2014 the Central Bank of Nigeria launched a centralized biometric ID system, the Bank Verification Number, to provide unique identification for account holders with all banks in the country. Banks in other countries with weaknesses in national ID systems have also developed such systems on a consortium model. Fingerprint authentication for banking transactions, including by biometric-enabled ATMs, has been used by financial service providers across a diverse set of countries for many years, including Bolivia (PRODEM), Mexico (Azteca), Opportunity Bank International (various countries), and Nepal (Siddharta and Everest banks) (Gelb and Clark 2013a).

Mexico's Banco Azteca, an early adopter of biometrics in banking, has been using fingerprints to register and authenticate clients since 2001. It registered over 8 million customers biometrically in the first five years and was processing over 200,000 fingerprint matches per day as early as 2006. The bank asserts that the use of biometrics has allowed it to provide access to financial services to poor clients without reliable official identification. Biometric authentication may not be the sole method of verifying customer identity, but it can provide additional security in settings where keeping personal identification numbers or deposit books under the control of the account holder may be difficult for sociocultural reasons (see the example of Opportunity International under target 5a).

Such programs can help to facilitate financial inclusion and protect the integrity of the banking system in the absence of secure and widely held government-issued identification. However, the banking industry must incur additional costs to register customers and maintain a separate system to identify them. This will be a deterrent to enrolling small clients and may prove financially unsustainable in the long term.

Improved Access to Credit through Better Credit Histories

Without reliable customer identification, it becomes far more difficult to maintain accurate credit records and enable customers to build credit histories. This can be a major obstacle to expanding access to financial services and providing economic opportunities to large segments of the population. One study concluded that, controlling for other factors, countries with functioning credit registries scored significantly higher on measures of financial development, with registries having a greater impact in countries that were less financially developed (Inter-American Development Bank 2004).

More research is needed on the impact of improving identification on financial development, but at least one experimental study provides a detailed picture of borrower reaction. Giné, Goldberg, and Yang (2012) tested whether recording borrowers' fingerprints during the credit application process in Malawi led to changed behavior in for low-income borrowers, starting from a situation where it had been widely assumed that weak ability to identify banking clients would limit the consequences of failure to repay debts. The study found that fingerprinting had little impact on customers who were already judged to be low risk, but that higher-risk customers borrowed more judiciously and increased their efforts and their own inputs into farming to reduce the likelihood that they would default. Such a change would reduce credit risk and costs for lending institutions, opening the way to greater financial inclusion (J-PAL 2011).

Kenya has been a pioneer among African countries in integrating information on the holders of financial accounts. All bank and mobile accounts are linked to the ID number of their holder, which provides the unique identifier across the system. In line with the 2012 recommendations of the Financial Action Task Force (FATF) to apply a risk-based approach, customer due diligence requirements are tiered according to the type and size of account; for larger-value accounts, financial institutions are required to check a central database to verify the validity of the ID card presented and to take further steps to confirm the identity of their customer. Banks, microfinance, and mobile money institutions are mandated to share data on nonperforming loans, and more recently on positive credit histories, setting the stage for a comprehensive credit information system (CIS Kenya 2015). Utility providers, retail outlets, and other nonfinancial firms that offer credit can also participate on a voluntary, reciprocal basis. The introduction of the system is reported to have been associated with a decline in the share of nonperforming loans as well as a decline in the proportion of loans secured by collateral (Kwambai and Wandera 2013).

What happens to borrowers who default on their obligations and how does identification affect their options and treatment by creditors? Solli and others (2015) report on interviews with 45 microfinance institutions as well as a wide range of experts across Uganda, India, and Peru. Even though the picture differed across the institutions, it mostly reflected cross-country variations in the local credit environment, including the area of identification. At the time of the interviews, Uganda still lacked a functioning government identification system and working credit bureau. Borrowers who could not pay often took flight and even changed their names. Anticipating this, lenders would take draconian measures at the first sign of payment difficulties, swooping in to seize collateral and selling furniture and other possessions on the side of the road to prevent them from being seized by another lender who also might be owed money. Such harsh tactics encouraged borrowers to decamp at the first sign of difficulty, perpetuating the cycle. The situation in India was less dire but still harsh. Most micro-loans were communal and debt contracts were enforced through sometimes overwhelming social pressure. In Peru, the situation was found to be different. The credit bureau held accurate loan records linked to borrowers through their unique national ID numbers. Credit histories were important for the possibility of accessing further finance, so that lenders knew that few borrowers would default willfully. According to the interviews, being able to reliably identify borrowers opened the way to more humane treatment and a staged process of engagement on overdue payments, often ending up in negotiated settlements where it was clear that failure to pay was not willful.[1]

These cases suggest that accurate credit registries, as enabled by unique identification, are an important element to promoting entrepreneurship and innovation, as laid out in SDG target 8.3. At the same time, they also contribute to individual income growth and with it to the achievement of SDG 1 (to end poverty) and target 1.4 through broadening access to financial services and economic resources.

---

1   Experience in a number of countries, including South Africa and Kenya, suggests another side to this story, a downside to increasing the leverage of financial institutions over poor borrowers through a shared system of credit information. Even if borrowers are more prudent, less prudent lending practices could lead to large numbers of excluded people, including those who may owe only small amounts.

Sustained Remittance Flows at Lower Costs

At a time when high perceived risks have led to the closure of many correspondent banking relationships, strengthening identity management systems is essential to achieving Target 10c: "reduce to less than 3 per cent the transaction costs of migrant remittances and eliminate remittance corridors with costs higher than 5 per cent." Building and sustaining banking relationships between countries including through correspondent banking, and through mobile money transfers, is essential for low-cost remittance flows as well as for cross-country payments more generally. The FATF (2012) has recognized the need for a risk-based approach that will not crowd out lower-risk clients and transactions with excessive KYC requirements, but to implement such an approach, financial institutions must be able to accurately identify their clients. Unique identity is particularly important to ensure that the use of graduated KYC regimes with less stringent requirements for small accounts and transactions is not undermined by "smurfing"—disguising large transfers by breaking them down into smaller transactions channeled through multiple accounts under different names. Of course, robust identification is only part of the challenge; another is to get greater clarity on the risk-based approach itself to eliminate excessively risk-averse behavior by banks (CGD 2015; CGD 2016; Gelb 2016).

Transitioning to digital payments, particularly mobile-to-mobile transactions, could also significantly reduce the transaction costs associated with migrant remittances. One study across nine remittance corridors estimated that moving to digital remittances would reduce the cost of sending money by 3.5 percentage points—from the current global average cost of 7.5 percent to 4 percent—resulting in $21 billion total savings to senders and recipients (Usman, McDaniel, and Schropp 2016). An official proof of identity is essential to taking advantage of these potentially lower-cost remittance solutions, as KYC rules require a verifiable identity for engaging in digital financial transactions, including mobile transfers.[2]

---

2 The cost of the digital remittance payment may not necessarily represent the full cost of the transaction if it is necessary to incur cash-in-cash-out fees in the source and receiving country.

Gender Equality and Empowerment

An inclusive identification system is an important stepping-stone to gender equality and women's unimpeded participation in economic and social life (Dahan and Hanmer 2015; Buvinic and O'Donnell 2016). Identification can directly enable women's empowerment by helping to secure women's access to products and services that cannot be obtained without an official proof of identity, and can provide women with greater control over economic resources. A recognized identity is needed for "agency"—the power to act independently. Identification is therefore an indispensable component of achieving SDG 5—gender equality.

Using similar language as target 1.4 (discussed above) but with additional emphasis on women's empowerment, target 5a calls for "reforms to give women equal rights to economic resources, as well as . . . financial services." In line with this aspiration, several social programs explicitly target women as the representative of the household, including Pakistan's Benazir Income Support Program (BISP), the largest social transfer program in the country. The Bamashah program in Rajasthan (India), which consolidates subsidies and social transfers into a single management system, recognizes women as heads of nuclear families—a revolutionary change in a previously male-dominated system.

Although virtually every country requires an official proof of identity to open a bank account, many women lack the required documentation. Globally, bank account ownership is over 10 percent lower among women than among men. Forty-two percent of adult women (or over 1 billion) are still unbanked, and the percentage of those with no access to financial services is much higher among the poor. Crucially, nearly one in six women without a bank account stated, when surveyed, that lack of documentation was a contributing factor to not having one (Hanmer and Dahan 2015).

To achieve equal access to all economic resources, including to property and inheritance, comprehensive and accurate marriage and death registration is also vital (O'Donnell 2016). This is in turn facilitated by robust national identification systems, including birth registration, and so inclusive rollout of these systems is a priority. Pakistan offers an example. Between 2008 and 2014, registration for the national ID card increased from 54 million to 98 million. The increase was especially large for women: a jump of 104 percent in enrollment versus 65 percent for men. In a country with long-standing social and religious objections to full female participation, this required special efforts, including women-only registration centers and mobile units (Malik 2014), as well as the incentive provided by linking the ID card to the ability to register with BISP for social transfers.

On a more limited basis, banks in countries with underdeveloped identification systems have deployed unique biometric identification to increase women's control over their own financial assets. Opportunity International was among the first financial institutions to roll out biometrics-supported banking for low-income customers across developing countries. It now serves over 3.5 million clients in 28 countries (Opportunity International 2014). In Malawi, where Opportunity International Bank signed up over 350,000 depositors, fingerprint-based customer registration and verification have been the norm since 2003. New clients are fingerprinted and issued a smartcard that includes a template of their biometric identifiers. Clients are then authenticated against the fingerprint scan stored on their bankcards at a teller's station or ATM, ensuring that only the account owner can access the funds. Anecdotal evidence indicates that women who previously were unable to stop male relatives from taking their savings books and accessing their savings have gained greater control over their funds (Campbell 2010). Not surprisingly, at around 84 percent, the proportion of female clients is far higher for Opportunity than for the financial system as a whole (Opportunity International 2011).

Access to Basic Services

Without a recognized proof of identity, many are barred from accessing basic (public) services such as healthcare or education. Identification can also help governments deliver health services to a greater number of people, and more effectively, by enabling the expansion of health coverage, tracking patients through courses of treatments, and gathering essential data to improve health outcomes.

Access to Education

A birth certificate or—where issued to minors—a national ID card is required to enroll a child in primary school in Algeria, Cambodia, Kenya, Nepal, Peru, Turkey, and many other countries. It is also often a requirement for further educational opportunities, such as sitting a school-leaving examination or enrolling in secondary school or university. Even where a birth certificate is not a formal requirement to access education (or if such a rule is not enforced), recent analyses point to important relationships. A 2014 Plan International report examining linkages between birth registration and children's rights in India, Kenya, and Sierra Leone found that in all three countries, children whose births had been registered were significantly more likely to attend formal education and to do so at the age-appropriate level (Apland and others 2014). For the Dominican Republic, a birth certificate is not required to enroll in primary school, and a study by Corbacho, Brito, and Osorio (2012) finds no relationship between enrollment and birth certification. However, a birth certificate is needed to sit standardized examinations, and, taking into account socioeconomic characteristics, the study finds a significant relationship between registration and graduation from primary school.

Should a child's right to education be denied because of a lack of identification? The answer is clearly no. Children have been enrolling in schools for decades in countries with weak civil registration and identification systems. The purpose of identification is to facilitate the SDGs, not to act as an obstacle. However, where children have established identities, education systems can work more effectively, for instance in providing resources through capitation grants or in tracking progress through the system, including through standardized tests. These findings do not conclusively prove a cause-and-effect relationship between identification and education, but they suggest how comprehensive identification can contribute to SDG 4, which seeks to ensure "inclusive and equitable quality education."

Access to Healthcare

Recent studies indicate a similar positive association between birth registration and childhood health, in particular with regard to vaccination rates (Corbacho, Brito, and Osorio 2013; Apland and others 2014). In countries as diverse as the Dominican Republic, India, Kenya, and Sierra Leone, children whose births had been registered were shown to have received more (and more timely) vaccinations for several highly contagious diseases such as tuberculosis, polio, and measles. Research on the Dominican Republic finds a relationship between birth registration and vaccinations, allowing for socioeconomic characteristics (Corbacho, Brito, and Osorio 2013).

In ongoing research, Oppenheim (2015) investigates the relationship between registration and identification in Kibera, a sprawling urban slum in Nairobi. Parental education and income had no significant effect, but children without birth certificates were 4.5 times more likely to be unvaccinated against polio and 10 times more likely to be unvaccinated against measles. Members of Kenya's Nubian community, who have long struggled to be recognized as citizens, were less likely to hold an official proof of identity or to have vaccinated their children. These results do not indicate a direct causal relationship between birth registration and immunization since the former is not required for the latter; they point, however, to the difficulty of delivering comprehensive health services when parts of the population "withdraw" from contact with the state because of a history of exclusionary policy.[3] An environment where the provision of identity services is seen to provide benefits to all children appears to be an important factor in "ensuring healthy lives," as outlined in SDG 3, as well as in combating the spread of communicable diseases (target 3.3).

Reliable identification is an enabler of target 3.8, which calls for universal health coverage and "access to quality, essential health-care services." The unique identification of healthcare users, made possible by the use of biometric technology, has been instrumental in providing over 100 million of India's poor with health insurance. The Rashtriya Swasthya Bima Yojna (RSBY) health insurance scheme, for example, uses biometric identification to minimize administrative burdens while also maximizing inclusion (Palacios, Das, and Sun 2011). The program covers costs of a list of specified procedures for those living below the poverty line (about 47 rupees, or US$0.70, a day). RSBY has grown to cover 41 million families and has subsidized 11.8 million hospital visits to date (RSBY 2016). Insurance companies compete to service each district and are paid according to enrollment. The winner registers eligible families, takes their fingerprints, and provides biometric insurance smartcards for a nominal fee (30 rupees) (Gelb 2011). If a beneficiary is hospitalized, the hospital verifies coverage using fingerprints and the smartcard and then submits claims to the insurance company. No cash changes hands and there are no lengthy claims forms to fill out. In contrast, inadequate identification has been a severe problem for some other health insurance funds that lack the scale of the RSBY and operate in countries without a robust national identification system. In some

3   "The Complainants have demonstrated that in order to acquire ID documents, significant burdens are placed on them merely on account of their ethnic and religious background. As a result of these burdens many individuals from the Nubian community face enormous hurdles in acquiring IDs. Without IDs, they are unable to enjoy a broad range of rights guaranteed in the Charter, such as the right to free movement, the right to education, the right to work under equitable and satisfactory conditions etc. The lack of IDs cards also effectively renders many Nubians stateless and liable at any point in time to expulsion or arrest." (ACHPR 2015, paragraph 32)

cases, they have investigated the possibility of a custom biometric system but concluded that the cost per beneficiary was too high.

Making an official proof of identity a condition for access to public services and programs has helped spur birth registration and demand for identification. As noted, in South Africa, linking access to generous child grants to birth certification boosted the rate of birth registration by 63 percentage points over a decade. Similarly, the opportunity to benefit from the BISP was an important factor encouraging enrollment into Pakistan's identification program, especially for women (Malik 2014).

Such policies must, however, be carefully balanced against the risk of increasing exclusion by making an identification requirement an additional barrier. Reuben and Carbonari (2017) offer some suggestive evidence for such an effect for the case of Peru, where enrollment of vulnerable infants in a health and nutrition program fell sharply after the introduction of registration requirements. Linking a proof of identity to benefits improves the state's capacity to deliver them; however, it also increases the premium on ensuring that registration be free and easily accessible to all. India's approach to financial inclusion offers a good example of a "carrot-before-stick" approach: customers have been able to open restricted bank accounts subject to an agreement to later register with their Aadhaar number rather than insisting on the ID number up front.

Fighting Epidemics and Providing Quality Care

To achieve SDG target 3.3, which calls for countries to tackle the epidemics of AIDS, TB, and other communicable diseases, it is important to be able to reliably identify patients through courses of treatment. A biometrically supported identification system, combined with on-site biometric verification of individuals at health facilities, can support such efforts, as illustrated by the smaller-scale projects below.

Patients of Operation ASHA, a nongovernmental organization (NGO) that provides TB treatment to the poor, receive their medication through a biometrics-based treatment administration system that is intended to improve adherence and prevent the spread of multidrug-resistant TB. This equally contagious but more difficult to treat strain of TB often develops in patients who skip or miss medication. Patients are registered via their fingerprints as they take their first dose of medication. For each subsequent dose, both the counselor (the ASHA employee) and the patient are required to provide their fingerprint. If the medication has not been dispensed on time, the e-compliance system associated with the biometric terminals issues a warning to the patient, the counselor, and the medical supervisor (Operation ASHA 2015). An interview-based evaluation of the program's implementation in 25 treatment centers across New Delhi and Jaipur reported that biometric monitoring made patients more likely to visit the health centers and take their medication on time. It also improved patient–health worker relations compared to traditional Directly Observed Treatment, Short-Course (DOTS) TB treatment programs (Bhatnagar and others 2012).

Evidence from two more recent studies using econometric analysis appears to support the benefits of biometric identification. Using data from a randomized controlled experiment in India, Bossuroy, Delavallade, and Pons (2016) find that patients are more likely to visit a health center and sustain their treatment if a center is equipped with biometric technology. Biometric monitoring was associated with 24 percent smaller probability of a patient interrupting their TB treatment before its completion. Similarly, in Uganda, Snidal and others (2015) show that patients are significantly more likely to be cured of TB when attending clinics where a biometric identification system is in place. As in the Malawi credit experiment, these cases suggest that monitoring identities can encourage more responsible behavior.

Customized systems may produce results but be less cost effective than common systems. Fingerprint-based tracking of antiretroviral drug treatment for HIV patients was piloted in South Africa under the U.S. Agency for International Development–supported DELIVER project (DELIVER 2007). Both patients and healthcare providers were issued with smartcards that were inserted into a smartcard reader simultaneously during health visits. The patient's identity was then verified with a fingerprint scan that matched it to the information contained on the smartcard. The patient's card also held data on diagnostics, laboratory results, and prescription information, while the provider's card stored details of the patient encounter temporarily and was uploaded to the healthcare provider's central database at the end of the day. The system worked well, but the high cost of the annual per site licensing fee ($1,450) for the proprietary software associated with the smartcard technology made the scale-up of the pilot program prohibitively expensive. This problem could be overcome with continued declines in the price of the technology and through more competitive and well-implemented procurement processes, but it would be still more cost-effective if programs of this sort could rely on a common national identification system rather than each developing their own.

In the fight against epidemics, biometric technology-assisted identification can be particularly useful in improving the effectiveness of vaccine delivery by enabling reliable repeat identification of patients. Unique identification for infants and very young children is still a challenge, although recent initiatives and advances in biometric technology suggest that it is not out of reach (chapter 4). Where direct identification of infants is not possible, being able to reliably and consistently identify their parent can still bring considerable benefits. Vaxtrac, an NGO providing technology-based support to vaccination programs in developing countries, has been using fingerprint scanners to register and track the vaccination records of infants in Nepal and Benin. Left and right thumbprints of both the mother and the child are captured and used to verify the vaccinations received during later visits. Given the low success rate in matching children's fingerprints, health workers rely primarily on the mother's biometric data.

Better Health Data

Comprehensive (civil) registration systems are crucial to improve the availability of health data on neonatal mortality, supporting SDG target 3.2 to "end preventable deaths of newborns and children under 5." Even though infant mortality is not an identification problem, the lack of comprehensive birth and death registration limits accurate data collection on both the number and the cause of deaths, making it more difficult to plan and implement prevention efforts.

Child Protection

Though certainly not sufficient on its own, an identification system that provides proof of age can play an instrumental part in eliminating child labor—an aspect of SDG target 8.7—which threatens the welfare of over 160 million children worldwide. Several countries have strengthened identification for children in an attempt to fight child trafficking; Peru is an example.

Stronger identification can also help enforce laws against child marriage and thus contribute to its elimination and the empowerment of women and girls worldwide, as envisioned by SDG target 5.3 (Hanmer and Elefante 2016). One study in Indonesia found that in the poorest 30 percent of households, 19 percent of girls were found to have married at 17 years or younger compared with only 2 percent of boys. The overall rate of birth registration was around 50 percent, with little gender difference, but fully 95 percent of these child marriages involved girls who did not have a birth certificate. Almost none (0.3%) of these married girls would complete 12 years of education (Sumner 2015). Although the study does not prove a causal relationship between lack of birth registration and underage marriage, its conclusions are strongly suggestive.

Labor Market Opportunities

To the extent that they can reduce transaction costs, well-functioning identification systems can foster job creation, entrepreneurship, and income growth. In the SDG context, identification is an enabler of SDG 8, which seeks to promote sustained and inclusive economic growth and full and productive employment.

Securing a Job in the Formal Sector

A well-administered identification system can help men and women gain recognized qualifications that are widely accepted as genuine by employers. This reduces transaction costs in hiring and improves the functioning of labor markets. Having an officially recognized identity is thus an important step toward SDG target 8.5—"achieving full and productive employment and decent work for all women and men."

Many countries, like Kenya and Malaysia, require a national ID or other official credential to be provided by students sitting school-finishing examinations and for other professional certifications. Examination and credential fraud poses a special risk in countries where there is no widely held credential to provide accurate identification. Custom systems, sometimes using biometric technology, can provide a partial solution but involve additional cost for the examining authorities. Faced with pervasive examination fraud in Nigeria—a country still without a widely held ID credential despite efforts to provide one—the West African Examinations Council began to deploy a mobile system in 2015 to identify and track candidates for national examinations (HID Global 2015).[4] Candidates were enrolled into the system while still in their regular classes in their own schools. The data were then consolidated and records assigned to examiners according to the identities of the candidates sitting the examinations in the individual centers. The biometric check is intended to both prove exam attendance and verify candidate identity.

---

4   Similar approaches had been tested in other West African countries.

Another example of an initiative to use identification technology to improve the integrity of the certification system is India's "digital locker" system, described in chapters 1 and 6. Its permission-based architecture allows ID credentials certified by the issuing authority to be shared directly with prospective employers or others, as permitted by the holder. Together with an Aadhaar verification at the time of sitting the examinations, such a system could guard against both examination fraud and credential fraud.

Safe and Regular Migration and Foreign Employment Opportunities

The role of accurate identification is perhaps most prominent in enabling the realization of SDG target 10.7 for "orderly, safe, regular and responsible migration and mobility of people." Free(r) movement of people across borders, facilitated by reliable and inclusive ID systems, can also expand access to economic resources and support the reduction of inequality within and among countries—as set out by SDG 10. Research by Clemens and Pritchett (2008) and Clemens (2011) has shown that small reductions in barriers to labor mobility could help increase the wages of migrating developing country workers to more than 10 times their current level.

A growing number of governments are issuing ID cards that conform to the standards for machine-readable travel documents (ICAO 2015), but these might not be necessary, or cost-effective, as a standard issue for poor countries. Both the Economic Community of West African States and the East African Community are working toward common identification frameworks to facilitate free movement of citizens across their national borders. Yet ultimately, the form of a document is less critical than the integrity of the ID process that supports it. Technology alone will not solve this problem. As shown by the extreme example of Somalia (chapter 2), citizens of countries that are less able to credibly confirm their identities face higher barriers to international travel, even when they are issued with ICAO-compliant biometric passports.

Social Protection: Grants and Subsidies

Robust identification systems can strengthen state capacity and provide governments with more effective tools to deliver programs and services. They can be used to support a wide range of programs, from delivering social grants and emergency aid to reforming wasteful subsidy programs.

By 2014 more than 130 developing countries were implementing at least one cash transfer program (World Bank 2015). The large and generally positive impact of such programs on the incomes and overall welfare of the poor has been comprehensively studied (Handa and others 2016; Haushofer and Shapiro 2013; World Bank 2009). They are often part of a country's broader social protection system, but cash payments can be a versatile and effective form of support in a variety of contexts, including in emergency settings or as part of a country's subsidy reform strategy.

Robust identification systems and the ability to uniquely and accurately identify intended program beneficiaries can be instrumental for the timely and cost-effective delivery of cash payments to poor and vulnerable members of society. They can thus be a valuable tool for governments seeking to achieve poverty elimination defined in SDG 1, together with the inclusive implementation of social protection systems—the aspiration of target 1.3. In turn, well-functioning social protection systems have been shown to reduce inequality within countries, in line with the aims of SDG 10 (World Bank 2015; Soares and others 2009).

Transparent and Reliable Delivery of Social Grants

Many social protection programs rely on communal processes to identify those most in need of assistance. Community monitoring is also used to ensure that disbursements are made to their intended recipients, typically at a designated time and location and in a communal setting. This approach may have some positive side benefits, since meetings are sometimes used for other purposes, for example in the Tanzania Social Action Fund program to impart information on child care and nutrition. The approach does, however, reduce flexibility for beneficiaries. It locks them into fixed payment arrangements and requires them to incur considerable time and transport costs each pay period; they also must hold relatively large quantities of cash between disbursements. Communal processes also become less effective as mobility increases and more people move to towns and cities, residing outside their traditional communities.

Many programs have been transitioning toward the use of digital payment systems underpinned by robust identification. These systems can accurately confirm the identities of beneficiaries, reduce the diversion of funds to "ghost" consumers or for other illegitimate purposes, and facilitate audits that can track funds from source to receipt by the individual recipient. As in Indonesia, community-based processes may still be used, together with centrally administered proxy means tests, to identify the neediest families. Countries that have used biometric systems to deliver social grants for some time include South Africa, Pakistan, and parts of India (Gelb and Decker 2011).

South Africa offers perhaps the earliest example of the use of this approach, at least in a development setting. Starting off as early as the mid-1990s in Kwazulu-Natal, provincial governments delivered pensions and social grants using a biometric system designed to work in areas with limited connectivity. ATMs were mounted on vehicles and linked to biometric readers. Each beneficiary's 10 finger scans were recorded on a smartcard, which also held that individual's benefit information, including the schedule for payment, the amount, and the date of last payment received. The vehicles proceeded from area to area, disbursing grants on the same day of each month.

Following the amalgamation of provincial offices into the South African Social Security Agency (SASSA), the social grant program, including pensions and child and disability grants, has continued to grow, to the level of some 3.5 percent of gross domestic product. About 17 million people, or one-third of the population, receive social grants, and for those at the bottom of the income scale these grants are the major source of income. With increasing connectivity, the payment mechanism has shifted toward bank and mobile accounts, but many beneficiaries still need custom payment arrangements because they are outside the banking system. The SASSA continues to rely on biometrics: in 2013 over 20 million social grant recipients were reregistered with their biometrics to streamline the recently centralized system (Bruni 2016). The reregistration is reported to have enabled SASSA to remove 650,000 social grants going to non-eligible individuals, which resulted in savings of over ZAR 2 billion (about US$165 million) annually (Ensor 2014). A new feature of the system is that all grant recipients must present a "proof of life" once a month—this can be done by scanning their fingerprints, but voice recognition is being considered as an alternative. Even though death registration is relatively complete in South Africa, this helps ensure that payments cease once a beneficiary has died.[5]

South Africa's system for the delivery of social grants became a subject of

5   The estimated completeness of adult death registration increased from 89 percent to 94 percent over the period 1996–2001. Although this is a high figure, this still leaves the possibility of a large number of cumulative unrecorded deaths, especially among the poorer parts of the population served by the social transfer system. (See Statistics South Africa's Statistical Release P0309.3 2011, available at http://beta2.statssa.gov.za/publications/P03093/P030932011.pdf.) With death registration rates far lower in many developing countries, voice recognition could become a key technology for social protection and pension programs.

intense and continuing debate in 2016 and early 2017 as the service contract with Cash Paymaster Services (CPS) approached its end-date. CPS is a subsidiary of Net1, the company that has long played a leading role in managing the identities of the country's social grant beneficiaries. SASSA had failed to develop its own capacity to deliver grants as it had committed to two years previously, leaving no option but to extend the contract on an emergency basis. The problem was not that the identification and payment systems were inefficient. It was rather that Net1's monopoly position and control over payments, as well as identification, allegedly enabled the company to push additional financial services to social grant recipients in a way that was widely considered exploitative, even if not illegal. This experience points to the problems posed by vendor lock-in and contracts that combine beneficiary identification and payments (chapter 5). It also calls for caution in seeing social grants as the entry point for financial inclusion in ways that can lock the beneficiaries into future payments.

Pakistan's BISP offers another important example, providing cash transfers to close to 5 million women from the poorest households. NADRA, the country's National Database and Registration Authority, partners with BISP to implement the nationwide National Economic and Social Register (NSER). The NSER covers all households and underpins the selection of beneficiary households for BISP, with the main disbursement arrangements for BISP being through banks. The program has been a major driver of financial inclusion (Malik 2014), and all account-holders must be identified by their national ID number. To improve the ease and security of withdrawals and increase competition by offering beneficiaries a wider range of choice, the disbursement system is being updated to enable wider point-of-service payments authentication using national ID cards and biometric identifiers. Initial assessments suggest that biometric authentication is not without its problems but that most beneficiaries prefer the new system because they at least get to draw out their own money, rather than having their debit cards and payments appropriated by male family members (Mott McDonald 2016).

Muralidharan, Niehaus, and Sukhtankar (2016) provide one of the few rigorous evaluations of the shift toward the use of biometric identification (pre-Aadhaar) and digital payments. Their study assessed the adoption of a new system by the Indian state of Andhra Pradesh to deliver pensions and wage payments from its National Rural Employment Guarantee Scheme (NREGS). As part of the reforms, NREGS and pension beneficiaries were reregistered, and their 10 fingerprints and a digital photograph were collected during the process. Registrants were then issued a smartcard, linked to a newly created bank account and containing an electronic chip that stored their biometric and biographic data as well as bank account details.

The study found that the move helped cut leakages and at the same time increased the amount of money collected by beneficiaries. The ability to verify the uniqueness of program participants, combined with an expanded payment collection network that relied on biometric authentication for withdrawals, helped cut leakages in both programs by over 40 percent and reduced the extortion of bribes at the point of payout. NREGS beneficiaries saw their incomes rise by 24 percent, and it took them 22 fewer minutes to collect their wages in areas where the biometric smartcard program was implemented relative to areas without the new system. Program implementation was also shown to be highly cost effective: the estimated leakage reduction ($38.5 million a year) from the NREGS program alone exceeded the cost of adopting the new identification and payment system ninefold. The transition to biometric smartcards was also popular with the beneficiaries: over 90 percent preferred the new system.

Timely and Accurate Provision of Emergency Aid

In addition to facilitating regular payments, robust identification systems can help ensure that emergency aid reaches affected populations swiftly in the aftermath of catastrophic events. Pakistan's rapid and effective response to devastating floods in 2010 provides an example of how they can help achieve SDG target 1.5., which sets out to "build the resilience of the poor and those in vulnerable situations" and help them cope more easily with income shocks and disasters.

After floods destroyed the livelihoods of millions in Pakistan, the country relied on its national biometric database to identify and authenticate citizens eligible for its national emergency cash transfer programs (Gelb and Decker 2011). The NADRA database helped to identify citizens eligible for assistance based on their registered address. The identities of targeted heads of household were then confirmed by comparing their fingerprints to those in the 96 million–strong database. This proved particularly useful to the many living in the flood-affected areas who had lost all other forms of identification. Over 1 million households were issued a "Watan" debit card, which could be cashed at numerous points of service and ATMs across the country (VISA 2010; Pasricha 2011). External assessments of the program concluded that beneficiaries received payments quickly and with little diversion, and had a generally favorable view of the compensation mechanism (Gelb and Decker 2011). Although disputed decisions required a lengthy grievance redress process, the problems reflected the selection of beneficiaries for the subsidy rather than identification and payment to those who were judged to be eligible.

Subsidy Reform That Does Not Hurt the Poor

Identification can also underpin efforts to reform inefficient government programs. Several studies suggest that unique identification is an effective tool to improve the administration of subsidies, including fossil-fuel subsidies, because it can enable the switch from price subsidies to (digital) cash payments (Radcliffe 2016). This shift supports the achievement of SDG target 12.c, and with it SDG 12's objective of "sustainable consumption and production patterns."

Consumer price subsidies tend to be inefficient, regressive, and prone to diversion. Energy subsidies are a particularly massive burden on public resources; an International Monetary Fund study estimated that in 2011 governments spent $480 billion, or 0.7 percent of global GDP, on pre-tax subsidies[6] for petroleum products, electricity, natural gas, and coal (Clements and others 2013). Although pre-tax subsidies have come down in the wake of falling world energy prices after 2013, they are still sizeable in many countries and could spike again if energy markets recover. In addition, successful action to combat climate change would require countries to impose "green taxes" on fossil fuels in line with their carbon emissions. These taxes would further increase prices for purchasers, often in situations where poor people are already net losers from the fiscal system—they are likely to have lower disposable income after taxes and subsidies because of indirect taxation on items they consume.[7]

6   Pre-tax subsidies represent the difference between how much consumers within a country pay for a given fuel and the international price for that fuel, adjusted for transport and distribution costs. A subsidy implies that consumers are paying less than the international price. Both actual government expenditures and foregone government revenues (from selling locally produced fuel at below the international price, though not necessarily below in-country production and distribution costs) are counted as pre-tax subsidies.

7   Fiscal incidence analysis for 28 low- and middle-income countries by Lustig (2017) shows that although fiscal systems are equalizing overall, the same is not always the case for measures of poverty. The extreme poverty headcount is higher in many countries after taxes and transfers than it would have been without them. The main reason for this effect is the indirect taxes levied on goods and services consumed by the poor. Even though poorer households might not be the highest users of fuels, imposing "green taxes" without offsetting direct transfers would exacerbate the situation. The problem cannot be resolved by reducing direct taxes, since poor households do not pay them.

If pricing reforms are to avoid an adverse impact on the poor, governments will need to implement compensatory mechanisms through one of two possible methods. As in Iran's reforms (Guillaume, Zytek, and Farzin 2011), compensation can be delivered to households through direct transfers that are delinked from energy consumption. Such uniform or progressive transfers can also eliminate the regressive impact of price subsidies, which tend to go to better-off consumers; a major objective of Iran's subsidy reform was to address this imbalance. This reform involved the creation of millions of new bank accounts, facilitated by a well-developed civil registration and identification system that allowed the government to accurately target the affected households. The other option is "lifeline pricing" that subsidizes a limited base energy allocation to each household—leaving richer users, who consume more energy, to pay the market price on purchases above the allocation. Either way, compensation cannot be effectively targeted and tracked without unique identification of recipients. As stressed by Radcliffe (2016), the combination of digital payments and ID technology provides new opportunities for governments to build capacity to implement subsidy reforms.

India's program to reform the subsidy system for liquefied petroleum gas (LPG) cylinders for household use offers an example of the lifeline model. Cylinders were previously sold to households at highly subsidized prices, but businesses were required to pay market prices plus taxes on commercial use. This fragmented pricing structure resulted in extensive diversions of cylinders from residences to businesses and encouraged fraudulent connections. The reform has eliminated the consumer price subsidy, replacing it with direct payments into bank accounts. Payments are based on the number of cylinders ordered, up to a current annual maximum of 12 cylinders per household. The initial stage of reform (Project Lakshya) involved a first clean-up of customer data based on biographic deduplication (unique names and connection addresses) and imposed a cap on subsidized consumption per household. As the reform evolved into the Pratyaksha Hastaantarit Laabh (PAHAL) program, it shifted toward using the Aadhaar to identify customers as well as to facilitate financial access—including to satisfy KYC requirements to open the bank accounts for direct payments. This made possible the transition to market prices, an important step to limit administrative diversion. The illicit gains from falsely booking cylinders to households not using their full quotas can no longer be directly appropriated by the dealers. Orders are placed through mobile accounts linked to the recipient households; because of the clear location of household connection points, it is not necessary to authenticate customers biometrically when

they receive cylinders. Later stages have included progressively tighter targeting, initially on a voluntary basis (the "Give-It-Up" campaign), and then by
curtailing subsidies to the better-off. The LPG program is being rolled out to
more households under the Ujjwala Yojana scheme as a cleaner and less environmentally destructive fuel to replace kerosene and biomass (with Aadhaar as
the established identifier), but it is already the largest energy price reform and
transfer program in the world.

The results of the program reflect a number of features—deduplication,
capping of subsidies, and progressive targeting—and are not easy to attribute
to its individual elements. Official estimates from the Ministry of Petroleum
and Natural Gas put the savings from identifying duplicate, fake, or inactive
domestic LPG connections at $2.2 billion in the financial year 2014–15 and
at close to $1 billion in 2015–16. The decrease was due to lower world energy
prices that reduced the size of the government subsidy per cylinder (Government of India 2016). Some details of these estimates are debated, including the
government's assumption that each shut-off connection would have used its
full allocation of 12 cylinders per year rather than the average consumption of
between 6 and 7 cylinders. Many consumers would probably not have given up
their subsidies in the absence of a program to identify them and provide subsidies in the form of direct transfers. Commercial (nonsubsidized) sales spiked
after the reform, suggesting a reduction in diversion (Barnwal 2016). But even
if the impact were considerably smaller than that estimated by the ministry,
the savings from the LPG program alone are far larger than the total cost of
the Aadhaar program, which to date had cost somewhere over $1 billion. Use
of the Aadhaar number as a common identifier for subsidies also has helped to
rationalize kerosene subsidies in line with the LPG rollout, since households no
longer receive kerosene subsidies once they have been provided with an LPG
connection.[8]

---

8   The debate about the savings from India's LPG subsidy reform reflects, in part, the dif-
    ficulty of establishing a clear counterfactual. The decline in global energy prices is a com-
    plicating factor because it reduces the unit subsidy and at the same time permits lower
    domestic prices that would be expected to stimulate consumption. Another complicating
    factor is the policy objective of expanding household connections to promote LPG as a
    clean fuel to replace kerosene. The number of household connections can be expected to
    increase for both reasons, together with the number receiving direct transfers; see, for ex-
    ample, Mukherjee, Gelb, and Diofasi (2016). The impact of the reforms on consumers also
    has been debated, but independent user surveys have reported high levels of user satisfac-
    tion with the PAHAL program (Sharma 2016). Another independent survey conducted
    by Microsave in 14 districts found a user satisfaction rate of 74 percent (Kumar, Sadana,
    and Sharma 2015).

The LPG program is only one among the vast number of social protection and subsidy programs in India that, in total, account for some $60 billion in annual spending. The Aadhaar number is now being seeded into program registers as the key identifier to record and deduplicate beneficiaries. Aadhaar is also increasingly being used at points of service to authenticate those receiving benefits. The Aadhaar-based identification and identity verification approach promises to bring about the biggest reform of subsidy and transfer programs in the world. States and districts are innovating, reforming programs at different speeds and testing out different approaches.

It is still too early to come to a definitive conclusion on the results of these reforms, on the efficiency gains from the new systems and how they relate to the different elements of the reforms, but more indications are beginning to emerge from the more advanced cases.[9] One implementation lesson is that reforms are not easy. Anomalies and inconsistencies have to be resolved as diverse schemes are restructured, merged (for example, into Rajasthan's Bamashah program), and seeded with unique ID numbers. Even programs supported by the most technologically advanced and sophisticated identification systems require committed leadership and sustained efforts to overcome inertia and resistance from individuals and groups who benefit from the existing system. Fair Price Shop owners who have largely depended on the diversion of subsidized products to secure a decent standard of living for their own families will require compensation if they are to remain in business. In recognition of this issue, it has been necessary to increase their small margins several-fold as the reforms have been rolled out. Mobile operators and banks may need to be pressured to increase coverage, including the threat of losing government business. It also has been necessary to drop unwilling businesses, and reassign licenses to new entrants that are willing to work with the new system.

Another lesson is that applying new technology in the field can require a period of experimentation before it is able to work smoothly. In Krishna District, one experiment involved the innovative introduction of antennae linked to point-of-sale devices to help boost connectivity; another innovation is the introduction of dual-SIM devices to enable field agents to switch between networks to take advantage of the strongest connection.

Yet another lesson is the importance of monitoring system performance to

9   The following comments draw on visits to Andhra Pradesh and Rajasthan in December 2016 and ongoing analysis of Krishna District.

be able to isolate points of difficulty and record technology failures, including problems with biometric authentication (chapter 4). Many users will require assistance to help them navigate the new systems and technologies. In Rajasthan, they can turn to a new industry of "e-Mitras"—some 44,000 small businesses that provide technical support in addition to operating as banking correspondents, but how helpful this commercial model is in providing assistance is yet to be determined. With diverse Aadhaar-enabled reforms proceeding at different rates across states and districts, India offers a laboratory to study the application of identification systems to development. Its experience should be of immense interest to other countries that are seeking to rationalize inefficient subsidies—as envisioned by SDG target 12c—without hurting the poor.

Managing Public Payrolls

Stronger identity management can reduce corruption by helping to verify both public sector employees and program beneficiaries, making it an important pillar for achieving SDG target 16.5—"to reduce corruption and bribery in all its forms." Many countries have been able to eliminate nonexistent workers from public payrolls, and some have found enormous fiscal savings even from limited applications. Nigeria and Ghana offer interesting examples—even though these two countries, despite their longer-term efforts, have had only modest success in rolling out their national identification systems. Identity management has also proved a valuable tool for managing payments to health workers in an emergency setting, during the recent Ebola outbreak in Sierra Leone.

Following a pilot in 2007, Nigeria's biometrically supported Integrated Payroll and Personnel Information System (IPPIS) was expanded to cover a number of federal public institutions; by 2014 it had unearthed over 60,000 ghost workers, equivalent to over 20 percent of the legitimate payroll of the agencies concerned. The cumulative savings over 2007–14 were estimated at $1.12 billion (Mede 2016; Nse 2014). The savings could have been higher if the system had been extended to the entire federal payroll, and even more if extended to state bureaucracies.

Ghana has long struggled to contain recurrent spending, which is high, relative to GDP, compared with other African countries. One objective of its e-Zwich payment system—"the world's first biometric money" (Breckenridge 2010)—was to clean up government payrolls through an indirect mechanism, by consolidating all salary payments into a single deduplicated system of bank accounts. The e-Zwich payment system captures customers' fingerprints during enrollment and stores the template on a smartcard; for each withdrawal, the fingerprints are checked against the template stored on the card. Plans to expand the mandatory use of e-Zwich to other government agencies have encountered opposition on the grounds that the system decreases the convenience of public employees. Rollout has been increasing, but at a slower rate than projected. However, one single modest application, to Ghana's scandal-plagued National Service System, has reportedly been able to remove 35,000 fictitious employees—almost half the initial payroll of 75,000—saving the Ghanaian government $35 million a year (Yeboah 2016). This figure alone indicates a high rate of return on the investment in the e-Zwich program.[10]

Accurate identification can also be a valuable tool for payroll management during national and global health risks, including in emergency settings, as promoted by SDG target 3d. During global health emergencies, such as the recent Ebola outbreak in West Africa, keeping track of the number of health workers and ensuring timely payments to the existing and newly recruited workforce poses a great challenge. In early 2015 a United Nations Development Programme–supported biometric payroll system was introduced for Ebola response workers (ERWs) in Sierra Leone, registering all 30,000 ERWs employed by more than 10 different NGOs and government entities (UNDP 2015a). The registration underpinned the rollout of mobile payments for ERWs, which ensured secure and convenient delivery of payments, including a "hazard pay" bonus for those at greatest risk of contracting the disease. These added incentives, coupled with an effective payment system, helped avert strikes and kept ERWs motivated despite the difficult conditions. The new system also helped to remove 3,500 duplicate records and identified many ERWs who received payment for the same work from two different entities (UNDP 2015b).

10 The e-Zwich system was provided by Net1, a South African company that is also responsible for the biometric system used by South Africa's social security system. Net1 was paid an upfront fee of $20 million with the provision for an additional payment of $3 per card. Payment for coverage of 1 million people—roughly the current coverage—would therefore have amounted to $23 million, and wide coverage, projected at around 7 million cards, would involve payment of $41 million (Gelb and Clark 2013a). These figures do not include all of the costs of implementing the e-Zwich system, but they are indicative.

Tax Collection

Accurate identification can also strengthen public institutions in other ways, for example through bolstering the state's ability for tax collection, as advocated by SDG target 17.1. Unlike some other SDG applications, improved tax collection requires an identity management system that can use a common number to link individual records across diverse databases.

One example comes from Argentina, where the use of a common identifier to integrate income and asset-related data across 24 databases (the SINTE-SIS project) helped to reduce benefit fraud and increase revenues (Gelb and Clark 2013a). Pakistan presents another example, at least of potential gains; its widely held unique national identifier allowed datasets containing information on property and vehicle ownership, utility consumption patterns, and banking and travel records to be consolidated, to identify 3.5 million potential taxpayers, a multiple of the approximately 800,000 who actually were paying direct taxes. The potential revenues from an expansion of the taxpayer base of this magnitude were estimated at $1 billion over only three months (Malik 2014).

Clean Elections

A clean, up-to-date voter registry is crucial for reducing fraud at the polls and ensuring the overall integrity of the electoral process. It is the backbone of free and fair elections and is integral to "responsive, inclusive, participatory and representative decision-making at all levels," as expressed by SDG target 16.7.

One example of the potential electoral impact of an identification system with strong biometric controls is Pakistan's actions to update its voter roll for its 2013 election. The new roll was based on the simultaneously updated population register maintained by NADRA, the national identification authority. As well as updating the register itself, the exercise resulted in the removal of 40 percent of the voter roll, eliminating 15 million voter entries without verifiable identities and an additional 13 million entries with invalid identities, as well as 9 million duplicates. The exercise also added 36 million new eligible voters. The voter roll was "liberated" to enable people to check their entries using cellphones: millions took advantage of this opportunity (Malik 2014).

However, from wider experience, this area has been one of the more problematic applications of identification technology. The first difficulty is that the use of technology does not necessarily improve electoral integrity and credibility. "Black box" processes implemented by vendors often fail to build trust, the programs may be ineffectively implemented, or other systematic problems may affect the voting. In Côte d'Ivoire, for example, the main electoral disputes have revolved around who is really a citizen and eligible to vote. Electoral fraud comes in many shapes and forms, and modern ID systems and technologies can address only a fraction of the potential issues. Voters may be intimidated or opposition parties banned long before an election, preventing any possibility that it will be recognized as free and fair. Paper ballots may be destroyed, and results falsified or ignored. Technology cannot help unless the basic preconditions are in place, including recognition by both the incumbent party and the opposition of the value of a credible election. But there are a number of positive cases where ID technology has contributed to cleaner and more peaceful elections. Despite reported difficulties with authenticating voters, Nigeria's biometrics-assisted voter registration system is widely credited with helping to curb fraud and to improve the accountability of the polarized 2015 elections, to the point where the results were accepted by all parties without violence.

The second problem with identification technology in elections is that the costly one-off voter ID programs launched by many countries are a wasteful and unsustainable approach to identity management. The costs of these programs can be high—sometimes as much as $20 per head, a multiple of what identity management should cost in a poor country (Gelb and Diofasi 2016a)—partly because comprehensive voter registration requires vast numbers of enrollment stations to blanket the country in a short window of time. Incumbent governments have used the high costs of elections in order to justify postponing further scheduled elections and remaining in power. In 2015 legislative elections in Chad were postponed, citing the lack of a biometric voter roll; they were finally held a year later, in April 2016 (Freedom House 2016). In addition, voter registration often leaves little or nothing behind in terms of sustained identity management assets, including for future elections. By eliminating the need for such wasteful exercises, strong, credible, and independent national ID systems with continuous registration would have a large and immediate payoff in many countries.

The other side of the equation is the high cost of violently contested election results, in terms of loss of life, assets, and economic production, as well as the credibility of the resulting government. Even with rough estimates, a cost-benefit comparison suggests that reducing the probability of serious postelection violence by only a few percentage points can produce benefits that cover the costs of voter registration (Gelb and Diofasi 2016a).

The lesson for SDG target 16.7 is that technology alone often will not be sufficient to guarantee credible elections and that one-off registration programs, whatever their contributions, are not a sustainable approach. However, the costs of violently disputed elections indicate that credible and inclusive identity management can have a high payoff at particular junctures in terms of political stability.

FOUR

Identification Systems: Innovations in Technology and ID Provision

Countries seeking to improve their identification systems and expand their capabilities to support development outcomes have many options to choose from, whether they want to see incremental changes or visionary innovations. Even if the choices may be limited by legacy systems, social traditions, institutional mandates and legal frameworks, or capacity to deploy particular technologies, some governments have been able to introduce improvements into their systems or even to transform them completely over relatively short periods of time. This chapter considers innovations in two broad categories: those driven by advances in digital technology and those taking place on an institutional level, changing the way identification services are provided and how identities are managed. It does not cover every possible option or innovation, but selects a few critical issues.

First, it looks at the implications of biometric technology, which has revolutionized the provision of identity services in developing countries, particularly those with weak underlying civil registration systems. Digital biometrics are certainly not a solution on their own, and they introduce their own concerns and vulnerabilities, but their use is instrumental to achieving many of the identification-linked development outcomes described in chapter 3.[1] Remark-

---

1 The use of blockchain technology for identity management is not considered here, since at the time of writing it was not clear that it had transformative potential. For more on potential development applications of blockchain, see Pisa and Juden (2017).

ably, the use of digital biometrics for unique identification and identity verification has made it possible to separate identification from any other entitlement,
program, or service, as well as national status. Identification then becomes a
true foundational service for all purposes. This "identity first" approach, pioneered by India's Aadhaar program, facilitates speedy and inclusive enrollment, so that the system can rapidly be deployed to increase efficiency and save
fiscal resources. Even if other countries might not want to adopt the full Aadhaar model, it offers important lessons for the design of ID systems. Steadily
advancing technology is also disrupting the identification of infants and young
children by making it possible to "lock in" identification at ever-earlier ages to
provide a unique "identity for life." This has the potential to strengthen identity management and reduce fraud arising from registration later in life, while
also increasing the importance of ensuring that civil (birth) registration and
identification work in an integrated way.

Turning to innovations and good practices in the architecture identification
systems, the chapter reviews current institutional arrangements for providing
identification services, both civil registration and national identification. These
differ greatly across countries: ID services may be housed centrally, under the
aegis of a government ministry; they may fall under the responsibility of local
municipalities; or come under the remit of the country's electoral body. In an
effort to streamline ID services and build trust in their provision, a number of
countries have established autonomous public agencies with the specific and
limited mandate to provide foundational national identification. There are advantages to having the service provided by an entity with such a focused mandate, but this arrangement raises important questions about the governance
structure of the ID system and how it should be financed if not as part of a
government ministry.

The final aspect considered is that of integration—the degree to which the
country operates a single integrated identity management system—and how
to get there. Most countries have already taken steps toward an integrated
system, in which individual programs may still each maintain their own client
or beneficiary register and issue a program-specific identifying number, but
these identifiers can then be linked to a common number. In practice, many
countries operate several disconnected systems, each with its own ID credential
and number, with no link to any common database. Some countries are working to integrate their systems through "reverse engineering"—whereby one or
more high-coverage functional ID registries are transformed to become the
basis for a multipurpose, foundational program. This approach further raises

the importance of common technical standards. Even if much current frag-mentation is transitional rather than a coherent policy choice, countries may still have different views on how integrated their ID system(s) should be, given the perceived privacy risks surrounding this issue.

Biometrics in Identity Management

Digital biometric technology has been central to the accelerated rollout of iden-tification systems in developing countries. Like other technologies, it is not a "silver bullet"—the use of biometrics cannot guarantee that a particular ID pro-gram will deliver on its desired outcomes, or that it will be development friendly or cost effective (see box 4-1 for a comparison with Integrated Financial Man-agement System projects)—but it has greatly expanded the capabilities of ID systems. Almost all new programs incorporate biometric technology, as do most of the established ones. Out of a sample of 117 established national programs listed in the World Bank's ID4D database, two-thirds (78) used biometric tech-nology. In the past 10 years, at least 50 countries have added biometrics to new or existing programs. In addition, many countries have changed the type or count of biometric identifiers. Programs that previously recorded only limited biomet-ric data, for example by including a picture of a thumbprint on a card, have been increasing data capture, typically moving from one or two fingerprints to taking a full 10 prints and sometimes adding a digital face or iris scan.

Digital biometric technology is moving toward a "commodity industry," with standards for devices and for data capture, storage, and transmission. At the same time, the industry is still in a phase of intense innovation. In addition to fingerprints, face, and iris—the standard biometrics used in identification programs—a widening range of physical and behavioral biometrics has been developing in recent years, and several other modalities are now used com-mercially on a large scale. More esoteric biometrics include ear-patterns and tongue-prints, 3-D and thermal face-prints, echocardiograms and electroen-cephalograms, gait and lip movements, smell, dynamic signature, and keystroke or mouse patterns. Some of these modalities are meant for specialized use or are at a more developmental stage, but Japanese banks, for instance, extensively use infrared finger vein patterns to authenticate clients at ATMs. They are difficult to capture without the cooperation of the holder and authentication is hygienic, with no need to touch the sensor. About 140 countries reportedly use voice biometrics for different purposes, including to provide "proof of life" for

BOX 4-1   Technology Is Not a Silver Bullet:
A Parallel with IFMIS

As large-scale technology-intensive projects, modern identification systems have some parallels to Integrated Financial Management Information Systems (IFMIS) projects. Although IFMIS projects are smaller, with an average cost of around $25 million, many have been rolled out; 87 by the World Bank alone between 1984 and 2010 (Dener, Watkins, and Dorotinsky 2011) and more by other development banks. Like national ID systems, IFMIS projects involve the use of digital technology to increase the effectiveness, efficiency, and transparency of public functions.

IFMIS has often been promoted as the "silver bullet" solution to governments' financial management problems, but the record of these projects has been mixed. The implementation of Iraq's IFMIS was halted because of poor planning and lack of consultation with ministries. Given the lack of buy-in from local leadership, they continued to operate their old systems in parallel or never even tried to implement the new one. A diverse set of countries have had similarly disappointing experiences with IFMIS implementation, but their difficulties are often rooted in the same issues: lack of sustained political commitment, inadequate preparation, misplaced priorities and sequencing, and inadequate domestic capacity (Cangiano, Gelb, and Goodwin-Groen 2017).

pension and similar payments. Voice may be used overtly as an identifier, or less transparently as "background" to customers' conversations with an operator to provide backup identity assurance. It is reported that after about 30 seconds of conversation, it is often possible to confirm with a low margin of error that the caller on the phone is actually the intended customer (Warman 2013). Voice identification reportedly is becoming quite common practice especially as such calls are openly and routinely "recorded to monitor service quality." The aim is not necessarily to identify every caller but to handle most cases to free up human resources to deal with the remainder.

The introduction of digital biometrics has been revolutionary for several reasons. First, they allow unique identities to be established even among very large populations. Within a matter of seconds, likely duplicate enrollments can be flagged for further manual examination to ensure that each person had been registered only once—that each identity is (statistically) unique. As highlighted in chapter 3, being able to screen out multiple registrations is a major step forward in terms of robustness, and central to many applications such as the cleaning of voter rolls to help combat electoral fraud or improving the efficiency of public administration by removing ghost workers or beneficiaries from the rolls.

Second, biometric technology allows for people to be authenticated with high accuracy against their claimed identities, whether "offline" against data stored on barcodes or QR cards or smartcards, as used in most countries, or "online" against a central database, as in the card-less Aadhaar system. This process helps to ensure that only the person entitled to access a service or benefit or authorized to transact can do so. The high level of identity assurance provided by biometric authentication may not be necessary for all applications; sometimes a visual check against a picture ID card might be all that is required, especially if the numbers on the card have already been deduplicated.

A third revolutionary aspect of the use of biometric technology is the ability to reduce reliance on extensive biographic documentation to identify a person. Many other attributes, such as detailed familial relationships or national status, can be filled in later. This approach can, of course, increase the risk that the initial identity presented at enrollment is not the "real" identity; a due diligence process is always needed for confirmation. But the discipline imposed by uniqueness is a powerful deterrent against misrepresentation, since the individual concerned will never be able to register again under any other identity. The use of biometrics to lighten the need for documentary evidence can speed up enrollment and make it more inclusive, especially for those who find it difficult to provide extensive documentary evidence of who they are.

Creating a new identity baseline in this way will have limited value in cases where there are serious concerns about establishing "real" identities for security-related reasons and grounds for thinking that some people may misrepresent who they are to gain privileges or access. This concern may be less pressing for settled populations and those who are able to return to their communities for supporting evidence, but will continue to be a serious problem for refugees, particularly those from countries considered to house terrorist organizations. Biometrics can help provide unique identification after registration and help displaced people to rebuild identity profiles by supporting a single, continuous identity, but unless the identity can be linked to trustworthy records from the country of origin, no technology can resolve this problem.

The use of biometric technology in ID programs and other applications will only become more common in the future. In recent years, standardization and competition among suppliers has made hardware and software costs fall sharply, a trend accelerated by the competitive, standards-based procurement launched by India's massive Aadhaar program. Costs for biometric registration and authentication devices continue to fall as readers are integrated into mobile phones and computers. Custom iris cameras, for example, cost between $100 and $400, but the cameras are now being incorporated into mobiles and tablets at an incremental cost of only $3–$4 for large-scale mass production. Some mobile applications that use face recognition do not require any additional hardware, since they rely on the mobile's existing camera. Small plug-in fingerprint scanners are also dropping in price (Gelb, Mukherjee, and Diofasi 2016).

Incorporating biometric capability into mobiles will enable a massive expansion of the biometric ecosystem. The technology can piggyback on the rapid spread of mobile technology without requiring costly dedicated devices. With expanding connectivity, direct online authentication against a central database is becoming possible almost everywhere, save in the shrinking parts of the world beyond the reach of mobile networks. Countries can offer this as an alternative, even if they choose to maintain a card-based system.

Performance

Distressingly little public data are available on the field performance of some of these biometrics and the programs that rely on them—for example, how many people cannot use them, or whether they actually can deduplicate enrollments as well as they claim. Vendor claims can be misleading, and the National Institute for Standards and Technology (NIST) and other testing bodies have evaluated only a limited number of technologies and devices.[2] Many factors can cause field performance to differ from the results of controlled tests, especially if the target population has distinctive characteristics. Older people, manual

2   NIST assessments have mostly covered fingerprints and iris and face biometrics. A major assessment of voice biometrics is soon to start. There have also been a number of studies of the effect of aging on biometrics; for iris, see for example Browning and Orlans (2014). While these do not indicate serious stability problems over a number of years, data on very long-term effects are still limited.

laborers, and farmers—all of whom are of particular importance for social protection and other programs—often have fingerprints that are less easy to scan. Biometrics are sensitive to ambient conditions, such as dirt and humidity (fingerprints), lighting (face), and connection quality and language (voice). Tests by Simprints, a nonprofit technology company from the University of Cambridge, show that normally well-performing devices and algorithms can record far higher error rates for particular groups and under difficult conditions (Storisteanu and others 2016). High-quality data capture and transmission is essential for these technologies to work as expected. Other nontechnological factors, such as the training and experience of individuals conducting the data capture, may also influence the results.

Enrollment. Accurate enrollment is possible for large populations. In a series of papers in 2012, the Unique Identification Authority of India (UIDAI) released proof-of-concept performance data on the inclusiveness and accuracy of biometric enrollment for a gallery of 84 million people using fused scores[3] from a combination of fingerprint and iris scans (UIDAI 2012c), and followed this up with large-scale studies of authentication (UIDAI 2012a; 2012b). These findings provide reasonable lower bounds on performance as technology is continually improving. They demonstrate that it is now possible to provide "unique" identity with a high level of precision in very large populations. This requires extreme accuracy, as every person needs to be compared with every other person in the database; the number of bilateral comparisons increases in line with the square of the population. Based on the UIDAI results, the probability of mistakenly confusing a new enrollee with an individual who has already registered is only 6.7 in 1 trillion (Gelb and Clark 2013b).

To illustrate what this level of accuracy means, it is worth looking at the UIDAI results on the scale of a more representative-sized population than that of India. Assuming a total enrollment of around 30 million adults (comparable to the number in Tanzania), the failure-to-capture data from UIDAI suggest that around 42,000 people would not be able to provide sufficiently high-quality fingerprint and iris data for the system to capture. They would need to be enrolled using biographic data and provided with alternative mechanisms to authenticate themselves for services. The number of false rejections, an erroneous indication that the subject had already enrolled requiring manual follow-

3 Fusion algorithms combine data from a number of biometrics, such as multiple fingerprints or fingerprints, face, and iris, to create a composite match that can be far more precise than any one of the separate biometrics. For more information, see Maltoni and others (2009) and Hicklin, Ulery, and Watson (2016).

up, would only be about 3,000. And even if as many as one person in a hundred tried to register twice, the low probability of successfully acquiring two identities (the UIDAI study used a "false acceptance" rate of 3.5 in 100,000) would result in only around 100 false acceptances or dual identities. Including face as a third biometric, which was not used for the UIDAI tests, would reduce all of these probabilities of failure considerably.[4]

Authentication. The emerging field evidence suggests reasonable accuracy but more difficulty with single fingerprint authentication in field conditions. In UIDAI's proof-of-concept reports on authentication, using a single finger and a false acceptance rate of 0.01 percent (the security level provided by a 4-digit personal identification number) resulted in a total rejection rate of 5 percent, defined as the sum of failure to capture fingerprints and false rejections following several attempts to take the print. The failure rate for each individual attempt to confirm a fingerprint could be considerably higher. In these tests, iris was far more inclusive and more successful, with dual-capture iris showing a total rejection rate of only 0.55 percent for the same false acceptance rate.[5]

Still-emerging data from the reform of India's public distribution system points to the importance of providing alternative options for people to authenticate themselves. Information released on the Andhra Pradesh Benefit Disbursement Portal suggests that the failure rate for individual attempts to authenticate fingerprints could be as high as 17 percent, although with three successive tries the rate could be reduced to around 2 percent.[6] In one audit in Andhra Pradesh of five Fair Price or ration shops with Aadhaar-based point-

---

4   The UIDAI results are supported by less formally released information from Indonesia's program that used the same technology as well as face.

5   For more detailed summary of the evidence from these tests, see Gelb and Clark (2013b). Iris was also more inclusive and easier to use than fingerprints in tests carried out by UNHCR. Hopkins and Hughes (2014) report on a field test in Malawi, which included 16,849 adults and young children. Regarding speed and ease of use, both operators and participants clearly preferred iris to fingerprints. Among the latter, 80 percent considered iris as "easy" relative to only 15 percent for fingerprints. Thirty-five percent of participants rated fingerprints as "difficult" versus none for iris. Face occupied an intermediate position. Failure-to-capture rates were also lower for iris.

6   For the complete data, see the Authentication Success Ratio Analysis at http://appost. aponline.gov.in/PostalWebPortal/UserInterface/Portal/Reports/DoP/DopAuthSuccess-Ratio_New.aspx?SC=AP. Another study of ration shops suggested a first-time authentication failure rate as high as 30 percent due to worn fingers and faulty connectivity (Yadav 2016). In some states, ration shop owners have been permitted to take photographs of food ration recipients in lieu of fingerprint authentication where the latter has repeatedly failed.

of-sale identity verification, about half of those beneficiaries who did not collect their rations cited nonmatching fingerprints as the reason (Scroll.in 2015).

It is especially difficult to authenticate fingerprints for groups that work with their hands. A study of Aadhaar-enabled fertilizer distribution by Microsave (Giri and others 2017) reports success rates of 35 percent, 70 percent, and 73 percent for three successive attempts to authenticate farmers, with 7 percent failing to be authenticated at all. This is more than a minor inconvenience, especially when the fingerprint problem is compounded by connectivity failures and delays. Farmers rush in to purchase fertilizer immediately after rain, so that speedy processing of transactions is essential. If the system is too slow, as it still appears to be, it will be circumvented at times of heavy demand. These problems can be eased by operator training, introducing establishing alternative biometrics or linking the identity number to a mobile number so that the mobile becomes an alternative credential.

Point-of-service biometric authentication for every service can also be overkill. For many purposes it may be enough to establish a deduplicated identity baseline with unique numbers and rely on less rigorous authentication at the point of service depending on the level of identity assurance that is needed (chapter 6). India's massive PAHAL and Ujjwala programs to provide direct transfers to households that purchase liquefied petroleum gas cylinders for domestic use do not require the recipients to provide their biometrics at the time of delivery, even though Aadhaar is now the basis for ensuring clients' unique identity. The connection address and link to the designated number of the mobile that is used to place the order provide adequate assurance that the correct beneficiaries have ordered and received the cylinders.

Vulnerability. Standard error data do not convey the level of resilience of the technology to possible "spoofing" attacks through the creation of artificial fingerprints or irises.[7] Unlike the hacking of data stored in a central facility, the spoofing of an individual biometric is a time-consuming process requiring specialized skills, and is not easy to undertake on a mass scale. However, this potential vulnerability has led to several developments, including the incorporation of liveness detection in fingerprint and iris readers; greater interest in

---

7   Such artificial biometrics can be created without the cooperation of the subject through recent advances in "capture at a distance" technology for face, and more recently fingerprints and iris, through the lifting of latent fingerprint images or the reengineering of a synthetic iris from a stolen template. The last process was widely believed to be impossible until such an iris was reengineered using a genetic algorithm (Zetter 2012).

"hidden" biometrics, such as infrared vein pattern recognition, that cannot be remotely lifted without the knowledge of the subject; and ongoing efforts to develop "revocable biometrics" so that a compromised template can be cancelled and reissued. It can also be helpful to store some personal identifying data "on card" (if a card is used) and under the direct control of the holder to provide an alternative in case the central database is compromised.[8]

Because no single approach is totally foolproof, security is best ensured through multiple independent identifiers. Especially for high-value transactions, biometrics should be used as one of several factors, together with other mechanisms such as tokens (what you have) and PINs (what you know), in multifactor authentication.

How Acceptable Is the Use of Biometrics?

Attitudes to the taking of biometric data vary across countries and sometimes across cultures. There has not been a comprehensive global survey, and most of the information available comes from high-income countries. The approach is complicated by the variety of biometrics and applications. For example, the involuntary taking of face prints by remote cameras (a topic not addressed in this book) raises different privacy issues than the conscious registration of a fingerprint on a scanner. As a broad generalization, the technology itself appears to be widely accepted despite some pockets of resistance to taking biometrics—on religious or cultural grounds, because of a traditional association between fingerprinting and criminality, or because some people have concerns over the hygiene of contact scanners. Mobile use is changing perceptions of the technology. In many countries where fingerprints have carried the stigma of their long association with law enforcement, they are now used for convenience, whether to unlock mobiles or even to enter amusement parks.[9] Direct contact may soon become a relic of the past, as a new generation of contact-less fingerprint scanners is emerging.

8   The Biometrics Institute provides guidelines on many issues relating to biometrics, including privacy and vulnerability to spoofing. See the institute's website at www.biometrics institute.org/.

9   Walt Disney World now uses the Ticket Tag system to scan fingerprints on entry to help prevent ticket fraud. The scan generates a number that is associated with a ticket for the period of its duration. The company asserts that no images or templates are stored. For more information about the Ticket Tag system, see the frequently asked questions page at https://disneyworld.disney.go.com/faq/my-disney-experience/my-magic-plus-privacy/.

Opposition usually relates less to the technology itself and more to concerns about the purpose of the identity system enabled by biometric technology, the potential misuse of personal data, and the difficulties of using the system. Nevertheless, religious and social traditions must sometimes be accommodated through special administrative arrangements. One example is the deployment of all-female enrollment facilities for women in socially conservative areas of Pakistan.

Convenience is key. The limited information to date suggests that people are pragmatic when confronted by new technology. If it is expected to deliver services more efficiently, it will be accepted, often with hope and even enthusiasm. If identification is seen as yet another bureaucratic obstacle, or if the costs of adapting to the new system and using it are high, the perceptions will be very different. A survey of border management by Accenture (2015), covering 3,000 people from several European countries, offers useful insights.[10] Overall, 80 percent of those surveyed were willing to share at least one form of biometric. For British travelers, 82 percent were willing—this from a country that has strongly opposed proposals to develop a centralized national identification system. German respondents were the least supportive, but even so 74 percent responded positively. Security and convenience were both important factors: 73 percent considered that biometric capture of everyone crossing the border would make their country more secure. Favorable responses were higher for those that had used biometric e-Gates than for those that had not, since most of the former had found them faster than manual gates.

The Accenture study also illustrated a general lesson—the importance of having a fast and effective mechanism to deal with technology failures. Travelers were comfortable with automated e-Gates provided that an attendant would be at hand to respond to any problems. Even if the e-Gates do not work every time, if they succeed in processing most passengers rapidly and smoothly they can free up resources to deal with a smaller number of failures in an expeditious way.

The Placebo Effect versus the Need for Greater Transparency

Why is there not more open information on performance? Considering the association of biometrics with law enforcement and security, a degree of secrecy is not unexpected. There may also be an element of self-fulfilling prophecy in the mystique of great accuracy. If people believe that the system is infallible,

---

10 The basis for sample selection is not clear so that results are offered only as suggestive.

fewer will try to cheat it and the percentage of errors and failures will be lower.

This "placebo" effect of biometrics has been acknowledged, for example, when referring to the practice of fingerprinting of infants in Uruguay as a deterrent to child abduction and trafficking, even though their prints often are not of useful quality when taken with standard equipment.[11] Rader (2016) provides a noteworthy example of the unwinding of such a virtuous circle during the 2008 registration of voters in Somaliland. The National Election Commission failed to run the deduplication software during biometric voter registration because of cost and planning problems. As people began to realize that duplicate registrations were not being flagged, more and more people took advantage of the loophole, not necessarily with the intention of voting multiple times but to acquire multiple identification cards that might be of use after the elections. "I registered five times," Rader reports a registrant in Hargeisa saying, "and I told everyone I knew to do the same."

Even recognizing this argument, from the perspective of the SDGs, lack of transparency on performance is problematic. It raises the risk of exclusion when it comes to dealing with actual performance failure, for example to verify the fingerprints of a genuine beneficiary, since the onus falls heavily on those affected by errors and failures to prove a supposedly "infallible" system wrong. Those more likely to be affected will be disproportionally from disadvantaged groups, such as poor manual workers and the elderly, whose biometrics are of lower quality and who are also more likely to be in areas with poorer connectivity.

More transparency in this area would therefore be highly desirable, both for the public and also for donors that may be asked to support such programs. India is ahead of other countries in disclosing information, not only by publishing its 2012 reports but also by beginning to make authentication success and failure rates available on public websites. It can go further by providing more detailed information on the incidence of failures to authenticate, as well as on the speed and effectiveness with which such failures are being resolved. Other countries and programs need to follow India's lead to ensure that the new identification and service delivery programs are held accountable for performance.

Far more systematic research is needed into the experience of using the new

---

11 This deterrent effect was discussed by Cristina Tello, project coordinator at the Office of Planning and Budget in the Presidency of the Republic of Uruguay, during a World Bank seminar on September 17, 2015. The link to child abduction is also mentioned in a video about Uruguay's civil registry on the Inter-American Development Bank website; see www.iadb.org/en/news/webstories/2011-09-19/uruguay-strengthens-civil-registry,9539.html.

systems. The still-emerging evidence shows that it is important to offer a range of options for authentication, including for those not able to provide biometrics of adequate quality to use the automated systems. Offering a wider set of authentication options than simply fingerprints would leave fewer people unable to authenticate themselves. Once the base identity is securely and uniquely established there are many alternative options—iris, PINs, or one-time passwords sent to mobile SIMs linked to unique identity numbers. The Fair Price Shops in Krishna District, Andhra Pradesh, for example, now have iris scanners to back up fingerprint readers when the latter fail to authenticate beneficiaries after three attempts. Iris still needs to be tested in the dust-laden atmosphere of fertilizer distribution centers.

Effective and responsive grievance processes are essential. Even with iris, biometric matching is a statistical process, and even the most advanced system will have inevitable errors. The importance of having access to human help is stressed by the Accenture study. Especially in the early stages, it is important to support those who are less able to navigate the system. The needed support services should be funded out of the savings generated by the programs. Technology will not solve all problems, but if it frees up resources by making service delivery easier and cheaper for most people (as in the e-Gates study) some of the savings should be used to serve those who are not able to navigate the system.

"Identity First": An Alternative to National ID?

India's Aadhaar program shows how recent advances in digital biometrics pave the way for alternative approaches to rapid and inclusive nationwide identification programs. The Aadhaar program is remarkable in many ways. It offers a multitude of lessons for other countries, even if they might not want to adopt every one of its features. The treatment here is brief; chapter 6 offers more detail.

Reflecting UIDAI's strong and specific inclusion objective, Aadhaar enrollment is both voluntary—as reiterated by numerous Supreme Court judgments—and open to all residents. Available documentation is scanned at enrollment and biometrics are taken, but the program requires no detailed biographic data or documentation. Like eligibility to drive a car or to receive subsidies, the entitlement of an identified individual to citizenship can be left for later, to be adjudicated by the National Population Registry if and when it becomes necessary to do so. This approach has enabled spectacular rates of enrollment, so that the system has been rolled out for use far more quickly than possible for many other identification systems. The "identity-first" approach differs from the more traditional national ID programs and agencies discussed in the previous section.

The program issues no card, only a number as a unique identifier. Although a basic picture card is widely held, the system does not depend on the physical credential to function. The true identity asset is the biometrically supported central register against which the identity of each holder of an Aadhaar number can be remotely authenticated independently of any card by providing fingerprints or iris. This provides full digital ID—a technological leap over many systems—and saves on the costly and difficult task of producing and managing cards. That said, the system does require connectivity to function.

Aadhaar is therefore not a national ID card or even a national ID. Nor was it created as a functional ID such as a voter card, ration card, or a driving license, where identification is linked to a particular purpose. It was established as a mechanism to give people the opportunity to register and authenticate themselves and to provide e-ID services for any program or purpose that can use them. It is a truly unique foundational ID program or mechanism. Such a program, delinked from the detailed requirements for documentation and providing unique identity on the basis of minimal data, would not have been possible without the use of digital biometrics. They provide unique identification and authentication of an individual based on physical characteristics alone—no cards and no other documentary evidence required.

Aadhaar has been revolutionary in other respects as well. One is the use of standards and competitive procurement to hold down costs while achieving massive scale. Enrollment is contracted out to a decentralized network of 50,000 agents who are employed by banks or other companies and paid on the basis of successful enrollments. UIDAI, which manages the program, does not maintain a vast network of service points. Especially considering its success in registering almost all of India's adult population—and now extending to children—it is a remarkably compact organization.

Another innovation is its use of Aadhaar as a platform to deliver a range of more advanced services through innovations built on top of the authentication function (the "India Stack"). These currently include e-KYC, the "digital locker," and payments applications that go well beyond the facilities offered by systems (chapter 6). With Aadhaar open to developers who wish to build on its capabilities to create new applications, the range of uses is only just at its beginning.

From the perspective of development and the SDGs, the "identity-first" approach has many advantages. The rollout of the system can be both inclusive and much more rapid than traditional national identification programs, especially in cases where complex nationality laws and processes create hurdles to enroll. The Aadhaar model can help to close the "identification gap," but it requires a radical rethink of identity management mandates, priorities, and processes. Other countries can learn from Aadhaar's "identity first" approach, innovative organization, and use of technology, even if they do not adopt all features of the Aadhaar model.

Lifetime Identification and Young Children

Infants and very young children are a frontier population for identity management systems. New advances in identification technology promise to strengthen the early entry point into lifetime identification and build a closer relationship between civil registration and identification. With the digitization of birth records and civil registries, birth certificates are becoming easier to authenticate, helping to cut down fraud further down the ID chain. Accurate biometric registration of very young children remains a challenge, but the latest technologies now allow children as young as six months to be reliably identified by their thumbprints. The rapid progress in this area also presents challenges: advances in technology that enable infants to be uniquely identified and enrolled into nationwide ID programs shortly after their birth could disrupt the relationship between civil registration and national identification, raising the risk of duplicative parallel systems. The enrollment of young children in (voluntary) ID programs also raises questions about the meaning of "informed consent."

Birth Registration as the Entry Point for Identity

Birth registration, long neglected in many countries, is beginning to be addressed by increased focus and finance, collaboration between registrars and health service providers, and the use of digital technology to communicate the details of births to registry offices. But paper-based birth certificates—the "breeder documents" for identification systems—still are an area of vulnerability for later identification.

At the most basic level, the coverage and timeliness of birth registration to establish an entry point for identification needs to be increased. Coverage is a continuing challenge in many countries (chapter 2), as is achieving registration soon after the birth. Some advocate for registration "right from the start" as a human right,[12] but others feel that mandating tighter global standards is discouraging to the many countries still low on the standard indicator of registration by the age of 5. From the perspective of ensuring the integrity of identity management, the earlier that birth registration can be performed (with links to parents' ID numbers), the better. Issuing the national ID number at birth can help to ensure the continuity of identity management over the life cycle. Botswana has done this since 2003; it is also the practice in other countries such as Uruguay, Peru, and Thailand.

A second priority is to standardize and secure birth certificates. Certificates come in a bewildering variety of forms; a study of birth certificate fraud (DHHS 2000) estimated that some 14,000 varieties of birth certificates, few with any security features, were in use worldwide. It is difficult for any authority to be sufficiently familiar with such a wide range of documents to readily detect fraudulent ones. Actions are needed to strengthen their security features and improve the quality of registries so that certificates can less easily be forged and more easily be authenticated. Spurred in part by a number of incidents and scandals, some jurisdictions and countries have taken steps in this direction, but global progress is still limited.[13]

Digital technology could help. With "digital lockers," as introduced in India, authorities can upload certified documents and end-users—in this case, parents and the children themselves—can share these virtually with other public and private entities for identity verification. This could reduce birth certificate fraud in the future. However, the widespread use of such sophisticated digital infrastructure is still likely a long way off for many poorer countries and their residents.

The third priority is continuing to address the technical challenge of authenticating people, including both adults and very young children, against the identities claimed on their birth certificates. These documents often were issued years before the need to establish identity; they include no photos or

12 See, for example, UNICEF (2002).

13 The problem is not confined to developing countries. In one assessment, some 10 to 15 percent of new French biometric passports were estimated to be held by an unauthorized individual owing to forged or substituted supporting documentation, including birth certificates (*Le Parisien* 2011). In 2010 all birth certificates issued by Puerto Rico had to be invalidated and reissued with security features in an attempt to curb rampant identify fraud (Wilhelm 2012).

other identifying data.[14] Young children cannot be expected to remember PINs or passwords but can be identified through something they have—parents with established identities—provided that the parents are at hand and that their testimony is trusted. A promising innovation is to provide unique identifying bracelets at birth, but these are vulnerable to loss or damage and may not be helpful in later life.[15] Another promising invention is an electronic necklace that includes in its chip the name and particulars of the child as well as a copy of its medical record. These can reportedly be produced for as little as $1 (Akpan 2014).[16]

What Role Can Biometrics Play?

The alternative to "something you know" and "something you have" is "something you are." DNA is a theoretical possibility but is neither technically nor financially feasible nor likely to be useful for routine applications. A swab could be taken shortly after birth and a set of identifying markers incorporated into the birth record, but the routine and wide-scale use of this option is not practical with current technology. The cost has come down but is still around $10 per identity for batch DNA (laboratory time 4–8 weeks) and $100 through rapid DNA (90 minutes). Even if costs fall further, they will not see the remarkable reductions that have occurred for digital technology. DNA is therefore not suitable for routine authentications, for example to check whether a child has already been vaccinated.

The use of DNA as a biometric for identification raises its own privacy concerns. Even the few pieces of data extracted from DNA for forensic ID purposes can reveal sensitive personal information, especially on familial relationships and—by comparing against a wider database—possibly on ethnicity. The data are drawn from a tiny subset of the genome; they consist of a sequence

14 It is noteworthy that birth certificates on their own do not receive much weight in GOV.UK Verify's approach toward verifying identity (chapter 6). One reason, no doubt, is the difficulty of proving that the certificate is being presented by the legitimate holder of an "active" identity.

15 One such system is the Bubble ID bracelet; see Morlin-Yron (2016).

16 Implanted microchips and digital tattoos are now routinely used to identify pets and are being tested as possible approaches to electronic human recognition. They are beginning to be used by some companies as an option to identify employees and might, in principle, work for infants and very young children. However, their routine use (if ever) appears to be well in the future. See Eng (2017) and Cellan-Jones (2015).

of 26 numbers each denoting the number of random sequence repeats at particular sites. It is understood that, on their own, the numbers reveal virtually nothing directly about the subject's health status or any other personal characteristics. However, relatives share more of their DNA than unrelated people; first-degree relatives such as siblings, parents, and children share on average at least half their DNA. A high percentage of matching in a forensic DNA comparison using the 26 numbers therefore signals that a relationship is likely. As a result, DNA testing can reveal paternity. In a criminal investigation, it can also lead investigators to individuals who are unlucky enough to have close relatives with DNA on file, perhaps because these relatives have previously been arrested. Since the frequency of arrests can be different across different ethnic groups, there is a greater probability of tagging members of some groups than members of others. This has raised concerns that even apparently innocuous DNA identification can exacerbate racial inequality in the workings of the justice system.[17]

Recent advances in other biometric technologies are closing the gap. The normal age for registration into national ID and similar programs is usually between 15 and 18, but younger children have been successfully enrolled using fingerprints and iris. India's Aadhaar program has begun to register children from birth, linking their number to their birth record and also to the Aadhaar numbers of their parents (Gupta 2016). Biometrics are taken from the age of 5, with reregistration at the age of 15. Registration is now being required for children to receive midday school meals (Iyengar 2017). Other examples include Mexico, which initiated a program to identify young children using iris, fingerprints, and face in January 2011 to fight child trafficking, and Thailand, which issues identity cards to children at the age of 7.[18]

All of these advances still leave open the frontier problem of infants and children below the age of 5. Iris and fingerprints have been tested, as well as palm- and footprints. Jain and others (Jain, Cao, and Arora 2014; Jain and others 2015) summarize a number of studies and note that operational efforts to identify children through fingerprints using standard approaches (for ex-

---

17 Seringhaus (2009) provides a useful summary of the features of DNA-based identification and the debate on racial bias and the use of familial search in criminal investigations. To level the playing field, he proposes the radical alternative of a universal DNA database. The technique appears to have been pioneered in the United Kingdom (BBC 2016). For ongoing debate on the use of familial search, see Rosenberg (2017).

18 The Mexican program reportedly registered some 14 million people before being halted due to nontechnical reasons.

ample, by VaxTrack) generally have had to revert to using the mother's fingerprints because of the difficulty of obtaining high-quality prints from the child. The difficulty in registering very young children in a refugee setting using standard equipment is also evident in Hopkins and Hughes (2014). High-quality fingerprints (and iris scans) were obtained from only 4 percent (14 percent) of children from newborn to age 3, compared with 87 percent (98 percent) of those age 4 and older.[19] As in the results from India's UIDAI, iris appears to be a more inclusive technology, but neither biometric scored well for very young children. Still more recent technical advances are moving the biometric frontier closer to birth. Researchers at the University of Michigan led by Anil Jain can now identify infants as young as 6 months with 99 percent accuracy based on two thumbprints (Rutkin 2016; Jain 2017). The UIDAI recently launched an Android application to register children below the age of 5, taking face and thumbprints and linking them to the Aadhaar number of their parents (Kulkarni 2015).

Biometric technology is not yet at the point where it can deliver a robust unique identity over the entire lifecycle that can be quickly and easily authenticated at a point of service. However, it is possible to do this from the age of 5, well before a person becomes legally responsible and has the capacity to commit identity fraud. With current rates of advance, it could soon become possible to include very young children and infants. Easy, fast, and accurate identification would not only strengthen the foundation of identity for life but could also make the administration of vaccines and other services easier during a child's first years.

At the same time, the (biometric) enrollment of young children into identification programs raises questions about informed consent and whether registered children should be able to delete or at least deactivate their ID numbers and associated records once they have reached adulthood. Birth registration is compulsory in many but not all countries, and records cannot be deleted. It can be argued that these are instrumental for the state's basic administrative functions and, as the most basic building block of identity, vital for any future needs. However, in the case of voluntary ID programs that enroll children below the age of 18 (or below the age of majority), the requirements and spirit of "informed consent" could be satisfied by having a provision for withdrawal once a registrant reaches adulthood. UIDAI's current policy states that the fin-

---

19 There was also some slight deterioration in the quality of both fingerprint and iris images
    for participants over age 50.

gerprints and iris scans of infants and children enrolled in Aadhaar must be updated within two years of their fifth birthday, and then again at age 15. If these children fail to do so within this stipulated two-year period, their Aadhaar numbers will be automatically deactivated. However, there appears to be no procedure for a person's data and Aadhaar number to be permanently erased (Deshmukh 2014).

Managing Identification Services: Toward Autonomous Providers?

For historical, legal, and other reasons, arrangements for providing identification services differ across countries. There is no "one-size-fits-all" solution. Many alternative arrangements can work well, though each will have advantages and drawbacks. The quest to establish trusted providers, along with the increased reliance on technology requiring skilled specialists, may favor the use of autonomous providers that have a clear and limited mandate to provide ID services and are located outside of government ministries.

Table 4-1 depicts the institutional arrangements for managing civil registration and national identification programs for 169 governments. The close relationship between these functions might lead one to expect that they would always be integrated into a common system and performed by the same entity, but surprisingly this is not always the case. In a little more than half of the countries the two functions are both located in the same ministry, usually Home Affairs (77 countries) or Justice (12 countries). The ministry officially tasked with overseeing registration may have little real influence or knowledge about local registration processes. Data held in local offices are not always reported to a central database in a timely way. However, even this arrangement does not necessarily ensure that the functions are closely integrated. Examples as diverse as Kenya and Indonesia show that civil registration and identification can be situated in different departments of the same ministry, but still have distinct mandates, separate processes, and separate data systems. Registration into a family card in Indonesia, for example, does not automatically trigger birth registration; neither is there an automatic linkage in the other direction.

In 13 countries, civil registration is managed on a decentralized basis at provincial or municipal level or even by local communes. It is more common for the national ID program to be managed centrally, though there are ex-

TABLE 4-1 Institutional Arrangements for National ID (NID) and Civil Registration[a]

Primary civil registration entity	Primary NID entity						
	Ministry of Justice	Ministry of Interior/ Home Affairs	Electoral body	Subnational body	Independent NID org	Other	Total
Ministry of Justice	12	11	4	0	0	3	30
Ministry of Interior/ Home Affairs	0	77	2	0	1	5	85
Ministry of Health	0	6	1	0	2	3	12
Electoral Body	0	1	5	0	0	0	6
Subnational Body	0	7	2	2	0	2	13
Independent NID org	0	0	0	0	5	0	5
Other	2	3	1	1	2	9	18
Total	14	105	15	3	10	22	169

Source: World Bank ID4D dataset, 2017 edition; categories revised.

a. Categories and assignments have been revised from the original ID4D classification, in particular to separate out the category of subnational providers.

ceptions.[20] In Pakistan, for example, birth registration is the responsibility of the Union Council, the lowest-level administrative unit, while the national ID program is managed centrally. In Peru, births are registered by both the ID agency RENIEC and municipal civil registration offices, but measures have been taken to facilitate and incentivize reporting from the municipal offices into the central RENIEC database to ensure accurate recordkeeping (chapter 6).

One downside of institutional separation is unnecessary duplication, with civil registration and identification each operating its own decentralized office network. Integrating these functions could save substantial funding and improve convenience for the public. Kenya maintains 107 civil registration offices, a modest number for the size of the country. This sparse coverage imposes considerable time and travel costs on parents who must in some cases travel long distances to the registration office, with one visit to register births and another to obtain a birth certificate. At the same time Kenya maintains over 600 local offices of the National Registration Bureau that administers the national ID system. The imbalance in the number of offices is indicative of the relative emphasis on civil registration and national identification in Kenya. Starting from a situation in colonial times where only white births were registered, birth registration has continued to lag and its coverage is still only moderate. Compulsory identification, now universal, dates back as far as 1920, when the Native Registration Amendment Ordinance made it obligatory for African males above the age of 15 to carry an ID document known as the *kipande*. The kipande was a pendant worn around the neck that included personal information, one fingerprint image, and the wearer's employment record. Its purpose was to help control movement and manage the labor requirements of the colonial system.

In another pattern, the election commission or a similar body is responsible for the national ID program in 15 countries and for civil registration in 6 countries. These arrangements are more prevalent for countries in Latin America and the Caribbean, although some others, such as Bangladesh, have also located their national ID program in their election commissions.

Even if there is no golden rule for institutional arrangements, choices have consequences. Entities will be driven by their own mandates and concerns. For

20 Zambia's national identification system is administered on a decentralized basis. Germany issues a sophisticated national ID card but for historical reasons has resisted the creation of a centralized database. As discussed in chapter 2, Ethiopia's decentralized kebele ID system provides many of the same services as a (low technology) national ID system.

example, having the election commission responsible for the national identification program could reduce the incentive to register individuals who are not eligible to vote or to maintain a continuous registration process to serve those who come of enrollment age between elections. It will always be difficult to insulate the functioning of the system from the main interest of the organization mandated to implement it. Even if measures are taken to do so, there is still the problem of perceptions. One argument sometimes put forward to justify costly one-off voter registration exercises carried out under the authority of an independent electoral commission is that it is difficult for a voter roll to be seen as credible if it is based on a registration process located in the justice or interior ministries and is under the direct control of the government that seeks to be reelected.[21]

Toward Autonomous Providers?

Several countries task an autonomous agency with the clear mandate to provide registration and identification services. Three examples include the Registro Nacional de Identificación y Estado Civil (RENIEC) in Peru, the National Database and Registration Authority (NADRA) in Pakistan, and, more recently, Rwanda's National Identification Agency (NIDA). All three were established as part of nation-building processes or national reconstruction. India's UIDAI, another example, has been considered previously.

Peru's 1993 constitution established RENIEC as an autonomous entity. Its chief officer is appointed by open competition for a four-year term, and it does not depend on or report to any ministry, although it has direct coordination with Congress, the Ministry of Economy, and the Ministry of Foreign Affairs (Reyna 2014). An important priority for RENIEC's creation was to reintegrate a country severely disrupted by the Shining Path insurgent movement. The insurgency, which had extended over many years and affected large parts of the country, had destroyed much of the civil registration system. Moreover, many people born during the conflict had not been able to be registered at all, so that they lacked official recognition of their existence. RENIEC's inclusive mandate—to register all—involved extending registration to cover members of often remote indigenous communities, many of whom had never been in-

---

21 As an example, in October 2016 the main opposition party in Sierra Leone urged donors to cease supporting the civil registration authority out of concern that the government planned to require the independent National Elections Commission to draw on data collected by the civil registry. See Margai (2016).

cluded in national registration. RENIEC is also responsible for civil registration, although this is also carried out by offices under municipal authorities.

Pakistan's first registration office was established in 1973 at a time when there was little population information available to the government. As in the case of Peru, the motivation reflected security and nation-building concerns. Performance lagged, so that in 2000 the current form of NADRA as an autonomous organization was created by a NADRA Ordinance. This was introduced with the aim of reducing government interference in the management of the program so that registration could be accelerated (Malik 2014). NADRA's chairman and board members are appointed for a statutory term of three years but must retire at age 65.

As in Peru, many of Rwanda's civil registration records were destroyed during the country's civil war in the early 1990s. Efforts to restart civil registration began in 1998, but it was not until 2006 that the cabinet established a national identification project. In 2007 a successful registration exercise was held to establish a baseline for the country's National Population Register (Atick 2016). The National Identification Agency in its current form was established by law in 2011 as an administratively and financially autonomous agency, responsible for population registration, civil registration, and the issuance of the national ID card. Though it falls under the supervision of the Ministry of Local Government, it is governed by an independent seven-member board, appointed by the president for a three-year term.

Enrollment

In line with their mandates, all three entities have greatly expanded registration. Between 2005 and 2013, RENIEC increased the numbers on its register by 89 percent, achieving almost total population coverage (99 percent). From 2008 to 2014, NADRA's enrollment grew by 80 percent. Reflecting its strategic goal to extend registration to women, registration increased more rapidly for women (104 percent) than men (65 percent). Overall adult coverage might not be quite as complete as for RENIEC, but is nevertheless high. Rwanda's population register also offers close to complete coverage, with about 90 percent of the adult population holding a national ID credential.

RENIEC and NADRA are widely regarded as technically superior institutions with substantial in-house capacity. They have both used innovative approaches and a variety of strategies and arrangements to expand enrollment and to bring registration services to isolated and excluded groups. NADRA and RENIEC have employed mobile units in addition to fixed registration offices. In the case of RENIEC, mobile units were needed to reach out to isolated communities in the Amazon forests as well as to remote mountain communities. In the case of NADRA, operators carried man-pack registration kits to penetrate mountainous areas, sometimes servicing communities with no other central government presence. Social and cultural sensitivities also had to be addressed. To facilitate enrollment in Pakistan, registration units for women in sensitive areas were staffed only with female drivers and operators. Both NADRA and RENIEC encouraged people to enroll by linking registration directly with access to programs such as social transfers and emergency relief support, and to voter registration. NADRA also introduced a transgender category, a surprising first for a socially conservative country.

Unlike NADRA's and RENIEC's more gradual approach to registration, Rwanda's relatively small population size and strong but highly decentralized administrative structure made it possible for the authorities to register almost all of the country's population within a matter of days. In an effort to establish a baseline for its population register and provide all citizens with a proof of identity, Rwanda conducted a mass registration drive over a three-day weekend in 2007 (Friday to Sunday). After a period of careful planning, the government requested all residents to remain in their communities. Teachers were required to report to the schools, which were turned into registration centers. Thousands of civil servants distributed registration forms to the country's 12,000 communities, often using motorcycles to courier them to all parts of the country. The completed forms were returned to Kigali on Monday. About 9.2 million people were registered in that single weekend (Atick 2016). Even for a compact country, this was a remarkable achievement. This information was then entered into a computerized database to form the basis of the national population register. Those over the age of 16 were then processed for a national ID card over the next several months, achieving an estimated coverage of over 90 percent. In contrast to previous ill-fated identification programs that had categorized people by their perceived ethnicities, ethnicity data are not collected, and Rwanda's new cards carry only the designation "Rwandan."[22]

22 Most writers on the 1994 Rwandan genocide note the introduction of group classification on ID cards by the Belgian colonial government in 1933, an action that introduced a rigid racial concept of group identity that had not previously existed. Of great significance also, however, was the repeated decision by the postcolonial Rwandan authorities to retain the group classifications on ID cards. See Fussell (2001).

Governance

RENIEC and NADRA both have arrangements to represent user interests in their governance. NADRA's board includes representatives of sectors that depend on the identification system to identify their customers; these include not only government departments but also banks and other businesses. They are not the only systems to follow this approach—to take another example, the Dominican Republic created a "Social Cabinet" with representatives from a wide range of ministries as well as the election commission to oversee the strengthening of its national ID program (Gelb and Clark 2013a). NIDA too has a governing board that includes members from the private and public sectors; at least 30 percent must be female. Together with financial incentives for service, such arrangements can help to ensure that the system responds to the demands of potential users, whether banks, pension funds, or social protection agencies.

Without such feedback, it is all too easy for the identification agency to fail to take user needs into account. The decision not to include a signature on Tanzania's national ID card offers an example. It was made on the grounds that signatures were relics of less advanced ID systems and rendered obsolete by new approaches to authentication. Clients of ID services, notably commercial banks, opposed this decision strongly, arguing that, together with the photograph, a signature was an important check on the identity of the holder, especially as the infrastructure for reading the fingerprint templates embedded in the card's chip had not been rolled out. It was also necessary to have a signature to compare against existing documents. After four years of issuing ID cards without signatures, in 2016 it was announced that all cards were to be recalled and replaced by ones that did include them, at considerable expense (Linus 2016).

User representation on identification governing structures also acts as a check against the risk of predatory pricing. As is the case for any other statutory monopolist, the fee-based activities of an ID agency require oversight to ensure that ID requirements and charges for key services and documents are not excessive (chapter 5).

Financing

Like many other providers of identification services, RENIEC, NADRA, and NIDA charge fees for some services while ensuring that basic registration for the poor is available without charge. Most of RENIEC's budget comes from verification fees collected from private sector entities, notably banks, as well as charges for the issue of ID cards, but it also charges other government agencies for service in cases where they charge ("you charge, I charge") and receives an annual performance-related payment from the central government budget to support services to the poor. Providing these services can be costly on a unit basis, especially as enrollment is extended to encompass remote communities.

NADRA has taken the fee-driven model further. It receives no regular budget allocations and funds its operations through charges for fast-track services and premium products for individuals (such as smart ID cards) and fees from banks and other business entities that need to authenticate their clients. NADRA's offices do not follow regular government hours but have autonomy to remain open for longer periods if the employees see opportunities for more business and higher bonuses. It also receives fees for projects undertaken for other parts of government, such as the Benazir Income Support Program, and it competes successfully for external contracts to provide identification services on a commercial basis. NADRA has won many of these contracts, including for services in Bangladesh, Kenya, Sri Lanka, and Sudan.[23] Its total revenues tripled over 2008–13, enabling higher salaries and an increase of 60 percent in staffing. The proceeds are used to cross-subsidize outreach to remote communities and the free registration and provision of ID cards to the poor.

NIDA reportedly covers its full operating costs from fees charged for ID issuance. Registrants are charged about US$0.72 for the basic national ID card, while fees for driver's licenses, passports, and expedited applications can be as much as 100 times higher (Atick 2016). Those who are unable to pay the fee for basic ID can receive it for free. Unlike NADRA, NIDA does not charge other government agencies or banks for identity verification services. It has been exploring the possibility of producing secure documents, such as diplomas or professional certificates for other entities, as a way of generating additional revenues.

The possibility of such a commercial model—which is made more viable by the growth of demand for e-ID and remote authentication—raises the question of whether identification should be considered as a public good or as a service like electric power or water to be provided by a public utility subject to cost recovery. Should investment in a nationwide identification system be treated as a public investment and required to provide a reasonable financial rate of return? (Chapter 5 considers this question in more detail.) The public

---

23 A public company was formed, NADRA Technologies Limited, registered with the Securities and Exchange Commission of Pakistan. It is wholly owned by NADRA and able to bid for contracts outside the country and earn revenues to support its operations. Income from foreign projects was $17.6 million in 2013 (Malik 2014).

good model seems more appropriate when identification is approached from the perspective of human and legal rights, and it is also essential to ensure that the poor are not excluded from programs and services because of costly ID requirements. At the same time, the experience of RENIEC and NADRA, and possibly NIDA as well, suggests that including service fees in the funding mix can offer some advantages in terms of helping to sustain the system in the face of short-term fiscal pressures and ensuring that the system is responsive. Both inclusion and sensitivity to user needs are important to harness the full development potential of ID systems.

A Direction for the Future?

Separating out identification services and locating them in an autonomous public entity with a clear mandate and some commercial incentives for service appears to offer potential advantages. Locating the system in a distinct institution could help ensure trust and facilitate the effective use of technology. Especially as digital technology, including biometrics, becomes a more central feature of identification, it may become more attractive to locate registration and ID services in an entity with strong technical capacity and a clear but limited mandate to register the population and provide ID services. NADRA, RENIEC, and NIDA (as well as UIDAI) are all widely regarded as effective institutions with strong track records in delivering ID services.

The governance structures of the agencies themselves may also partly insulate them from government pressures. In Peruvian opinion polls, RENIEC has emerged as the country's most trusted institution, ahead of even the Catholic Church (chapter 6). By including users in the governance structure and building in financial incentives for performance, identification agencies could increase responsiveness and convenience for end-users. If, for instance, the autonomous approach sufficiently increased confidence in the independence and professionalism of the national ID program, it could eliminate arguments for costly one-off voter registration programs—a large saving for many countries.

Integration between Registries and Programs

One number or many? Should identification services be provided by one single system or by many unrelated systems? Must identification always flow logically onward from birth registration, or can it be based on functional systems set up to serve particular needs? How can information be updated if not through the civil registry?

Even when countries have committed to supply identification services through a centralized system based on continuous civil registration, immediate demands for stronger identification have created vastly different architectures. Figure 4-1 sets out the comparative features of several country systems. As in figure 1-2, the components include the civil registration system, the population register and its associated national ID program, and the separate program registers used for social transfers, voting, or other purposes. The relative sizes of the boxes and cylinders correspond to the coverage of the respective programs. Solid lines connecting the components indicate that the components are linked; namely, that the unique number issued by the ID agency is seeded into each individual record for the program. The figure's four country examples illustrate different levels of integration and interconnectedness among civil registration, national ID registers (population registers), and program registers.

Of the four selected cases, Peru has the most highly integrated system. Both RENIEC and municipal registry offices can register births and issue certificates. For institutional births, the infant's first ID is usually registered and issued within the hospital, through RENIEC's in-house auxiliary registry offices. Other births are often registered at municipal offices, and the municipal records are integrated with RENIEC's database, reporting at regular intervals. Civil registration therefore provides a continuous flow of data to the population register.

However, Peru's trajectory does not fit the "standard" model. National registration took precedence over civil registration during much of the previous decade, and it is only in more recent years that authorities have started to strengthen civil registration capabilities in underdeveloped areas and to coordinate the two sets of registries (chapter 6). In conflict-affected and geographically remote areas where records were destroyed or never existed, initial enrollment for the national ID could not rely on any civil registry. A phase of mass enrollment was needed to reestablish the identity baseline; only later did the civil registration system catch up.[24] Peru's national ID credential, the DNI, is also highly integrated into applications and used for virtually all purposes where identification is required: voting, education, healthcare, social transfers,

24 RENIEC and UNICEF data suggest that national ID coverage, at 99 percent, is still higher than the country's under-5 birth registration rate. Considering the total population, historical birth registration rates among adults are likely to be well below the current figure; many of those registered by RENIEC will not have had birth certificates.

FIGURE 4-1 Different Identification Architectures

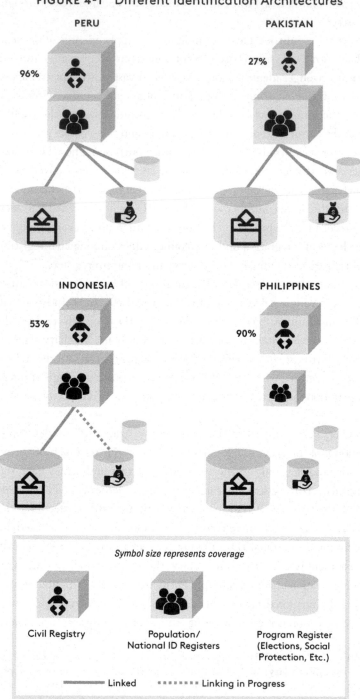

PERU

96%

PAKISTAN

27%

INDONESIA

53%

PHILIPPINES

90%

Symbol size represents coverage

Civil Registry

Population/
National ID Registers

Program Register
(Elections, Social
Protection, Etc.)

Linked ▪▪▪▪▪▪▪ Linking in Progress

banking and many more. These applications maintain separate databases, but all can identify individual participants through the same unique national ID number.

Pakistan also implements a national identification system with high coverage and all-purpose use, but is less able to rely on civil registration data than Peru since both birth and death registration rates are lower. As in Kenya and other countries in a similar situation, separate registration and enrollment exercises need to be undertaken for the national ID in order to include many individuals who have never previously been registered. Without a continuous flow of information from the civil register, such systems face a continuing challenge in updating the population register. Family and household registrations are even more difficult to maintain. These are needed, in addition to the individual ID records, because many NADRA-supported programs deliver benefits or services at family or household level.

NADRA's experience shows the importance of continuous use to keep the information current (see figure 1-2). To update its registers, NADRA draws on information as the identification system is applied, whether to register voters, to provide emergency relief to displaced people or flood victims, or to distribute social transfers. The 2015 voter reregistration exercise, for example, provided an important opportunity for NADRA to update its own database in the course of house-to-house visits. NADRA is also an implementing partner of the BISP, which with 5.4 million beneficiaries is the country's major social protection scheme. To identify beneficiaries, BISP draws on the National Socio-Economic Registry (NSER); this covers all households in Pakistan and is updated every few years. For more continuous updating, BISP has developed a data-sharing protocol to formalize arrangements to share data collected by other programs that might also require such information. In return for access to the data, the using agency agrees to submit updated and corrected information to improve data completeness and accuracy.[25] Pakistan's cycle of use and feedback shows the importance of continuous use of identity data to create incentives to update it and opportunities to do so.

Indonesia, the third country in figure 4-1, operates a dual regime, with the

---

25 The NSER is a national registry developed to create a single database to store information on individuals, households, and families—including, for instance, to identify poor households through a proxy means test. It can help target beneficiaries of multiple programs and facilitate research on the needs of the beneficiaries. Data are shared with organizations, individuals, or institutions that are granted access at different security clearance levels. In return, data users are required to provide updates and corrections. See BISP (2016).

SIAK population registry (Sistem Informasi Administrasi Kependudukan) co-existing with a less-comprehensive civil registry. This dual system results in an inconsistent approach toward identification and creates considerable difficulties for the poor (see Sumner 2015 and chapter 2). Relative to Peru or Pakistan, the national e-ID system is less widely integrated into applications, and the roll-out of an authentication ecosystem to use its advanced electronic ID card, the e-KTP, is less highly developed.

The fourth country, the Philippines, has a disconnected identification eco-system with multiple unrelated functional ID programs. Unlike most other countries in this situation, the Philippines has a comprehensive birth registra-tion system with over 90 percent coverage. This broad coverage could provide an effective entry point for a widely held national ID, with the identifier based on or even identical to the birth number. Even with repeated efforts to push the national ID program forward, and acknowledged gains in efficiency and convenience, data privacy and surveillance concerns (in addition to a range of probable vested interests in the existing arrangement) appear to have been pow-erful enough to stymie the rollout of such a program. As a result, each major government service or program operates its own system and issues its own ID credential. Consequently, the Philippines reportedly has at least 28 separate identification registers and cards, although a single individual will hold far fewer of these credentials.

Integration as a Social Choice?

Shifting from multiple functional program-specific identification systems toward a single nationwide foundational system has many practical advantages, although not all of the SDGs considered in chapter 3 require the use of a single system or a common number. People will only need to register once to acquire a multiuse credential. Identification systems are significant investments, espe-cially if they each incorporate the technology needed to ensure that enrollments are unique. This increases both fixed and variable costs. Separate systems will require duplicative local facilities. They will not be able to rely on shared infor-mation to update their records—for example, in the case of NADRA, the use of voter registration drives and social programs to update information that is relevant for both purposes. Unique and integrated ID is essential for an inte-grated social registry (Leite and others 2017).

However, the concerns expressed over identification systems also tend to be stronger for highly integrated systems. Privacy International has argued against the integration of social registers across multiple programs on the grounds that this coerces poor people to enroll in databases and systems with a wider scope and reach than any benefit they may be seeking (Hosein and Nyst 2013). Another possible risk is exclusion, if a nationality or residence test is required to enroll in the common system (chapter 5). Although the Aadhaar program does not impose a nationality or residence test, as noted earlier, it has faced similar criticisms that linking it to benefit programs for poor people with few options involves an unacceptable element of coercion. On data security, the argument is less clear, since multiple poorly protected databases that combine personal identifying information with other data might not be more secure than a well-managed central system that holds only the minimum identifying information needed.

Objections to integrated systems can also reflect more self-serving concerns. Those who are able to avoid taxation because of the difficulty of integrating income from different sources, or who benefit from leakages of subsidized goods or multiple identities or illegal access to multiple programs, will be concerned about the potential to tighten identity management and to consolidate incomes and benefits around each individual. The strength of the vested interests against such uses of identification cannot be discounted. The example of Pakistan (chapter 5) shows how vested interests can block valuable uses of an integrated system, especially when they threaten elites' discretion and privileges. In addition, government agencies have a natural tendency to defend their own mandates and ID systems. Moving to a central system not only threatens their power but removes high-value ID technology procurements out of their control. They often resist integration on the grounds of the transitional costs of moving away from their legacy systems.

Integration by Reverse Engineering

Several countries have sought to reverse-engineer national identification programs from functional programs. Bangladesh has taken steps to convert its voter registry into a national ID. The Bangladesh Election Commission biometrically registered over 92 percent of the voting-age population ahead of the country's 2008 elections; after the elections, the National Identity Wing was established in the election commission to administer the national identity system using the newly collected voter data. National ID cards were issued to the 85 million citizens registered in the database. Bangladesh is currently upgrading this system and issuing a biometric smart-ID card including a unique identifier, and aims to issue this card to all Bangladeshis by the end of 2017

(World Bank 2016b). In a similar effort, following its 2015 elections, Tanzania has initiated a process to issue national ID numbers to registered voters who will later be processed for national ID cards. The aim is to integrate about 15 million of the 22.3 million voter records into the National Identification Authority database to accelerate the rollout of the national ID (Lamtey 2016). Nigeria, too, is seeking to integrate several sources of identity data, including from banking, voting, mobiles, and immigration, into its national system managed by the National Identity Management Commission.

Considering where some countries are today, the reverse-integration approach seems attractive, but it is not without challenges. Legislative approval may be required before data can be shared. Agencies may resist losing control over their data. Even if these hurdles can be overcome, the information may not conform to common technical and quality standards. The datasets might not include comparable biographic information; biometric data might not conform to common standards and formats that enable the information to be merged. Systems also may have different quality standards, with hasty registration in some areas, such as SIMs or voter rolls, resulting in lower quality data. Sustainability is also an issue: a one-off boost to registration from merging the systems can speed up the process of creating an identity baseline but does nothing to solve the problem of updating the population register. There will be little opportunity or incentive to update these registers unless the system is rapidly put into use. Otherwise, the national ID database will be out of date before the next election.

FIVE

Confronting the Risks

W hile robust identification systems can help achieve many development outcomes, they can also give rise to a number of risks or exacerbate existing vulnerabilities. Most have been flagged in earlier chapters but have not been considered in an integrated way. This chapter provides an overview with an emphasis on risks relating to development impact. It does not consider specialized technical issues of data protection or the production of secure documents. Rather, it focuses on how ID systems can be applied in ways that run counter to the aspirations of the Sustainable Development Goals—or waste, rather than conserve, valuable resources—and how to mitigate the risks of such adverse applications. It is helpful to group the many different varieties of risks into three categories: exclusion risk, privacy risk, and cost risk.

Regarding the first category, exclusion risk, the formalization of identification through stronger systems may exclude vulnerable individuals or groups from participation in social and economic life or from essential services. They may be excluded because they are poor and deterred by the fees and charges required to enroll in the system or to use it to access services or benefits; they may also need assistance to navigate new technologies and approaches. Women or members of particular groups, such as ethnic minorities or remote communities, can face particularly large difficulties in accessing and using the system. A large but undetermined number of people face discriminatory exclusion from opportunities, services, or benefits when more rigorous identification is associated with the determination of national status.

The second category, privacy risk, is the possibility that personal data collected by identification systems may be misused to track the activities of individuals, invade their privacy, or steal their identities. This is not to say that advanced digital ID systems are inherently antithetical to privacy. In some circumstances, digital technology can be a less intrusive way to deliver benefits or services than traditional approaches. Also, identification is only one aspect of the digital revolution that is sweeping through rich and poor countries alike and raising other, more serious risks to privacy. The risks are likely higher in poor countries, however, because of the more limited stage of data privacy and protection laws as well as weaker systems of political checks and balances.

The third category of risks concerns the cost-effectiveness of large investments in identification systems. Even though there is mounting evidence that investing in a robust ID system can yield a high rate of return in a developing country context, the field is littered with cases of wasted investments and low-productivity programs. Some problems lie on the supply side—failures in strategy or design, or corrupt procurements that create redundant systems or boost the costs of acquiring technology. In other cases, the limiting factors lie in the demand for the use of the system. Even well-conceived investments in ID systems will fail to be productive if they are not used in appropriate ways, including to support the SDGs, whether because of implementation failures or because powerful vested interests block their most productive uses.

Any assessment of the balance of benefits and risks is complicated by the possibility that the role played by an identification system and the purposes for which it is used are liable to evolve in response to changing policies and needs. One notable example already flagged in chapter 1 is South Africa: Breckenridge (2005) describes how its ID system has evolved from helping to enforce discriminatory residence laws during the apartheid period to underpinning the rollout of large inclusive social grant programs under post-apartheid governments. Another example is that of Spain, and its history of using ID systems to discriminate against Moors and Jews. Cases show how the same ID system can help some poor people claim essential services and benefits even as it simultaneously excludes others. The rollout of the ID system in the Dominican Republic, for example, was promoted as helping to integrate poor Dominicans into the national social safety net—which it may well have succeeded in doing. But, as outlined below, the process was also used to exclude many residents of Haitian origin from Dominican citizenship, rendering around 200,000 of them effectively stateless.

All three risks—social and economic exclusion, loss of privacy, and wasteful investments—are present to varying degrees, even where no national or nationwide identification system exists. They will pose less effective threats to citizens of states with robust democratic institutions, strong legal frameworks, and enforcement capacity. However, in weak or repressive states, ID systems can increase opportunities for malfeasance and exacerbate existing threats and harmful practices.

Exclusion Risk

Exclusion can be a result of several risk factors and vulnerabilities, but in practice there is often overlap among them. Poverty often is associated with a lack of previous identity documentation, which can complicate registration and make it difficult for individuals to prove their status as a national. Those unable to prove their status as a national or even a legal resident will, in turn, be less able to take advantage of economic opportunities, locking them into poverty. Countries with laws or sociocultural norms that restrict enrollment possibilities for women will also be more likely to discriminate against women in other areas, such as the ability to pass on their nationality to their children, a factor that can increase the risk of statelessness and the associated lack of formal identity documentation, resulting in further social and economic marginalization.

The poverty barrier. Costly or difficult registration requirements are an obstacle to poor and disadvantaged populations. As well as financial cost, barriers can include long distances to registration centers, long wait times to enroll in the system or to pick up identity documents, requirements for prior documentation, or administratively complex registration processes. Countries that have successfully boosted enrollment, such as Malaysia, Pakistan, and Peru, have often used mobile units to reach poor registrants in isolated areas or empowered a decentralized network of contracted enrollment agents (as in the case of India's UIDAI). Issuing the first ID for free, at least to the poor, is also important to ensure that the identification system is inclusive. In many countries, authorities levy fees for the issuance of a birth certificate, and late registration can carry particularly large costs due to penalties and increased administrative requirements. As highlighted in chapter 2, costs for late birth registration can be as high as $1,000 in some developing countries, effectively barring the majority of the population from obtaining an official proof of identity if they were not registered very soon after birth.

The gender barrier. Although, on average, the gender differences in birth registration rates are small, women in some countries and conservative communities face legal or customary barriers to obtaining official identification, as well as participating more generally in economic activities. There is little systematic data on the gender breakdown for enrollment rates in national or functional identification programs, but some examples illustrate the problem. In Nepal, women's access to identification is hindered by custom and administrative regulations that require the presence of male relatives for obtaining an official ID. A survey of 20,000 Nepalese residents found that only 74 percent of eligible women—compared to 87 percent of eligible men—held citizenship certificates, the country's primary identity document (FWLD 2014). Without a citizenship certificate, women cannot register land or home ownership, obtain employment, or access a range of financial or other public services. Citizenship laws are also discriminatory; they limit women's ability to pass on their citizenship to their children and spouse. These gender-based barriers are not confined to Nepal. In several other countries, including Afghanistan, Iraq, and a number of Middle Eastern states, a woman cannot register without the presence of a male relative or at least the male relative's ID documents.

Social norms can provide powerful disincentives for registration, sometimes spanning generations. The children of unmarried mothers, or mothers in traditional or religious marriages that have not been registered with the civil authorities, can face stigmatization when their birth certificates are issued without the name of the father. The mothers therefore may choose not to register their children at all (Sumner 2015). In some cultures, spouses and other family members may discourage women from obtaining an official ID for fear that it could enable greater access to services and greater financial independence. Such independence may be seen as increasing the decisionmaking power of the female household member and even increasing the risk that the marriage could be dissolved.

The technology barrier. As digital technology is incorporated into identification systems, there is the risk that some will be left behind. Older people especially can have difficulty navigating new technologies. Systems that require connectivity for online authentication pose a challenge for those in poorer and more remote areas where connectivity is more likely to be weak or variable. People in these areas will be at least seriously inconvenienced, and at worst disempowered, without a ready offline authentication mechanism. Some occupational groups have greater difficulties providing high-quality fingerprints; so do older populations, since print quality deteriorates with age. Services that require authentication at the point of delivery increase the challenge for aged or disabled people who previously could rely on others to collect benefits on their behalf. As noted in chapter 4, alternative authentication mechanisms need to be available to ensure that all can use the system. Some technologies can help; for example, voice recognition can be used for proof-of-life requirements to ease difficulties for pensioners who are not able to travel easily.

The nationality barrier. As outlined in chapter 2, national status is not particularly relevant for many of the SDG-related applications of identification systems. Indeed, the example of the Aadhaar shows that identification need not require any determination of national status or even legal residence in order to help people be included in subsidy and benefit programs, strengthen the administration of these programs, and facilitate financial inclusion. Nonetheless, this does not imply that nationality is irrelevant to legal identity in the context of development. The universal framing of the SDGs has caused development aspirations to align more closely with the human rights agenda. People without clear legal status will be seriously disadvantaged in many SDG areas. As noted by Gelb and Manby (2016), a person who is an irregular migrant may have only the most basic rights to due process and freedom from deliberate abuse if they are to be deported. Stateless persons—who are not recognized as a national by any state under the operation of its law—may have severely limited opportunities with no rights in any country at all and may be regarded as irregular migrants even in the country of their birth and lifelong residence.

Many countries are formalizing legal identity, a process that could render stateless an undetermined but potentially large group of people, many of whom have no plausible links to any other country. This has already happened deliberately in at least three cases, the Gulf States, Mauritania, and the Dominican Republic (Mahdavi 2016; IRIN News 2014; *New York Times* 2015). In the case of the Dominican Republic, a retroactive reinterpretation in 2004 of "temporary status"—a category previously applied to people present in the country for only short periods—denied birthright citizenship to children of "non-residents," notably persons of Haitian descent who had been born in the Dominican Republic, sometimes to parents who had been born there as well. Many had considered themselves to be Dominican citizens; some had even held Dominican passports. As the identification system was reformed, lifelong residents of Haitian descent were refused national ID documents (*cédulas*) unless they were able to provide documentary evidence of legal Dominican residence going back multiple generations. Without ID documents, they faced statelessness, were denied access to education, political participation, and the justice system, and also were unable to register the birth of their own children (Open

Society Institute 2010). In 2013 a constitutional court ruling further entrenched the exclusion of residents of Haitian descent, ordering a review—effectively a repeal—of Dominican citizenship status going back to 1929, which put an estimated 200,000 Dominicans of Haitian descent at risk of statelessness (Blake 2014). Subsequent revisions in response to intense international pressure have restored citizenship to a modest number and opened the theoretical possibility of citizenship to many more, but only subject to costly and complex administrative requirements that very few will be able to fulfill. This transition from "legal statelessness" to "administrative statelessness" (Hunter 2017) leaves the situation of many residents in limbo.

The uncertainty surrounding citizenship rights in the Dominican Republic is neither unique nor quantitatively the largest example. Only about 30 countries, mainly in the Americas, grant citizenship automatically on the basis of jus soli, birth on national territory. The remainder impose a variety of tests and criteria based on ancestry, length of residence, and birthplace that may require complicated and expensive legal processes to confirm citizenship. Nationality laws often have provisions that leave the question of citizenship open for interpretation by local officials; the authority in charge of registration and identification thus becomes the de facto court for adjudicating claims to citizenship. Legislation may directly discriminate against certain vulnerable groups, such as ethnic or religious minorities or women. Twenty-seven countries grant no or only limited rights to women to pass on their citizenship to their children or spouses (UNHCR 2014a). Increased statelessness therefore looms as a risk as identity is increasingly formalized. The United Nations High Commissioner on Refugees' official statistics indicate that the worldwide population of stateless persons is at 3.7 million, but UNHCR estimates the true total figure to be about 10 million because data are missing in many areas (UNHCR 2016; UNHCR 2014b). Stateless people may not be formally undocumented, since statelessness is itself a recognized status, but their political and economic participation is heavily constrained.

Myanmar offers an example of the complexity. Citizenship is divided into three categories, with acceptance into each category relying on a different set of criteria and each category of citizen assigned different rights. Only those with "full" citizenship can run for political office or establish political parties. Members of the two other categories—"associate" citizens and "naturalized" citizens—are barred from 14 liberal professions, including medicine, law, and engineering (UNHCR 2015a). The 1.2 million members of the Rohingya minority group, living mostly in the northern state of Rakhine, have for decades been denied any form of citizenship. Some have been issued temporary identification documents—"white cards" and, more recently, "green cards"—but these provide no right to state protection or access to public services, and further entrench differences between their status and that of recognized citizens (Aung and Mar 2015).

Africa is said to have over 720,000 formally stateless persons, but experts regard this figure as a dramatic underestimate of the number of people with unclear national status. Relative to those in, for example, most of Latin America, African nationality laws are exclusionary: over 20 countries have no provisions regarding a child's right to nationality or a path to citizenship for those with foreign-born parents (Manby 2016). Only three African countries automatically confer citizenship from birth to those born on their territory. Several countries still grant greater rights to men than women to pass citizenship to their children or spouses. Citizenship by naturalization is often almost impossible to obtain in practice, and many countries allow naturalized citizenship to be withdrawn on arbitrary grounds. Half of African states even allow revocation of a person's birth nationality.[1] Recognizing the increasing risk of marginalization, the African Union has called for a Convention on African Nationality in its report *The Right to a Nationality in Africa*; however, progress in this area has been slow (ACHPR 2015). Statelessness is an urgent problem that, if left unattended, could complicate the process of formalizing identity in both developed and developing countries around the globe.

Mitigating Exclusion Risks

Countries' experience offers many lessons on how to ensure that the formalization of identity supports inclusive development rather than greater exclusion. Governments can eliminate fees and charges for birth registration and the first issue of a national ID. They can use technology and mobile units to reduce the barrier of distance and women-only registration units to overcome the gender barrier. They can build in incentives for registration, both for the system (payment per registration) and for people (linking registration to health services or social transfers). They can review their requirements for identification to

1 Some countries base nationality directly on racial criteria. For example, only people of African ancestry may obtain Liberian citizenship.

ensure that these are not excessive in relation to the risks. Not every service or transaction requires "gold-standard" identification to the highest level of assurance (chapter 6).

Social nongovernmental organizations have played a facilitating role in some countries, intermediating between people and registration authorities, helping them to gather evidence, negotiate complex forms, and respond to questions. As an outstanding example, in Indonesia the Female-headed Household Empowerment Program, PEKKA (Perempuan Kepala Keluarga), has played a major role in supporting civil registration, including by helping to convene "one-stop shop" rural registration fairs and clinics staffed by paralegal members (World Bank 2012; Gelb, 2015; Sumner 2015). Registration fairs may include a party for the children, helping to communicate that birth registration is something to be celebrated rather than just another administrative process. In India, the Aangaan Trust works with Community Protection Volunteers in six states to help families without Aadhaar numbers navigate the application process and ensure that they receive benefits from the social protection programs they are entitled to. Through its community outreach, Aangan has helped more than 20,000 children and their family members enroll in the Aadhaar program and access Aadhaar-linked benefits (Donger and Mehrotra 2017).

Donors can also encourage outreach by funding each additional registration on a pay-for-performance basis, as has been done in some countries, subject to controls against multiple registrations.[2] Pay for performance needs to take into account the dramatic increase in the unit costs of registration as enrollment is extended to remote communities. In Peru, each registration in the Amazon region involves a multiple of the cost in mountain communities, which, in turn, involves a multiple of the cost in dense urban areas.

Technology should not be a barrier for those who are less able to use it. Offline authentication should be an option, especially in areas with poor or unreliable connectivity. Programs also need to allow for people who cannot register or authenticate themselves in the regular way, whether because they are not able to provide biometrics of adequate quality or not able to recall personal identification numbers and other identifiers. Multimodal biometrics can enhance inclusion by offering more options, but there will still be a small percentage of people who are unable to provide either quality fingerprints or iris

---

2   For example, civil registration support in the Dominican Republic included funding to upgrade the system and $5 per additional registration. Such an incentive scheme requires effective measures to prevent multiple registrations.

scans. Older people in particular may need help to navigate new systems. All programs should set up a system to monitor registration and authentication failures and a responsive grievance mechanism to resolve them.

As countries strengthen their identity management systems, often with the support of development partners, the risk of increasing statelessness can be mitigated in several ways (Gelb and Manby 2016). First, to prevent people from being denied access to key services, all residents should be provided with a proof of identity. This can be through an Aadhaar-type approach or, in the case of a country where identification is based on a national ID, by offering it to "residents," a category whose legal status in the country may not be fully resolved. This approach can also accelerate enrollment; experience in a number of countries, including compilation of voter rolls, shows that ID programs can be rolled out rapidly if they do not require too much documentary evidence at the time of registration.

Second, in applications, it is important to minimize discrimination based on legal status. Certainly, governments should not be expected to confer documents confirming nationality without proof that the conditions are met, but there is no good reason to use legal status in a country as a barrier to prevent people from holding financial assets, purchasing a SIM card, or registering property, or to bar children from going to primary school. Without a clear understanding on this issue, development partners could find themselves supporting an exclusionary identification system rather than an inclusive one.[3]

Third, development partners engaged in supporting identification programs can help mitigate exclusion risks by reviewing states' practices in determining nationality against both their own laws and international legal commitments. Practice may diverge considerably from laws and commitments. For example, almost all African states are party to the 1990 African Charter on the Rights and Welfare of the Child, which provides for states to grant nationality on the basis of birth on national soil if the child has no other nationality. This provision is also included in the 1961 International Convention on the Reduction of Statelessness, which additional countries have ratified in recent years. Implementing this commitment would eliminate statelessness within a generation. In some cases, national courts or constitutional bodies have found governments in violation of their own laws, but the rulings have

---

3 To the extent that birth registration requires details of parents' nationality in the birth record, such as by incorporating their national ID numbers, it raises similar concerns about nationality-based exclusion.

not been implemented. There also needs to be a credible grievance process backed up by independent judicial review; at present, decisions are often made by administrative officials without a clear system of appeal. In the most extreme cases, court challenges are specifically excluded in relation to decisions on entitlement to nationality.

Finally, recognizing that countries are sovereign, they should be encouraged to review their own practices, laws, and international commitments, with a view to increasing inclusion. This can best be done through encouraging participation in collaborative processes; UNHCR is the leading international agency in this regard. For example, in the case of Africa, countries could be encouraged to review their laws against the General Comment on Article 6 of the African Charter on the Rights and Welfare of the Child ("right to a name and nationality"). The global thrust toward stronger identification needs to be complemented by a global push to reform nationality policies.

"Exclusion assessments" of countries' laws and practices that covered these aspects would be a valuable complement to the privacy impact assessments recommended below, to help ensure that investment in identification systems supports the SDGs. Especially in extreme cases where the system is likely to entrench discrimination, development partners need to weigh carefully the arguments for and against involvement.

Privacy Risk

Digital identification systems are only a part of the wider digital revolution that has expanded the quantity of all types of personal data and raised a range of privacy issues. Should encryption of digital communications be permitted? Under what conditions should official access be given to cellphone records? Should individuals have "the right to be forgotten"? Should entities such as Facebook, Google, LinkedIn, or internet service providers be constrained in how they collect and commercially exploit personal data—including through the use of face recognition technology—and if so, how should this be done? What about the widespread use of other monitoring tools like closed-circuit televisions—now one for every 11 people in the United Kingdom? The privacy risk associated with ID systems is only one of many areas of concern. It could be argued that citizens of the European Union (EU), with its more comprehensive privacy legislation, enjoy greater personal data privacy rights than U.S. citizens, even though most EU countries have national ID programs while the United States does not.

Identification technology can be seen as an intrinsic risk to privacy or as privacy enhancing depending on the protections built into systems, the nontechnological alternative, and what is understood by privacy.[4] Accessing a service or program by submitting a fingerprint or iris scan may be seen as less intrusive than responding to a long list of questions to confirm identity or requiring testimonials. In Pakistan, one motivation for the use of biometric smartcards to support internally displaced populations was to avoid their humiliation from having to stand in lines for cash support (Malik 2014). The digital payment of benefits determined on the basis of proxy-means-test results may be less intrusive than community-based support programs that rely on scrutiny by neighborhood committees. This is not to argue one way or the other, but it points to the need to consider the pros and cons of alternative arrangements.

Digital systems can also be used to segment personal information to provide only the attributes needed for a particular purpose in ways that are difficult to do using only physical cards or tokens. For example, a simple yes/no answer to a question on age might be enough for permission to consume alcohol; there is no need to reveal name, address, gender, or such other personal details as might appear on a card. This type of capability could be provided by an Aadhaar-like system, where the end-user, authenticated by a fingerprint, authorizes the system to respond to such a question. To the extent that technology can constrain the release of information to that legitimately required by any service provider, proponents note that it may enhance privacy. In the case of the "federated model" described in chapter 6, the service provider receives only an authentication, without any identifying information.

Nevertheless, integrated identity management systems can facilitate access to personal information and make it easier to link individual records and transactions across disparate data registers through a common identifier. Some groups are especially vulnerable. A more integrated identification system for refugees, an objective of UNHCR, could help these displaced persons re-create their identities and facilitate their movement (UNHCR 2015b). However, it may not be easy for refugee agencies to resist requests to share personal data

4   In the present context, "data privacy" is best understood as referring to the right of an individual to have access to and control over the use of her or his personal data. India's Supreme Court has recently issued a thoughtful judgment on the right to privacy, including the complications posed by ever-increasing reliance on digital technology (see chapter 6).

with host countries ill-equipped to safeguard sensitive information. These data can be particularly sensitive because of risks to family members remaining in their countries of origin.[5]

Data Privacy Laws: Are They Sufficient?

As the number and coverage of identity systems expand, more countries are implementing data privacy and protection measures. In 1980 the Organization for Economic Co-operation and Development developed a set of Fair Information Practices (FIPs) codified in the OECD Guidelines on the Protection of Privacy and Transborder Flows of Personal Data. These guidelines form the basis of many modern privacy agreements and national laws and are an essential starting reference point for assessing the legal frameworks of different countries (Dixon 2008).

In one of a series of surveys, Greenleaf (2013) cataloged 99 states and territories as having a framework for data privacy legislation in 2011 that conformed to the widely accepted OECD (2013) FIPs guidelines.[6] Table 5-1 shows the percentages of countries with data privacy laws in place in 2011 by income group. As expected, the coverage increases sharply with income level, from 12 percent of the low-income group to 76 percent of the high-income group. This is an evolving picture as more countries are adopting data privacy laws. Greenleaf (2015) finds that two to three countries have been passing such laws every year since the 1940s, with an acceleration to five new countries covered by laws per year in the 2010s alone. Nevertheless, the rapid spread of identification programs to lower-income countries means that the coverage of the laws still lags that of the programs.

The spread of data privacy laws is welcome, but is it sufficient? Such laws might not offer much comfort in a country where there is little technical or institutional capacity to implement them or where the rule of law is generally

5   See for example Hosein and Nyst (2013) and Lindskov Jacobsen (2015). Currion (2015) argues that government guarantees of privacy are not useful. He observes that even though the European Commission promised that its EURODAC database of asylum seekers would be protected in 2012, it allowed Europol and other law enforcement agencies to access the data.

6   Inclusion requires that the country has designated an identifiable data controller and enforcement mechanisms, in addition to having an acceptable legal framework. Greenleaf notes several important differences between the countries, such as whether data privacy laws apply to the public sector, the private sector, or both. For a review of the OECD principles as applied to identification, see Gellman (2013).

TABLE 5-1 Data Privacy Laws and Rule of Law by Income Group

	Number of countries (percent of group)				
	LIC	LMIC	UMIC	HIC	Total
Countries with data privacy law	4 (12)	15 (32)	22 (41)	44 (76)	85
Countries with data privacy law + rule of law above mean	0	3 (6)	9 (17)	42 (72)	54

Sources: Greenleaf (2013), Worldwide Governance Indicators (2012 edition) (https://data.worldbank.org/data-catalog/worldwide-governance-indicators); World Bank, World Development Indicators (2013 data) (https://data.worldbank.org/data-catalog/world-development-indicators).

LIC = low-income countries; LMIC = lower-middle-income countries; UMIC = upper-middle-income countries; HIC = high-income countries

weak. Angola and the Kyrgyz Republic, for example, are classed by Greenleaf as having data privacy laws, but at the same time their rule of law indicators are among the lowest in the world. Table 5-1 also shows the distribution of countries that had both data privacy laws and a rule of law indicator above the global mean. Far fewer lower-income countries passed the threshold under this composite criterion; in 2011 no low-income country had both a data privacy law and a rule of law indicator above the global average. It is in this group of countries where the coverage of formal identification systems has been expanding most rapidly. The problem of ensuring the privacy of personal data is deeper than simply whether a data privacy law is on the books.

As another warning sign, the cross-country distribution of data privacy laws in 2011 was strongly associated with measures of the level of political rights and civil liberties as well as with gross domestic product per capita (figure 5-1).[7] As identification systems are rolled out in more countries, they increasingly will need to be implemented in less democratic contexts. Even where data privacy laws support their rollout, this suggests an uphill struggle to ensure that citizens' data will not be used for unlawful purposes and for the ID management entity to emerge as a trusted institution.

The lack of trained information technology and data management person-

---

7 The association between data privacy laws and political rights and civil liberties remains after controlling for the income group of countries. This suggests that the issue is not simply related to income.

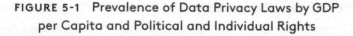

FIGURE 5-1 Prevalence of Data Privacy Laws by GDP
per Capita and Political and Individual Rights

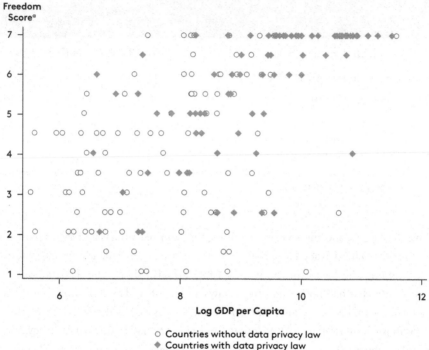

○ Countries without data privacy law
◆ Countries with data privacy law

Source: Greenleaf (2013); Freedom in the World 2013: Democratic Breakthroughs in the Balance
(https://freedomhouse.org/sites/default/files/FIW%202013%20Booklet.pdf); World Bank, World
Development Indicators (2013 data) (https://data.worldbank.org/data-catalog/world-development-
indicators).

a. The Freedom Score is the average of Political Rights and Civil Liberties score. The scoring scale
has been reversed from its original formulation, so that a higher rating (closer to 7) indicates more and
freer opportunities to exercise political rights and civil liberties.

nel poses a further challenge to the effective implementation of ID systems in a
number of lower-income countries. Countries often will need to rely on outside
vendors (private companies) to manage the enrollment process as well as for the
longer-term operation of their identification system. Many lack the capacity to
effectively monitor the work of these private entities, leaving them to handle
the personal data of citizens and residents unsupervised. This lack of supervision can undermine registrants' trust in the system and make countries and
individuals vulnerable to their data being held hostage by a private company.

Mitigating the Privacy Risks

Some commonly agreed-on safeguards can help minimize the privacy risks associated with any identity database (Gelb and Diofasi 2016b; Principles 2017). Especially when legal protections are weak, the system's design will be the first line of defense. Personal data collected and retained by the system should be minimal and restricted to what is essential for the use case. Particularly sensitive data such as ethnicity and religion should not be collected, and certainly not displayed on an ID credential. In the past, information such as community of origin or location of residence may have been helpful in matching credentials with their holders, but such information can help to profile people by providing indicators of tribal affiliation or ethnicity. With new authentication technology, it is less useful today. Learning from the bitter experience of civil war and genocide, Rwanda's ID system data and documents do not include ethnicity—all are simply "Rwandan."

Similarly, traditional identification numbering systems often reveal considerable personal information such as date of birth, gender, community of origin, or point of enrollment. Some numbering systems, such as Soundex, commonly used for driver's licenses, incorporate phonetic algorithms to reproduce the name of the holder. These systems may have been useful in the past to provide a rough check that the characteristics of the person presenting an ID card matched the data on the card, but are also redundant with the more precise authentication methods now available. If personal information is included in the number, it can create difficulties when identifying attributes such as gender change, since it should never be necessary to change the number.[8] The trend is therefore toward the use of random numbers, including a check digit to help guard against errors.[9]

Transparency and accountability to end-users are also important in mitigating privacy risks. People should be provided with information and control over their data: they should be able to query what information is held on them, how their data will be used, who can access their data, and who has accessed

---

8   There are exceptions in exceptional situations, such as enrollment in witness protection programs that require new identities.

9   Most modern ID numbers include a check digit, computed algorithmically from the other digits in the number to help spot errors in recording or transcription. These systems can detect most common errors, such as a mistake in a single digit or the reversal of two adjacent digits. The final digit of credit card numbers is usually a check digit.

them. They also should have simple means to correct inaccurate data free of charge and to update their information.

Countries have taken several approaches to mitigating the risks associated with integrated identification systems. One approach is to provide for multiple identifiers while still ensuring that identity itself is unique. This corresponds to the idea that a single, unique individual should be able to be identified in different ways for different purposes. In Austria's distinctive system, cryptography enables users to access multiple government services using a single e-ID while ensuring that transaction records cannot be matched across the different databases using a common number. Each e-ID card includes a unique personal identifier, the Source PIN, which is stored only on the card and cannot be held by any government body or private entity (Rössler 2007). When a cardholder wants to access a service using the card, a unique sector-specific identifier, called the sector-specific PIN or SS-PIN, is generated from the Source PIN using a one-way cryptographic function. The SS-PIN is different for each service and also for different private sector applications. It is not possible to derive one SS-PIN from another, for example, to generate the tax SS-PIN from the social security SS-PIN. Neither can an SS-PIN be used to calculate the Source PIN.

This unique system enables cardholders to use the same credential to authenticate themselves for all purposes, but prevents their records from being consolidated across different databases using a common number. Of course, it does not prevent the use of matching by names or other biographic data to consolidate records. The generation of SS-PINs without the card is only possible for the Source PIN Register Authority and is only permissible when personal data are to be processed or transmitted in conformity with the Data Protection Act 2000.[10] The federated model of GOV.UK Verify (chapter 6) provides another example of an approach that enables people to access multiple sources to authenticate digital identities while not relying on any particular credential or number for all transactions.

Another line of defense is to limit the sharing of information through technology and system design. Countries can combine the advantages of a single unique base identity with segregated functional databases. In Estonia, the databases of each department and service provider are held separately and are connected through the X-Road data exchange layer that manages the exchange of

10 See the Austrian E-Government Act, Federal Act on Provisions Facilitating Electronic Communications with Public Bodies (10/2004), at www.digitales.oesterreich.gv.at. Data can still be matched across different registries using other information such as names and addresses, but the process is more laborious and less accurate.

information as needed by each program. Security is further enhanced through the match-on-card identity credentials provided to each person enrolled in the system (chapter 6). Transparency can be increased, as in Estonia, by logging each data access request submitted to the system and making the consolidated log available only to the individual concerned.

Integrating Privacy Impact Assessments (PIAs) during the planning phase of the identification system could help to identify vulnerabilities early on. Some of the risks can be mitigated both through the system design and the rules established for its subsequent use. Many countries have not yet reached the stage where large quantities of personal data have been digitized, but this change can happen relatively quickly. Where donors are involved in strengthening ID systems, provisions for extended support to data protection and data privacy should be built into their programs.

Membership organizations, such as the Multilateral Development Banks, the United Nations, or the African Union, could help members overcome capacity constraints and reduce their vulnerability with regard to private identification management firms. They could offer independent technical assistance to help oversee and monitor vendors and to design systems that meet the data privacy and protection recommendations outlined in the Principles on Identification for Sustainable Development.[11]

Identification as Investment: Do the Benefits Justify the Costs?

Like any public investment, spending on identification systems should yield an acceptable rate of economic or social return. This does not necessarily mean a direct financial return; even if they may charge fees for passports and expedited services, many governments see civil registration and national identification as intrinsic and essential functions of the state, to be funded through general revenues. Nevertheless, the considerable expenditures on ID systems made by many countries and often supported by development partners raise questions of financial sustainability and the balance between the costs of the systems and their quantifiable benefits. There is not much systematic information on the costs of establishing and operating ID systems, and it is even more difficult to

11 For the full list of principles and their detailed interpretation, see Principles (2017).

place a monetary value on many of the benefits.[12] Illustrative examples, such as those below, are the best current source of such information.

Costs of National ID Systems

The costs of establishing and maintaining an ID system depend on many factors. One is its scale—every system has fixed costs, including those required to establish a data center, train a core of operators, and set up an office and communications network. Is the target population large enough to attract providers? Technology companies are less interested in small contracts and tend to offer less favorable terms. Another is geographic density—is the country densely populated, or are people widely scattered across remote and inaccessible communities? This can greatly affect the costs of achieving universal coverage. For Peru, the unit costs of enrollment in rural areas are eight times higher than in urban areas. Unit costs will also depend on program-specific factors, not least of which involve the technology—whether cards are issued, whether they are costly smartcards with chips or cheaper barcoded or QR cards, and what security features they possess. Enrollment costs may also depend on whether the system can draw on a strong civil registry for baseline data or whether it will need to start registration from scratch.[13]

Labor costs constitute a substantial part of the total costs of rolling out and operating an identification system. The absolute unit cost might be expected to be lower in poor countries where labor is cheaper, but formal labor is costly relative to GDP in some poor countries, particularly in sub-Saharan Africa. Yet technology costs will be as high in poor countries as in richer countries or possibly even higher, especially for small systems that are unable to procure at scale. Even if the overall unit costs are lower in poor countries, they may be higher relative to levels of GDP per head.

One approach to costing is Atick (2014), which draws on a number of cases to offer ranges of typical costs for nationwide identification programs in poor countries. The initial costs associated with enrollment are distinguished from those of maintaining and operating the system (table 5-2). These estimates do

12 One example of a cost-benefit analysis is that conducted by the U.S. government for its Real ID program (Department of Homeland Security 2007). This, and other studies done for the proposed identity card scheme in the United Kingdom, shows how much easier it is to quantify the costs than the benefits. The World Bank has launched a study on the costs of systems and their components, expected to be published in 2018.

13 For estimates of the costs of scaling up civil registration, see World Bank/WHO (2014).

not include point-of-service devices for authentication such as card or finger-print readers, since in most cases these devices would be supplied by users, such as banks or program administrators, who need to authenticate their clients. According to these estimates, the unit costs to enroll and to issue cards are between $4.15 and $11 per head. Taking a midpoint estimate for a low-income country with a GDP per head of $670, where half of the total population (the adults) is covered, the enrollment costs would be around 0.6 percent of GDP.

After mass enrollment, the system would settle down into a steady state, with most expenses going for operations and maintenance (including the need to issue replacement cards) and a small part reflecting the need to enroll new entrants. The long-run steady state costs therefore depend on, among other factors, the rate of growth of the target population. Taking into account population growth as well as the need to respond to some degree of international mobility, a reasonable estimate for new enrollments could be around 5 percent of the number already enrolled. This would yield a steady state cost of around $1.50 per person, or 0.1 percent of GDP for the low-income country.

When identification programs are implemented as part of the activities of government ministries, it can be difficult to isolate their total costs to compare with these benchmarks. It is easier to do so when programs are managed by autonomous agencies with clearly defined budgets. Considering two cases described in chapter 4, the annual budget of RENIEC in Peru has been around $4 per head, or 0.065 percent of GDP. This figure includes much of the civil registration system as well as identification. For NADRA in Pakistan, the annual budget has been around $1.20 per person registered, or 0.060 percent of GDP. These countries have higher income levels than a typical low-income country, so that even though their absolute costs are higher than the benchmark, as expected their costs relative to GDP are considerably lower. These comparisons suggest that the benchmark estimates may not be an unreasonable place to start, but that many countries can probably do better.

Relative to the benchmark range, India's Aadhaar program stands out as a low-cost outlier. It operates at extremely large scale, procures competitively, collects a minimum of biographic information, and does not provide cards for offline authentication. Through its high-intensity phase, the unit cost of enrollment was only around $1.16 per head. Although the marginal cost of enrollment will increase after the mass registration phase, the total projected budget is only $2.2 billion for a potential coverage of 1.3 billion people (*Economic Times* 2015). Other countries will have difficulties in matching the low cost of the Aadhaar system. India operates at scale and has therefore been able to drive a

TABLE 5-2   Costs of e-ID Systems

Component	Description	Investment
Enrollment (investment)	Capturing identifiers at points of enrollment including biometric and biographic data	$3–$6 per person (Aadhaar low case, $1.16)
Register (maintenance)	Database management and maintenance, updates, deduplication, other checks	+15%–25% per year
Authentication (investment)	Issuing smartcards (if used) or other credentials	$1.15–$5 per ID card depending on features +$0.50 for digital certificates
Authentication (maintenance)	Card maintenance, replacement	+$0.05–$0.10 per year per card for maintenance/replacement

Source: Atick (2014).

hard bargain with technology providers. It is also, in general, a low-cost country even considering its income level.[14] Nevertheless, Aadhaar points to the possibility of establishing a unique digital ID system more cheaply than previously thought feasible.

Drivers of excessive spending. Beyond "regular" expenditures for enrollment, system maintenance, and authentication, other factors can contribute to excessively high costs of identification programs, including inadequate consideration for user demand, vendor lock-in, and corruption. Competing parts of government can continue to press for their own systems—each with its independent biometric database and deduplication capability—resulting in high-cost fragmentation of the ID ecosystem (Gelb and Clark 2013a: Nigeria, Mexico). On the supply side, systems can be overdesigned in response to vendor pressure to incorporate costly features, particularly into cards, that represent little added value over less high-tech and less costly alternatives.

Vendor lock-in can drive up expenses, with proprietary technologies or data storage formats reducing countries' ability to improve the efficiency of their

14 Data from the 2011 round of the International Comparison Project shows India with a purchasing power parity (PPP) of 31.8 (United States = 100). This is 35 percent less costly than a representative PPP for countries at the same nominal income level (Gelb and Diofasi 2016c).

systems and reduce costs. Identification systems may be linked to particular programs in ways that make it difficult to introduce competition. For Kenyan social protection programs, the financial institutions responsible for payments to the intended beneficiaries were also the ones to implement the biometric systems for identity verification. Similarly, in the South African social security system both identification and payments are locked in to the vendor (Net1) and its subsidiary (Cash Payments Services), which also enjoy a monopoly position in offering additional financial services to beneficiaries. There would be a substantial cost of switching to new intermediaries even if they offered better service.

Procurement quality and competitiveness can also influence costs greatly. Corruption continues to plague procurement processes and has often contributed to excessively costly systems, sometimes not well suited to local conditions. Although the details are usually obscure, some well-documented cases illustrate the scope of the problem.

Kenya is a particularly egregious case as the preexisting national ID actually formed the basis for voter registration for its 2013 election. A report by the Office of the Auditor General (2014) provides a critical assessment of the procurement process for biometric voter registration kits. It was opaque from the start and lacked a clear decisionmaking framework (Gelb and Diofasi 2016a). The 29 proposals from the first round of bidding were assessed by four different committees, and they arrived at three different conclusions with regard to the proposed winner. As a result of the controversy, the tender process was eventually terminated and no winner was selected. After the termination, the Independent Elections and Boundary Commission signed a contract with the Canadian Commercial Corporation for $75 million to purchase 15,000 biometric voter registration kits from Safran Morpho—without an open or competitive selection process (Office of the Auditor General 2014). Owing to delays in the procurement process that compressed the enrollment period, 5,250 more kits had to be ordered than originally envisioned to cover the entire country. The purchase was financed through a commercial loan, which increased the total costs by $31.2 million (including loan insurance and interest) to the astonishing figure of over $106 million (or $7.40 per voter) for equipment alone. In 2016 the Public Affairs Commission investigated the election commissioners on charges of questionable procurement (Ngetich and Ayaga 2016).

In a more recent case, several high-ranking officials in Indonesia were indicted for embezzling funds from the country's e-ID (e-KTP) procurement.

Losses to the state are estimated at $230 million (La Batu 2017); they represent close to 40 percent of the total project value, suggesting that Indonesia's system cost almost twice as much as it should have. The Democratic Republic of Congo's biometric passport scheme, which charges passport applicants US$185 (one of the highest charges in the world), also raises red flags. The true cost of supplying the passport is reported to be about US$60; the government receives US$65 as additional revenue, while the remaining US$60 goes to a mysterious company registered in the United Arab Emirates, supposedly owned by a close relative of the country's president (Lewis 2017). These and other cases show the importance of having a sound governance structure for identification systems that include users as an interest group.

Benefits. Quantifying the benefits is even more difficult than estimating the costs, since many impacts of strong identification will be diffused throughout the economy and difficult to isolate. Estonian experts have estimated the time that citizens have saved by using the country's advanced e-ID system, from eliminating the need to be physically present for many services and transactions to reducing the use of paper forms. The savings are substantial—on the order of one week in a year—but there is no rigorous basis for their estimates. There have also been some estimates of the global savings from e-ID systems; analysis by Boston Consulting Group (2014) indicates that e-government services, enabled by digital ID systems, generate gains in efficiency and convenience that could yield global taxpayer savings of up to $50 billion per year by 2020.

It is more feasible to estimate financial savings with regard to specific applications such as removing ghosts and duplicates from public payrolls and reforming subsidy programs. Some of these cases, described in chapter 3, suggest that the returns to effective identity management can be high. In Nigeria, the biometrically supported Integrated Payroll and Personnel Information System eliminated over 60,000 ghost workers in the public sector, for a cumulative savings of $1.12 billion over its eight-year implementation period. Ghana's government was reported to have saved an estimated $35 million a year by introducing a digital identification and payment system for government employees. Such savings—and there are probably many more in other countries—would indicate high rates of return on these countries' ID investments.

The Case of Aadhaar

Evidence on the fiscal savings from India's Aadhaar-enabled reforms is only starting to accumulate, but it confirms that the rate of return on unique identification could be high. The savings announced by the government on only the liquefied petroleum gas reform over one or two years would be sufficient to fund the Aadhaar program. These estimates are sensitive to the level of world energy prices and to the estimated costs if the program had not been implemented, and not all savings can be attributed to any particular element of the reform, but even far more modest gains, including on the program as it is rolled out further, would provide a good financial rate of return (chapter 3). In this case it should be noted that the objective was less to save resources and more to rationalize subsidies so that the LPG system could be rolled out more widely. Regarding the public distribution system, field visits to the most advanced implementation site, Krishna District in Andhra Pradesh, suggest that the savings could be considerable. Local officials estimated that deduplication of beneficiaries and the closing of avenues for diversion of unclaimed rations from the Fair Price Shops has saved around 8 percent of the cost of the program, one that was previously considered to have been relatively well administered. More, and more rigorous, assessments would be desirable.

Cost-benefit projections. In 2012 a cost-benefit analysis was conducted for Aadhaar (National Institute of Public Finance and Policy 2012), projecting costs and benefits over a decade. Costs included both those related to the identification system itself (which peak over the intense 2012–17 enrollment period and then gradually fall) and expenditures needed to integrate the Aadhaar into other subsidy and benefit schemes throughout the decade. Benefits were estimated as the annual savings from reducing leakage and diversion in each of the programs; they rose continuously over the period as the percentage of beneficiaries covered by Aadhaar increased from 2 percent at the start of the period to a projected 100 percent by 2019. The internal rate of return came out at 53 percent. Although these estimates have been debated, halving them would still yield a 20 percent return; the rate would not come down to zero until the benefits had fallen to one-third of their projected value.

It is not possible to compare the 2012 projections with realized costs and benefits since no detailed accounting is yet available. In a March 5 statement from the Ministry of Electronics and Information Technology (2017), the savings from reforms in India's subsidy and benefit programs over the previous two and a half years were announced to be Rs 49,000 core (about $7.6 billion).

Not all of this can be attributed to Aadhaar of course, but the amount is astonishingly high, about twice the savings projected by the 2012 analysis up to the
end of 2016–17. Further assessment waits on more detailed information on how
the savings are estimated and attributed.

Even if profitable, is Aadhaar an exception? Aadhaar is a particularly
low-cost program relative to many others, and is being applied at scale to massive subsidy and benefit programs that account for some $60 billion in annual
spending. Even modest savings across these programs would provide a substantial fiscal return. Other countries might therefore face more of a challenge to
generate similar rates of return from their programs.

Nevertheless, to offer a more representative picture, civil service salaries are
typically on the order of 6 percent of GDP in developing countries (they can be
considerably higher, as in Ghana) and general government wages are around
9 percent of GDP (World Bank 2011). For total government payments to individuals, one can add public pensions (in Kenya, for instance, the number of
civil service pensioners exceeds the number of active civil servants) and social
transfers (in South Africa, around 3.5 percent of GDP) (Bruni 2016). Public
payments to individuals will therefore usually be at least in the range of 10 to
15 percent of GDP. Based on the cost estimates in table 5-2, to provide a reasonable financial return on investment, an effective registration and identification
system will need to generate savings from eliminating leakages, diversions, and
corrupt payments to ghost recipients equal to around 2 percent of the total
value of these payments.[15] Such savings seem modest compared to the impact
seen in a number of cases. In addition—as discussed in chapter 4—user fees
and charges may be able to cover a substantial part of the costs. But these are
only speculative estimates, and they also do not take into account other possible
fiscal benefits, such as stronger tax administration. Much more information is
needed on the social and economic, as well as financial, costs and benefits of
identification, including net benefits or costs to recipients in terms of convenience, to provide a stronger basis for assessment.

In a number of countries, one of the greatest benefits of a robust and inclusive identification system would be to eliminate the need for costly one-off
voter registration exercises. These programs are often expensive, and although
information on the breakdown is woefully incomplete, the use of biometric
voter ID technology appears to account for around one-third of the total costs

---

15 The internal rate of return assuming no benefits over the first two years would be 5 per-
    cent over a 10-year period.

(Gelb and Diofasi 2016a). Enormous numbers of voter registration kits need to be purchased to register all voters within a short timeframe, along with thousands of printers if voter cards are to be produced on the spot. In several countries, a credible and well-functioning ID system would have saved much spending on separate, one-off voter registration exercises. To the extent that effective identity management can contribute to credible elections—with caveats, as in chapter 3—it can also reduce the likelihood of seriously disputed results and postelection violence, which can cause economic and social disruption as well as loss of life.

Mitigating the Cost Risks

Addressing all of the issues that bear on the cost-benefit calculation is beyond the scope of this chapter, but several items stand out. The first is the importance of taking a strategic approach to the architecture of identity management systems rather than focusing on individual systems in isolation. Countries and their development partners need to place a heavy emphasis on how systems are to be used rather than simply focusing on the resources and technology needed to create them. The SDGs provide a useful checklist—if the system is not used to help achieve SDGs and their targets, it is unlikely to be a sound investment.

Supply. World Bank/World Health Organization (2014) estimates suggest that it would be cost-effective to move to continuous civil registration as the basis for the population register.[16] In many countries, it will be some time before civil registration processes can supplant periodic enrollment drives and engagement-based approaches to updating the registers, but to ensure long-term viability, governments will have to strengthen and modernize the civil registry to provide the base for an integrated identity management program.

To avoid excessive costs from vendor lock-in for identification services and associated payment systems, countries and their development partners should separate ID services from payments services and support a standards-based approach—building on the pioneering approach of UIDAI—to help guard against lock-in by proprietary systems or technology.[17] The most sophisticated

16 These civil registration costs do not include costs such as smartcards or biometric registration, which make up a major part of the costs identified in table 5-2.
17 For more details, see World Bank (2018a, forthcoming). This will provide a guide to relevant standards, mostly developed by the International Organization for Standardization (ISO) and International Electrotechnical Commission (IEC).

systems are not always the most cost-effective. For example, particularly if mobile access is expected to be widespread, it may be better to deploy simpler QR cards than expensive smartcards. There is no need for the ID to also function as an electronic wallet or debit card if mobile money is already widely accessible through private service providers.

Demand. Systems that are not used to deliver results cannot be cost-effective. Political will may be lacking to drive the rollout of a national system to the point where it covers enough of the population to render competing systems redundant. Coordinating supply and demand to focus on high-value operations can help, such as by prioritizing the use of the system for payroll, pensions, subsidies, and transfers. A second stage can include property registration and tax administration, other areas with potential for large fiscal gains. It is not necessary to wait until coverage is 100 percent before applying the system to such applications.

The Political Limits of Identification

In the last resort, the successful deployment of identification systems to help achieve development goals depends on the political economy of the country. Elites may resist the implementation of a system in high-value areas if they believe it might threaten their privileges and range of discretion, for instance by increasing transparency or dismantling corrupt practices. The political limits on the use of the system need to be realistically assessed as part of any cost-benefit calculation—whether, for example, a country will actually apply such a system to eliminating ghost workers. Technology is usually not the binding constraint. Vested interests have resisted the broader rollout of biometrically supported identification and payment systems in both Ghana (e-Zwich) and Nigeria (IPPIS) despite, or perhaps because of, their proven ability to eliminate fictitious workers from government payrolls and generate savings to the government and taxpayers.

The experience of NADRA in Pakistan provides a further sobering example. In terms of contributing to the SDGs, NADRA is a leading and successful example. It has boosted enrollment, making special efforts to reach underserved populations such as tribal groups, transgender populations, and women. It has pioneered many large-scale applications, including the use of smartcards to support populations displaced by conflict, the Watan Card flood relief program, and the BISP for social transfers to poor households. In these areas, strong identification has underpinned both inclusion and improvements in state capacity. But success has been more limited in areas that threaten the privileges of the elite.

Tax reform. Pakistan's tax system is notoriously weak, with less than 800,000 registered taxpayers in a population approaching 200 million. Under an agreement with the Federal Bureau of Revenue, NADRA questioned a wide range of databases to identify an additional 2.4 million potential taxpayers as well as 1.2 million individuals with tax numbers that were not filing returns. Although the exercise was publicized to encourage potential taxpayers to come forward, the results were not used aggressively to target tax offenders.

Pensions, payrolls, and prisons. NADRA identified ghosts in public service and pensions. Some people were receiving pensions three times over and some were ineligible, while others were falsely excluded from the system. The project stalled because of strong vested interests (Malik 2014). Fingerprint matching also revealed corruption in the justice system. It revealed that many prison inmates were proxy prisoners, engaged by well-connected individuals to serve out sentences on their behalf. After a brief news flurry, attention subsided. The exercise was not completed before the then-chairman of NADRA resigned and left the country.

Free and fair elections. Pakistan's 2013 election provided a major opportunity for NADRA to update its database and reconcile it with the voter roll. The initial roll was found to include 15 million people without identities, 9 million duplicates (in some cases with multiple entries), and 13 million invalid identities. These 37 million voters, 45 percent of the voter roll, were expunged from the system. The roll was augmented with 38 million new voters, either people who had registered with NADRA in the previous three years or citizens who had previously registered but had not been included in the voter roll. The new voter roll was made available to the public for checking through SMS; some 55 million voters checked their registration through this service.

Cleaning the voter roll shifted the focus of electoral fraud to the polling stations. Identity checks revealed examples of large-scale vote rigging. One man was found to have voted 310 times, and from a women-only polling station. The election tribunal recalled the result and ordered a new vote, which was won by the challenger. However, NADRA's chairman was forced to resign and leave the country following death threats to himself and his family.

Balancing the Returns and the Risks

As is clear from the examples, identification technology and systems are multipurpose; they are driven by multiple factors and, depending on social and political context, can be used in many differing ways. The potential benefits, set out in chapter 3, are arguably greatest in countries with less existing administrative capacity, but this depends on the political will to use ID systems for good purposes. The risks associated with them are already present to varying degrees in most countries, but in weak or repressive states they can increase opportunities for malfeasance and exacerbate existing threats and harmful practices. The challenge to the development community is how best to support their use in ways that promote the achievement of the SDGs while at the same time mitigating the risks. The design of the system, as well as the rules governing its use, can play a significant role in mitigating these risks—including by following the 10 principles on identification for development laid out in chapter 7—but cannot eliminate them entirely.

SIX

Five Frontier Cases in Digital Identification

In response to the challenge of providing identification, a number of states have developed innovative solutions. In some cases, their national identification programs go back several decades, but are noteworthy for the way they have been implemented and used—innovation can relate to institutional arrangements as well as to technology. Other programs are at relatively early stages of implementation, but the novelty of their approach has already started to garner attention and in some cases to produce impressive results. The private sector's increasing role in identity management—whether "retailing" government-issued ID credentials, helping to authenticate official identities, or even establishing new forms of digital identification—has also come under the spotlight.

This chapter considers five "frontier" cases of identity management. The first four look at government programs: the national ID systems of Peru and Estonia, India's foundational Aadhaar program, and the United Kingdom's GOV.UK Verify remote digital identification program. The fifth case discusses the potential of social networks, such as Facebook and other online communities, to provide a form of digital identification. Table 6-1 provides an overview of some features of these programs.

The first three identification programs, those of Peru, Estonia, and India, are all centralized systems. However, their approach to providing ID services and their mechanisms to deliver unique digital identity for multiple uses differ considerably. Peru operates a relatively traditional system and is only one among several Latin American countries with a strong and inclusive ID system. However, it is an outstanding example of a country that saw identification as a national priority and created innovative arrangements to extend it to all, using financial incentives to spur outreach and boost enrollment, as well as to integrate civil registration and the ID authority. Estonia has been the global leader in providing digital identity to its citizens. Estonians can access a wide range of private and public services online from any corner of the globe; they can sign documents, fill in government forms, and request official records, all electronically. More recently, Estonia has extended its digital ID service to those who are not physically resident on its territory through its e-residency program, the first case of "global" digital identity. India's Aadhaar program is revolutionary in many respects, including the way in which it conceptualizes "identity" and uses technology to provide it, and it is also unique in how it has been implemented. Its use in government programs is accelerating, but it is still at an earlier stage of application than the other two cases. It is also the lowest-cost ID system in the world by a wide margin. Relative to its potential use and impact, the Aadhaar program has barely scratched the surface. Each of the three cases offers valuable lessons for other countries that are developing or strengthening their identification systems.

The last two cases are very different. The GOV.UK Verify and Facebook cases illustrate the possibility of a future progression from centralized management of identity services toward a "federated" authentication model, and still further toward the "electronic village" mode of digital identification (see figure 6-1). Neither of these cases provides first-stage "foundational" official identity; they are probably better seen as complements, rather than alternatives, to centrally managed government systems. GOV.UK Verify is multipurpose, but it draws on government databases and state-issued "functional" identity documents (such as a driver's license or passport) as well as supporting information from private databases. And whether an individual has a Facebook or LinkedIn account and a given number of "friends," "likes," or endorsements will not be sufficient, for example, to satisfy the existing Know-Your-Customer requirements for banking. It is difficult to imagine a full range of services being provided through network-based identification without any reference to state-issued identity credentials, and there are still questions regarding the potential for a business model to provide this type of identity service. Rigorous identity screening may not be compatible with a network approach where

TABLE 6-1 Summary of Select Features of the Five "Frontier" Cases

Case	Motivation	Managing entity	Provides official, primary ID	Biometrics for registration	Biometrics for authentication	Authentication	e-ID? (remote access)	Coverage
Peru	Nation-building and reconstruction; social and development programs	RENIEC; an autonomous public agency	Yes	Yes	Possible; not widely used	Based on ID card; can also authenticate against RENIEC database	In process	30 million or 99% of combined adult and child population
Estonia	Nation-building and administrative control; efficiency in service delivery	Information System Authority (coordinated with police and border guard)	Yes	Yes	No	Remote authentication based on digital certificates and PINs	Yes	1.2 million or 94% of population above age 15
India (Aadhaar)	Subsidy reform, financial inclusion, digital economy	UIDAI, an autonomous government agency	Yes	Yes	Yes	Remote authentication via biometrics (iris or fingerprint)	Yes	1.1 billion or 98% of adult population (86% of total)
UK.GOV Verify	Efficient and convenient online access to public services	GDS, a government agency, in cooperation with certified private identity providers	No	No	No	Certified entities verify identity to standards using public and private registries	Yes	950,000 or 2% of adult population (just out of pilot phase)
Facebook	Network services (not essentially related to ID); business driven	Facebook, a for-profit corporation	No	No	No	Identity not officially verified; algorithmic checks; users of flagged accounts may need to submit official credentials	Limited to entities accepting Facebook login	1.8 billion or 23% of global population (32% of world above age 15)

value is enhanced by including as many members in the network as possible. Nevertheless, these new forms of managing identities are significant in important ways and they will only become more powerful as the volume of digital data increases and their algorithms improve. They can draw on additional evidence to supplement official, government-issued credentials; this can include "dynamic" records (such as banking or mobile activity, credit cards, or local library borrowing habits) that confirm the existence of claimed identities over long periods of time. A particular contribution has been to increase attention to levels of identity assurance—"gold-plated" assurance is not needed for every use-case. The new network-based models may be far superior to some of the ad hoc methods still used in some instances, such as seeking a confirmation of identity from one or two friends or neighbors.

These five cases are not the only programs of particular interest. Malaysia's MYKAD is another frontier case, as the first system to issue a multiapplication smartcard (Wehr 2004). A number of other countries, including several in Africa, have gone on to implement such a model. Pakistan's national ID program is another leader in terms of innovative and widespread use, and shares some institutional features with Peru's national ID program (Malik 2014). It has been cited frequently in previous chapters and so is not included here. Some other cases are astonishing for their context, as in the efforts to roll out not one but two high-tech biometric programs at the same time in Somaliland (Rader 2016).

Peru: Registration and Identification as a National Priority

The universal provision of legal identity became a national priority in Peru following the end of the decades-long political violence of the Shining Path insurgency and the transition to democracy in the early 2000s. The new, comprehensive population registry and the issued national ID credential, the Documento Nacional de Identidad (DNI), were seen as integral parts of a larger process to restore citizens' trust in state institutions, as well as to facilitate the rollout of social protection programs (Reuben and Carbonari 2017). Rebuilding the country's identification system was a monumental task. During the conflict, many civil registry records were destroyed and large parts of the population, particularly in remote and poorer areas, were never registered at all.

From some perspectives, Peru's identification system is relatively traditional. A physical ID credential (the national ID card, or DNI) containing the holder's photo and certain biographic data, compulsory at age 18, is used to enable inspection-based visual verification of a person's identity. The validity of the card can be checked against a central database. Recently issued e-ID cards offer the possibility of real-time biometric authentication, but not all service providers have this capability. As of the end of 2016, only a modest proportion of ID cards in circulation[1] had been replaced by smartcards.

At the same time, the Peruvian system has a number of notable and innovative features. As noted in chapter 4, its politically and in part financially independent public identification authority has had remarkable success in enrolling close to all of the country's residents, no matter how young, poor, or geographically isolated, and has managed to ensure the smooth and timely flow of information from dispersed civil registry offices to the central population register. Peru's ID system is also one of the most highly integrated in the world. The unique personal identifier, which is now issued upon registration at birth, is held by almost all the population. It is integrated into all relevant databases and used to identify individuals across virtually all government registries and transactions as well as for KYC and commercial purposes. Virtually no formal economic transactions are possible without it.

Innovative Institutional Arrangements toward a Fully Independent ID Authority

The Registro Nacional de Identificación y Estado Civil, or RENIEC, was established in 1993 and assumed its current responsibilities for national identification and civil registration in 1995. It was separated from the electoral commission with the mandate to establish and manage a centralized population registry and to enroll the entire population, providing unique identity. Registration during the first five years of the agency remained low, about 10 percent, but today it covers close to 99 percent of the population: over 21 million adults and 10 million children.

The governance and financing arrangements for RENIEC were distinctive. It is set up as an autonomous agency, with constitutionally guaranteed independence from government ministries and other political bodies (Reyna 2014). RENIEC does not directly depend on or report to any individual ministry, but carries out its identification work in coordination with Congress, the

---

1 Fewer than 100,000 as of September 2016.

Electoral Committee, the Ministry of Health, the Ministry of the Economy, and other government entities as needed. Its head is appointed by the National Council of the Judiciary for a four-year term, following a competitive selection process. Persons holding or having recently held political leadership positions cannot be considered for the post.[2]

RENIEC was set up to be financially independent, with all costs covered by fees for service. At present, it generates about 70 percent of its own resources through fees collected for the issuance of DNIs and replacement cards, as well as for providing identity verification services to private entities. The largest of these companies are financial service providers, but other businesses also revert to RENIEC to authenticate their clients—the individual end-users of RENIEC's services. Notaries, for example, are required to validate the identities of all parties to real estate transactions with RENIEC.

The rest of RENIEC's budget is covered by government funds allocated to subsidize RENIEC's services to poor and remote populations, where the cost of providing identification can be much higher and where fees may pose a substantial barrier to enrollment and continued registration. These payments were introduced as the unit costs for enrolling people into the system increased after the initial phase. Registration and issuance of a DNI at an ordinary RENIEC office cost the agency about $10 per registrant in 2014, while the cost of registration and DNI provision by mobile units could be as high as $40 in the mountains and $80 per person in the jungle regions of the Amazon (Reyna 2014). Government funds for subsidized ID services are disbursed to RENIEC using a performance-based model, conditional on the agency's achievement of pre-agreed targets in reducing the undocumented population and providing ID services to them.

RENIEC's clear mandate, independence, and strong technical focus appear to have helped to create the trust in the national identification program that policymakers had hoped for. In national surveys, Peruvians consistently rank RENIEC as the country's most trusted institution, even ahead of the Catholic Church (Reuben and Carbonari 2017). However, the fact that it now depends on public funds to a substantial extent poses a risk to its financial autonomy and therefore its institutional independence. With coverage now almost universal,

2 The National Council of the Judiciary is responsible for appointing RENIEC's head, following a "tender" issued by the RENIEC Advisory Committee. It also can remove the head in exceptional circumstances. RENIEC also has a three-member advisory council, with members appointed by the Supreme Court, Justice Ministry, and Interior Ministry, respectively, to provide oversight and monitoring.

revenues from the issuance of new DNIs are in decline, while the unit costs of "last mile" registration continues to be far higher for people in remote and isolated areas. RENIEC still collects most of its revenues from service charges on people, businesses, and other government departments that charge for their own services. Under the "you charge, I charge" approach, RENIEC gets a cut of the fees for driver's licenses and passports. But its experience suggests that the task of creating a commercial yet fully inclusive ID service is not an easy one in a country with many poor people.

Integrating a Lagging Civil Registry into a Robust ID System

A second innovative feature of the Peruvian system is the arrangements to integrate the civil registration system into the national identification system. In Peru, as in many countries, civil registration was traditionally the responsibility of municipal governments. Following the creation of RENIEC, civil registration and identity services were brought under the aegis of the same agency. However, the integration between the localized civil registries and the central population registry was fraught with challenges.

During the early years of Peru's democratic transition, it was sensible for the government to prioritize the establishment of the national identification system and the rapid expansion of ID coverage. It needed to enable large segments of the population to participate in the national elections as well as to improve the administration of social services. This push resulted in a robust, digitized, central population register that formed the backbone of the national ID. Efforts to incorporate the locally managed civil registries into a single national system led by RENIEC followed only some years later, too slowly in the opinion of some observers like Reuben and Carbonari (2017).

At first, RENIEC attempted to replace the decentralized municipal registries with its own facilities. It established some 400 of its own auxiliary registry offices, many within hospitals, to register births and issue birth certificates. However, this approach proved impractical because its network was not sufficiently dense. The majority of data collected on vital events remained decentralized, with births, deaths, and other relevant information still recorded at the municipal level through a network of almost 4,000 registry offices. Underequipped and unmotivated, these municipal registry offices often failed to transmit their records to RENIEC's central database, making it difficult to maintain an up-to-date population register against which citizens could validate their identities.

To fully integrate the two registries, RENIEC and the central government used a two-pronged approach. First, the Ministry of Economy and Finance made the timely transfer of local registry data to RENIEC part of its performance-based payment plan for municipal modernization. Municipalities only got paid if the civil registry entries were received centrally; in many cases, this required sending the entries weekly in paper form to the collecting agency. Second, RENIEC created an office dedicated to the integration process, to focus on strengthening the local offices' capacity by providing technological and digitization support and bringing remote offices online. These two strategies have helped link data from the "lagging" civil registry to RENIEC's central database and further improved the robustness of the system.

ID for All: Policies for Inclusion

Another noteworthy element of Peru's identification system has been its ability to provide close to universal coverage, including for children and for those living in isolated communities. The government, in cooperation with RENIEC's leadership, undertook several measures to expand coverage to remote and conflict-affected areas and to ensure the inclusion of vulnerable segments of the population, in particular indigenous groups.

Registration for many institutional births was made quasi-automatic through RENIEC's in-hospital auxiliary registration offices, which issue birth certificates on the spot. The issuance process for a child's first ID credential, the child DNI, is also facilitated at the same time. Most national ID programs only start enrolling their citizens in their mid-teens, but Peru begins in infancy: children are assigned a unique ID code and can be issued a child DNI within days of their birth. Even though they cannot serve as reliable biometric identifiers, children's footprints and photo are also recorded during the application process. The issue of a child ID in itself is not unprecedented; as discussed in chapter 4, it may become more prevalent, together with the taking of biometrics for infants and very young children.

To decrease financial barriers to registration, the first birth certificate is free for all, and all ID documents are free for those living in the country's poorest areas. Mobile units are also regularly deployed to remote areas to conduct first-time and continuous registration. In communities affected by the political violence, the documentary requirements to replace destroyed IDs and issue new credentials were relaxed.

As in Pakistan, South Africa, and some other countries, RENIEC has also increased demand for official IDs by linking it with access to services. The highly integrated identification system, where the provision of all government services, including social protection programs, healthcare, and pensions, is linked to the beneficiary's national ID, has helped spur demand for enrollment among wide segments of the population. However, Peru's experience with tying service provision to ID ownership also suggests that this policy can have unintended negative consequences. In 2012, when having a child DNI was made mandatory to access a noncontributory health insurance program, enrollment in the program dropped dramatically from 11,759 to 966 newborns in some of Peru's poorest districts. In turn, exclusion from health services appears to have led to a higher incidence of child malnutrition in the program areas. The requirement for a DNI might not have been the only factor, but the timing is suggestive (Reuben and Carbonari 2017). Regulations did allow for exceptions to the registration requirement, but these may not have been communicated to the local population or applied by local officials on the ground.

Toward the Future: Transition to e-ID

RENIEC and the Peruvian government are continuing to expand the functionality of the country's identification system and the ID card itself. Although service providers can contact RENIEC to verify the validity of an ID card, cardholders are usually matched to their claimed identity by a visual inspection of the photo on the card, since the infrastructure for biometric authentication has been very limited. This is likely to change once the process of updating the national ID card to an e-ID is completed, as this will enable match-on-card verification against a fingerprint template stored on the card (RENIEC 2016). As part of the update, all 10 fingerprints of applicants are now recorded, compared to two fingerprints previously. The new e-ID, known as the DNIe, will also enable users to transact and engage with government services remotely through its digital signature (e-sign) capability—a function that opens up the possibility for electronic voting.

Lessons from Peru's ID System

In most senses, RENIEC is a "traditional" identification program, but it provides a remarkably successful example of inclusive identification in a postconflict setting, one where a new robust identity base for facilitating public and private transactions has helped expand government programs to those most in need. Its accomplishments are grounded in an innovative institutional framework for ID provision that relies on strong performance-based financial incentives and a politically autonomous and independent ID agency with the clear mandate to expand coverage. Peru's efforts to integrate a relatively weak, decentralized civil registry into a more robust central ID system also offer insights to many countries struggling with consolidating the information flow from disjointed registries into the central identity management system.

At the same time, not all features of Peru's identification system may be suited for other country contexts. RENIEC's largely commercial financing model has supported its political independence, while the government subsidies and incentives it received to enroll hard-to reach populations has made Peru's ID program inclusive. Governments with scarce resources may find the idea of a commercial, fee-based ID model for ID provision attractive, yet it is important to balance the need for low government expenditures against the need for inclusive ID provision, including to extremely isolated and remote communities. In countries where large segments of the population live on less than $2 a day, or even $4–$5 a day, if universal coverage is the goal then full cost recovery will be difficult to achieve.

Peru also indicates the need to assess possible trade-offs when it comes to linking ID ownership to access to social programs. On one hand, linking IDs to tangible benefits and applications can encourage enrollment; on the other hand, making ID enrollment a prerequisite in areas with low coverage or where the target beneficiaries are members of a particularly marginalized group might become a barrier to achieving the program's development goals. A further potential concern for a highly integrated system is to ensure that its use does not compromise data privacy—an issue that is now receiving more attention in Peru.

Estonia: e-ID Pioneer

Since 2002 Estonia's e-ID system has provided its citizens and residents with the most comprehensive virtual identity and digital access to government services in the world (Secure Identity Alliance 2014; Roosna 2016). As the world's first true e-ID, it combines a physical ID card with a secure digital identity that provides remote, digital access to over 2,000 publicly and privately provided services. Estonia's case illustrates how robust identification programs—like those being rolled out in many emerging economies today—can serve as a stepping stone toward moving the majority of government-citizen interactions online through state-provided digital identities. The privacy and data protection features of the system, including credentials under the full control of the end-user and the design of a secure data exchange framework to link separate public and private databases, also offer important insights.

In the complex geopolitical space following its exit from the Soviet Union, Estonia needed to consolidate its national identity and to demonstrate its new government's ability to provide services economically and efficiently, including in relatively remote rural areas. The country's path to full digital ID started in 1992, with the creation of the Personal Identity Code, a unique number assigned to all residents (Pedak 2013). The current e-ID system was launched in 2000, with the first e-ID card issued in 2002.

Systems like Estonia's can only function successfully with a highly digitally literate population. At the time of the e-ID launch, the country initiated a public-private partnership to increase digital literacy and expand its population's access to the internet. Over two years, more than 100,000 Estonians were educated on the use of information and communications technologies, and the number of public internet access points increased from 200 in 2001 to 700 in 2004, a high number at that time for such a small country (Vassil 2015).

Nevertheless, the process of transitioning to electronic public service access and digital transactions using the new e-ID was a gradual process. It was only after five years and after more than 75 registries became accessible through the new system that its use became widespread. As with more traditional ID credentials, the uptake of Estonia's e-ID appears to have been closely linked to the number of services to which the ID provided access. This further underscores the idea that supplying identification is not enough; to galvanize demand, there need to be many opportunities to use the system. The inconvenience of venturing outside during Estonia's long winters may also have been one factor encouraging system use. Fifteen years after the e-ID system's inception, members of Estonia's highly computer-literate population can access virtually all public service providers online and perform numerous digital transactions, including signing documents and voting, with only a few exceptions. Weddings are one—brides and grooms have to be present in person since digital marriage registration is not permitted.

As in Peru, the e-ID system is underpinned by a state-held population database or national register, which provides all citizens and other residents with a unique 11-digit personal identifier. The database contains a limited set of information: name, date of birth, gender, address history, citizenship, and legally recognized relationships. Each person is also issued an email account to provide an official electronic address. State agencies and a number of private entities then can use this unique number to identify users and link them to their records within their respective systems, whether medical history, education or police record, or others. Information sharing between the different registries is facilitated through a simple yet innovative platform called X-Road, which currently enables secure data exchange between 170 databases and provides access to more than 2,000 services (e-Estonia 2016a).

Data protection has been a priority for Estonia's identification system since the start of the e-ID program. A massive public data leak in the 1990s (see box 6-1) made authorities mindful of the risk of unauthorized access from both within and outside of the system and wary of consolidating large amounts of personal information in one database. The system's notable emphasis on user control and secure and transparent data exchange reflects these early concerns.

Full Digital Identity under User Control

Although enrollment is mandatory for all residents, Estonia's e-ID program covers about 94 percent of its population above the age of 15.[3] Biometrics (face and 10 fingerprints) are taken on enrollment to ensure against duplicate registrations, but they are not used for authentication. Instead, remote digital authentication is facilitated through a smart ID card containing a microchip with two digital certificates; one to authenticate the holder with a personal identification number (called PIN1), and the other for digital signing (which requires a separate PIN2). PIN1 is a minimum 4-digit number and PIN2 is a minimum 5-digit number. Both are completely under the control of the user, and authentication is match-on-card rather than against the central population register.[4]

An Estonian digital identity is then the combination of three things: the

---

3   The "mandatory" requirement of an ID card can mean different things in different countries. Some impose a penalty, usually a fine, for not having one, while others do not. Even when there is no penalty, as in Estonia, the fact that the ID is mandatory means that it can legally be required for almost all purposes, which makes it difficult to function without one.

4   The system also provides for a third PIN, the PUK, which cardholders can use to unlock PINs blocked after several incorrect entries.

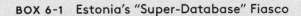

BOX 6-1   Estonia's "Super-Database" Fiasco

Estonia's decentralized digital registry infrastructure and the creation of its secure data exchange layer, the X-Road, are in large part the product of a major public data leak in the mid-1990s, which underlined the risks of a consolidated central database (Veldre 2016). A young programmer named Imre Perli was hired by several public and private entities, including the police, to establish and administer their respective digital registries. He managed to create a single registry, dubbed a "super-database" by the Estonian media, which contained virtually all relevant administrative information about Estonian citizens, including personal data from the population register, vehicle registration, traffic offenses, telephone numbers, and tax records. Perli then reportedly sold the database for around US$30,000–$50,000 to banks, insurance companies, and debt collection agencies (*Postimees* 1996). After the story about the data leak and the large-scale misuse of data became public, Estonia's government veered away from consolidating registries and focused instead on developing a secure approach for data exchange.

user-controlled PINs, the ID card and its digital certificates, and the database against which their validity is verified at the time of using the card. If the card is lost or the PINs are compromised, the certificates can be cancelled and the holder can reregister for a new card. Estonia's system therefore uses all three identifying factors: something you have (card), know (PINs), and are (initial biometrics for registration).

This system provides an unusual degree of control and protection to ID end-users because both the cards and their PINs are under the personal control of their holders. Even though no system is completely secure, it will be difficult to unlock the identity of a cardholder without them. This feature probably also helps to reduce the incentive to hack into the system because doing so would not give the intruder the ability to easily steal identities. In this regard, Estonia is far ahead of identity systems where users lack a "private key"—for example, the United States, where the Social Security number is widely used as an identifier even though it is relatively easy to steal.[5]

Estonian residents can verify their identity remotely online by connecting their physical ID card via a smartcard reader to their computer or (since 2007) by using a personalized digital ID-linked SIM card in their mobile phone. Digital signatures and authentication are legally equivalent to handwritten signatures and face-to-face identification in Estonia, and between partners upon agreement anywhere around the world. Once their identity is verified, ID holders can undertake a large range of activities online: they can review their personal records, such as medical, education, and employment history; they can also register changes in their legal status, file taxes, or start a new business. Estonians have embraced the system—as of 2016, the 1.27 million active Estonian e-ID cards in use had facilitated over 482 million electronic authentications and had been used to sign documents digitally in over 321 million instances (ID.ee 2016). On average, each cardholder provides 50 e-signatures per year. Estonians have been able to use their e-IDs for online voting since 2005, both in Estonia's parliamentary and European Parliament elections. In the last election, close to a third of voters cast their vote electronically.

Although there has been no rigorous assessment, the savings from the e-ID system and from moving government services online appear to be considerable. The Estonian government estimates that savings from "paperless" public administration could amount to over 2 percent of GDP (about US$500 million), including from saving over 115,000 working hours per day (e-Estonia 2016a; 2016b). Another estimate based on time savings suggests that online access to government services and digital signatures have saved over $140 million for Estonians and Estonian companies (Arm 2014). During the last elections, savings from e-voting were estimated at 11,000 working days and €500,000 (e-Estonia 2015).

---

5   On August 30, 2017, an international team of researchers informed the Estonian Information System Authority of a vulnerability potentially affecting digital use of Estonian ID cards (Republic of Estonia Information System Authority 2017). At the time of writing, it was not apparent that any identities had actually been compromised, but this reinforces the need for continued vigilance (Zorz 2017).

Secure and Transparent Data Exchange

Unlike the multipurpose Malaysian ID card, Estonia's card is used only for identification. For greater security, the various publicly administered databases are decentralized. Each government agency and service provider stores user data separately, and only what is necessary for its own purposes. Yet this does not mean that different registries (or rather, their administrators) have no way of communicating with each other. The databases are linked through a data exchange layer called X-Road, which enables the secure exchange of essential information between the state's information systems as well as private entities such as banks or employers. It also allows end-users to query the different databases following an authentication process using their e-ID.[6]

The system is designed to provide residents with maximum access and control over their data, while also making sure that sensitive information is protected. All authorized service providers have public key certificates and each data request is digitally signed and time-stamped to maximize transparency (Tonurist, Lember, and Kattel 2016). Estonians can verify what information about them is held in each government system and the reason why this information is retained (Herlihy 2013). They can check who has accessed their data and when, with the exception of queries related to criminal behavior and national security. Unwarranted snooping by public officials is punishable by imprisonment.

E-Residency: Toward a Global e-ID?

In a pioneering move, in late 2014 Estonia introduced an e-Residency program, which allows those not physically resident on its territory to obtain a government-issued digital ID. This is the first such initiative for a state to issue identity as a "third party" to individuals with no direct relationship to the country. Applicants need to fill out an online application and provide their biometric data and a proof of identity in person at an Estonian police and border guard office or embassy (e-Estonia 2014). The application receives similar scrutiny as would be applied, for example, to an application for physical visit or pres-

---

6   For another approach that uses cryptography to prevent the use of a single number from making it easier to share data in a country with a centralized identity management system, see the example of Austria in chapter 4.

ence. The current fee for establishing a state-verified digital identity is €100 (about $110).

E-residency does not convey any right to physically reside in Estonia; neither is the application linked to eligibility for a Schengen visa for persons who require one to visit the country. However, it enables the holder to perform a wide range of virtual transactions in Estonia, including to establish a company and to set up payment arrangements. For example, this can be done through PayPal, an arrangement that might not be possible in the country of physical residence. As of the end of 2016, Estonia had some 14,000 registered e-residents from 135 countries, who had set up over 450 new businesses digitally (e-Estonia 2016b).

In principle, Estonia's e-Residency program could provide a universal approach to third-party global identification. It remains to be seen how widely such an approach would be accepted as a credential in other countries, and for what purposes.

Lessons from Estonia's e-ID

Estonia provides an example of how the provision of an e-ID can facilitate more effective public administration. The use of multifactor authentication through unique identity in the population register, a physical card verified against a central register, and the use of match-on-card PINs known only to the user provide a high level of protection while ensuring that users retain control over the authentication process. Estonia's digital data-sharing framework, the X-Road, also offers lessons: it enables coordination between different public registries, and thus faster and more efficient interaction between different government entities, while maintaining control of the process and secure exchange of personal data. Citizen-government interactions are more transparent and less time-consuming. Identity management is centralized, but there is no all-encompassing database.

Is Estonia a model for developing countries? Large-scale digital access to services may seem far off for some with still-limited connectivity and information technology infrastructure. In addition, Estonia's system requires a highly computer-literate population, accustomed to using PINs and aware of the importance of not sharing them. In Estonia, this message is constantly reinforced, and it would be more difficult to maintain PINs secret in countries such as India, where family members are accustomed to sharing information with each other. But Estonia provides a glimpse into the (not-too-distant) future. Many of its capabilities, including the ability to sign documents digitally, are already being incorporated into identification systems in other parts of the world, notably India's Aadhaar program.

India: The UID (Aadhaar) Program

India's unique identity or Aadhaar program offers the most revolutionary and innovative approach to identification seen to date in a developing country context, and possibly in the world. Against the backdrop of low birth registration rates (though these have increased in recent years) and a weak civil registration and vital statistics system, the Aadhaar program relies on multimodal biometrics to establish a unique identity baseline and to authenticate registrants for transactions, including the delivery of subsidies, transfers and, services. Using remote authentication as an entry point, through the "Aadhaar Stack," it also serves as a platform for more sophisticated digital services than those available in any other country.

The Aadhaar is the only known identification program in the world that was not linked to any particular status or entitlement or use upon its introduction. Nevertheless, the launch of the program was justified by specific needs. There had been earlier interest in strengthening ID systems, but the prime expressed motivation for the program was the need to rationalize India's extensive and complex system of subsidy programs that, in total, accounts for some US$60 billion in government expenditures per year. These are often inefficient and poorly targeted. Estimated losses from leakages and fraud were enormous. A 2008 Planning Commission report showed, for example, that more than a third of grain intended for poor households was instead sold to non-poor households, and that over half of subsidized grains did not reach intended recipients because of various delivery and identification errors (Zelazny 2012). Ensuring that beneficiaries were uniquely and consistently identified was expected to reduce these leakages as well as to streamline the complex system of programs. Because there is a growing literature on Aadhaar, and it has been referred to frequently in previous chapters, the overview here is intended solely to bring out some central features.[7]

---

7   Zelazny (2012) provides a description of the Aadhaar program through its early stages. For more details on the initial stages of the program and the creation of UIDAI, see the Government of India's own UIDAI information page at https://uidai.gov.in/about-uidai/about-uidai/background.html. A study by IDinsight (Abraham and others 2017) provides

Launch and Progress

The concept of unique identification for all Indians was originally conceived in 2006 in the context of the National e-Governance Plan adopted that May (Sarkar 2011, Zelazny 2012). The plan envisaged multiple "high priority citizen services" offered by various government departments whose mode of delivery would change from manual to electronic delivery. The plan aimed to offer "a seamless view of Government" and to bring service delivery to citizens' doorsteps. Sarkar (2011) notes that the plan's approach combined a centralized initiative with a decentralized implementation model.

In January 2009 the Planning Commission of India created the Unique Identification Authority (UIDAI). It was elevated to a cabinet committee level and Nandan Nilekani, previously the chairman of Infosys, was appointed as UIDAI's chairman in July. The authority's goal was "to develop and implement the necessary institutional, technical, and legal infrastructure to issue unique identity numbers to residents all across India" and to "issue a unique identification number that can be verified and authenticated in an online, cost effective manner, which is robust enough to eliminate duplicate and fake identities."

Progress has been remarkable. More than 1.14 billion people, about 88 percent of the population, have enrolled in the program since its launch, even though registration is not mandatory. Adult coverage is almost complete, and registration is now being extended to children. Documentary requirements for registration are flexible to maximize inclusion, with many different credentials being accepted as proof of identity and residence. Those who do not have credentials of any type could be registered on the basis of testimony from a local "introducer."[8] The Aadhaar program is also remarkably inexpensive considering its size. Unit cost, at $1.16 per enrollment, has been the lowest of any identification program in the world, although it is bound to increase since the mass enrollment period is almost over.

---

a useful updated summary, including references to Aadhaar-related legislation. For insights on India's development and modernization, including the role of the IT sector, see Nilekani (2009). Aiyer (2017) provides a readable account of the creation and rollout of the Aadhaar program.

8   Enrollment data from April 2015 indicate that only 219,296 Aadhaar numbers (0.03%) were issued based on introducer-provided proof of identity. Most people were therefore able to produce some other evidence of identity, but this is not to say that they had consistent documentation able to prove unique identity. See *The Wire* (2015).

The unique Aadhaar number, a 12-digit random number that conveys no identifying attributes of its holder, is being seeded into an increasing number of program databases, in what is already the largest social sector reform in the world. The Aadhaar is now anchored in a broader national plan for economic empowerment, financial inclusion, and poverty reduction that includes the provision of "Jhan Dan" bank accounts to the previously unbanked, the use of the Aadhaar, and its linking to mobile numbers to enable remote authentication and mobile payments (the Jhan-Dan-Aadhaar-Mobile Trinity, or JAM). Some 220 million new bank accounts have been created, many using UIDAI-issued identification to satisfy KYC requirements and to serve as vehicles for MGNREGS (the Mahatma Gandhi National Rural Employment Guarantee Scheme),[9] pensions, scholarships, and other payments.

In line with the combination of centralized initiative and decentralized implementation set out in the National e-Governance Plan, the Aadhaar is being seeded into multiple program databases. At least 558 use-cases are documented by Abraham and others (2017), many at state level or even implemented as pilots at district level. Some programs, such as the Aadhaar-enabled reforms of the public distribution system, deliver in-kind benefits rather than monetary payments. Policymakers are now extending its use beyond the administration of benefit programs to areas as diverse as attendance monitoring for public officials, asset registration, and tax administration.

The Aadhaar program has attracted great attention and had a major impact on thinking about identification programs and the biometrics industry. It is a "frontier" case in several dimensions.

Identity First

Unlike other multipurpose national identification programs, the possession of an Aadhaar number is unrelated to national status and even to proven legal residence in India. The conceptual model separates the attribute of "unique identity" from all other attributes, such as proof of citizenship or legal residence or entitlement to subsidies. These can be filled in later, as needed, by the responsible agency. Seeding the Aadhaar numbers into records enables the

9 MGNREGS guarantees one hundred days of wage-employment in a financial year to adult members of rural households in exchange for unskilled manual work.

program to handle identification for any purpose. This essential feature of the Aadhaar program has not always been fully appreciated, even in India.[10]

As a unique program that separates identification from specific purposes or status, the Aadhaar has provoked some head-scratching in the development community. Functional programs are always created in response to particular needs—a driver's license to regulate driving, or a social transfer card to distinguish beneficiaries. Foundational national identity programs are multipurpose but invariably related to national status. The Aadhaar is therefore neither a traditional national ID program nor a functional program.

Biometrics and Number as Identity

UIDAI relies on biometrics for identification and online authentication. Fused fingerprints and iris scans, and now also digital face scans, are used to deduplicate enrollments across India's massive population, including children down to age 5. At the start of the program, it was not guaranteed that this would be possible because of the vast number of pairwise comparisons necessary and the poor quality of fingerprint images for many manual workers. Performance data released by the program in 2012 showed that deduplication was possible with a high degree of precision (chapter 4, and Gelb and Clark 2013b). This is only possible with tight quality control at the point of capture.

Even though there is frequent reference to the "Aadhaar card," the program is distinctive in that authentication does not depend on the use of a costly or sophisticated card.[11] This was a deliberate choice to save the costs of producing, distributing, and managing cards, and protecting against alteration or forgery. Although the central database is heavily protected and encrypted, it could be argued that this renders the system more vulnerable to fraud or mass data

10 For example, one concern that has been expressed by the Supreme Court is that Aadhaar numbers could be issued to undocumented or illegal residents. The program reflected the need to build an identity foundation in the face of the reality that most individuals had only fragmentary and often inconsistent ID credentials with no credential providing proof of legal status. Although it does not confer legal status, the Aadhaar actually offers a powerful tool for border enforcement. If an individual is found to have an Aadhaar number and is not a legal resident with an entitlement to it, the number can be blocked, making it more difficult for the person to reintegrate in India.

11 In practice, the Aadhaar card is widely held and used as less formal evidence of identity. Initially, people laminated the piece of paper informing them of their number and held this as a simple card; it is understood that the program now informs people of their Aadhaar numbers by providing them a simple picture card. Rigorous authentication is against the database rather than the card.

breaches than the match-on-card PIN approach used by Estonia. However, Estonia's approach is more costly and requires a highly computer-literate population. Recreating iris or fingerprint images is no easy task and needs to be done on an individual basis. And once the primary identity of the holder is verified by in-person authentication, there is nothing to stop financial institutions or other service entities from requiring secondary IDs secured by mobile numbers (one-time passcodes), tokens, PINs, passwords, or other biometrics such as the finger-vein ATMs in use in Japan. Two- or even three-factor authentication would be normal for large transactions made by high-value customers.

One limitation of a fully cardless system is that there is no offline local identity verification mechanism to fall back on in case of a connectivity or technology glitch. With no secure way to check the claimed identity holder, when connectivity fails all transactions must be halted or, if they proceed, they may not be able to rely on much in the way of graduated levels of identity assurance. Even when connectivity is perfect, individual authentication failures may be frequent (chapter 4). Although the failure rate after three attempts is lower, the need for repeated attempts can slow transactions.

Problems can arise in any new system, and some of these difficulties can be eased with experience and experimentation. Iris readers are being introduced to provide an alternative authentication mechanism; their costs are poised to fall rapidly as iris technology is incorporated into mobiles. One lesson from the Aadhaar is that to maximize inclusion and ease of use, systems should enable as wide a range of authentication mechanisms as possible regardless of their exact design. The type and frequency of failures should be monitored (as is done in Andhra Pradesh), and a fast and accessible grievance process must be in place.

Standards-Based Implementation and Decentralized Rollout

Another distinctive feature of the Aadhaar has been its certification process, implemented by the Standardization Testing and Quality Certification Directorate. Technology suppliers have to submit documentation and three sets of biometric devices for testing against performance standards. Once approved, certificates are valid for three years. Coupled with the huge size of the program, the use of standards (and the development of new standards where none had existed) has stimulated competition among suppliers. This has had a considerable impact on the biometrics industry; although its products are still highly differentiated, it has moved substantially toward a "commodity" industry. Standards-based procurement has greatly reduced the costs of the Aadhaar program. Computing equipment is off the shelf. Proprietary technology is used only for the purpose of deduplication, where three providers compete for market share.

The program's standards-based approach has also allowed for its enrollment to be decentralized. States and territories identify registrars who then outsource the function to enrolling agencies to create some 50,000 "empanelled" enrollment points. Decentralized enrollment is only possible with quality standards and tight monitoring. In addition to biometric and biographic information, every enrollment data package includes detailed information on the process, including the time taken to enroll and the number of repeat takes needed to capture biometrics. To eliminate the temptation to enroll an applicant multiple times to boost payments, agents are paid only on the basis of the number of successful enrollments. The three types of information—biographic, biometric, and process—are packaged and sent to the center for analysis. This provides continual feedback on the performance of devices purchased from different manufacturers and also on the performance of individual operators, some of whom have been disciplined for taking shortcuts or otherwise inappropriate operations.

The "India Stack": Paving the Way for Multiple Digital Services

So far, the most visible use of the Aadhaar program has been to provide authentication services to a wide range of government programs. The "India Stack" builds on the system's capabilities to offer a wider range of services, including digital KYC (e-KYC). New applications can connect with the system through open APIs (Application Programming Interface).[12] This opens up identification as a platform for a potentially unlimited range of applications, well beyond those offered by other ID programs and limited only by the imaginations of developers.

The first set of services came as early as 2011, when the National Payments Corporation of India launched the Aadhaar Payments Bridge and Aadhaar-Enabled Payments System. These services use the Aadhaar number to channel government benefits and subsidies to beneficiaries' accounts linked to the number. This payments facility was followed in 2016 by the Unified Payments Interface, a generalized system to facilitate payments between any two

12 For more information on the India Stack, see the associated website at https://indiastack.org/about/.

Aadhaar-identified accounts. Another type of service was launched in 2012, with e-KYC, formulated to enable banks and other businesses to satisfy customer due-diligence requirements without painstakingly assembling and copying identification documents. The objective was to reduce costs, increase convenience, and facilitate financial inclusion. After being authenticated, a potential customer requests e-KYC and authorizes the release of essential information to satisfy requirements. E-KYC has reportedly reduced the cost of onboarding a customer from around $5 to $0.70.

In 2015 e-Sign was launched. This application enables Aadhaar holders to sign documents digitally, a capability that is possible with only a relatively few of the world's most advanced identification systems (chapter 1). Another innovation is DigiLocker, a platform to issue and verify documents digitally. Each person is entitled to 1 gigabyte of storage. The "digital locker" can store verified official documents or any other records the holder wishes to maintain in a secure digital registry and can share them through a "consent-based" architecture, as desired by the holder (Ministry of Electronics and Information Technology 2016). For example, a job applicant will be able to authorize the sharing of a college transcript with a particular employer. Transcripts would be digitally certified depending on their source—a transcript originating directly from the issuing institution would be differentiated from a scanned copy uploaded by the applicant. This would make it difficult to submit fraudulent credentials. The widespread adoption of services of this type would be a large step toward eliminating paper-based systems. Further applications are in process.

The Debate on Use and Privacy

Since its inception, the Aadhaar program has seen a series of legal challenges to its use before India's Supreme Court. To some extent these mirror issues raised for identification systems in other countries, but they also reflect the unusual sequence of Aadhaar, where the program was created before the legislative basis for its use was established. The program was established by executive order, with legislation coming only after it achieved widespread coverage and a number of government programs had begun to use it for identity verification. Judging by the speed of its rollout and integration into services and programs, this approach has been highly successful and it may have been the only way to move forward in a country with as much diversity and many fractious interest groups as India. However, even though concerns around privacy, data protection, and the potential for the common number to link individual records across multiple databases apply to other systems as well, this unusual sequence has contributed to continuing debate on the program. Other countries may not want to follow a similar sequence.

One of the tensions has been between voluntary enrollment, a clear position of UIDAI reconfirmed by Supreme Court rulings, and requirements for the Aadhaar to access benefit and other public programs. Can a voluntary credential—in this case, a number and fingerprints or iris—be legally required to access benefits or subsidies that are widely considered to be entitlements? Can it be required for public-private interactions that do not involve benefits, such as registering property or filing tax returns? Can it be required for citizens to exercise their rights to vote? If the Aadhaar serves only to enable individuals to voluntarily authenticate themselves, can data held by UIDAI be required for security or law enforcement purposes? If the answer to such questions is yes, in what sense can Aadhaar truly be a voluntary program? The passage of the Aadhaar Act 2016[13] cleared the way for its use to identify those receiving subsidies and benefits. A more recent court ruling placed a partial hold on the requirement that Permanent Account Number (PAN) cards needed to file tax returns be linked to Aadhaar numbers; those who possess an Aadhaar must link it while those that do not are not required to do so. But this left unresolved the question of whether there were any limits on the use of the Aadhaar. In the views of some critics, even if the expressed motivation for the program may have been to reduce leakages in benefit programs, the true goal may be a much more pervasive use of the system (Dreze 2016).

In a landmark ruling on August 24, 2017, the court recognized privacy as a fundamental right of Indian citizens. At the same time, however, it asserted that, like other rights, this right was not absolute, and that there was a need for "a careful and sensitive balance between individual interests and the legitimate concerns of the state."[14] These legitimate aims "would include, for instance, protecting national security, preventing and investigating crime, encouraging innovation and the spread of knowledge, and preventing the dissipation of social welfare benefits." Use-cases that threaten privacy would need to pass three tests: proof of legality, demonstration of a legitimate need, and proportionality. The implications of the ruling for the various uses of Aadhaar,

---

13 Aadhaar (Targeted Delivery of Financial and other Subsidies, Benefits and Services) Act, 2016. For full details, see https://uidai.gov.in/beta/images/the_aadhaar_act_2016.pdf.

14 Writ Petition (Civil) NO 494 of 2012 Justice K. S. Puttaswamy (Retd.) Versus Union of India Part T, p. 265.

including to deliver social transfers and payments, remained to be resolved by subsequent judgments on whether the program and its uses satisfy these tests.[15]

As another example of the debate, when introduced, the Aadhaar's mandate was more restricted than that of a traditional national identification program. The use of identifying data held by UIDAI was explicitly limited to responding to authentication requests made by the individual concerned. Data could not be used other than for such one-to-one comparisons; neither could they be shared, even for law enforcement or national security purposes. This stance was supported by India's Supreme Court in a 2014 ruling in response to a petition from Goa. It was noted that data sharing would be "in breach of an individual's right against self-incrimination under Article 20(3) of the Constitution. No consent has been taken from citizens when providing their biometric information that it may be used in future potential investigations against them" (Patil and Desai 2014).[16]

Although sections 28 and 29 of the Aadhaar Act strongly support maintaining the confidentiality of data and records, section 33 introduces important exceptions for requests for identifying information or authentication records made under a court order or in the interests of national security.[17] Although the act provides for strict processes and for oversight, it introduces a significant chink in the armor of strict confidentiality around UIDAI's data. It was suggested that the constitutional validity of the Aadhaar Bill, were it to become law, would need to be tested against the established legal standards against self-incrimination and the standards of privacy in India (Patil and Desai 2014). It therefore remains to be seen whether the Aadhaar program comes to be used for the full range of functions typically served by a national ID. Pakistan's NADRA system, for example, is used for law enforcement and antiterrorism

15 The Supreme Court ruling was welcomed by the CEO of UIDAI, who argued that the uses of the unique identity number conformed to the reasonable restrictions and criteria set out by the court (Agarwal 2017).

   A number of breaches of data privacy reported in the press appear to involve Aadhaar numbers, as well as other personal data, that have become publicly available as a result of the disclosure of program lists by agencies. UIDAI maintains that the database has not been compromised. This raises wider questions of whether an identity number can be considered as secret or sensitive personal information rather than a unique name for digital systems. In India it has been traditional to publicly post beneficiary lists to facilitate community oversight, but some will see a difference between the physical posting of a list of names in a village and the digital release of data. See CIS (2017) and a response from Dr. Ajay Bhushan Pandey, CEO of UIDAI, in Singh (2017).

16 The implications of this judgment were widely disseminated, see Mishra (2014) and *Indian Express* (2014).

17 Aadhaar Act, Sections 33 (1) and (2).

purposes, including as a forensic tool to help identify perpetrators and victims of terrorism (Malik 2014).

Lessons from the Aadhaar

Aadhaar offers multiple lessons for other countries, even if they do not choose to take all of its features on board. Some countries may prefer to maintain card-based authentication systems as well, at least until stronger connectivity and mobiles become ubiquitous, but the Aadhaar indicates the value of developing direct authentication as an option to enable a future shift away from costly cards. Its technology has already provided a basis for the implementation of Indonesia's e-KTP identity program.

On the program itself, one lesson is the value of sequencing "identification" before "status" and the use of multimodal biometrics to lock in an identity baseline without requiring extensive documentation. Equally important are its implementation lessons, including the use of standards to drive competition among hardware and software providers and bring down costs. Standardization and a data-driven approach have enabled a wide range of entities to be empanelled in a decentralized enrollment network. Other countries that are less able to generate massive economies of scale may not be able to attain the Aadhaar's low unit cost, but the program offers a number of lessons for keeping costs down while maintaining high levels of efficiency.

The Aadhaar also offers many emerging lessons on the use of unique identification to reform benefit, subsidy, transfer, and other programs. The reforms go beyond authentication; they include the computerization of supply chains and changes in the way that subsidies are provided. Nonetheless, unique identification and the consequent direct program-to-client link are key underpinnings of the reforms.

The India Stack and its use of open APIs to encourage developers to build a layer of services should also be of great interest to other countries seeking to streamline administration, reduce costs, and open up new opportunities using digital platforms. E-KYC has great promise for countries that want to encourage financial inclusion and digital payments, including through the simplified payment arrangements enabled by linking ID numbers, bank accounts, and mobiles. Some of the more advanced services may take some time to become widely used; the case of Estonia suggests that a span of several years, if not a decade, is the norm for a new technology to become fully absorbed.

"Federated" Identification: GOV.UK Verify

The United Kingdom's GOV.UK Verify program makes use of government-licensed companies to verify (or "establish") residents' digital identity to allow them to access government services and transactions online.[18] Verification is based on information from multiple nongovernment sources as well as government-issued credentials. This arrangement points to the possibility that identification systems may evolve from the top-down centralized model toward more decentralized or "federated" models, including a marketplace for privately provided identity services. This model functions differently from the centralized systems of Peru, Estonia, and India.

The creation of the United Kingdom's digital identity verification scheme was motivated largely by a government-backed push for greater efficiency in the provision of public services. In April 2011 the Government Digital Service was established to support the implementation of its "digital-by-default" strategy, which would bring the majority of public services online. It was estimated that providing transactional services digitally would save the state up to £1.8 billion (about US$2.8 billion at the time) through shorter processing times, the reduced need for physical office space and staff, and less use of postage and packaging materials (GOV.UK 2012). Depending on the service, costs for a digital transaction were projected to be up to 50 times lower than for one where both parties had to be physically present. The government also felt that the convenience of accessing public services online would save British residents considerable amounts of time.

The idea of moving toward digital services and online citizen-state engagement was nothing new. Estonia's e-ID system already offered most of the functionality that the British government wanted to provide, and probably more. However, the United Kingdom's political and socioeconomic context and its underlying identity infrastructure was dramatically different. Crucially, the United Kingdom has no national ID card or any other official document whose primary purpose is to identify an individual (CESG 2014). The last national identity program in the United Kingdom was introduced during World War II and was repealed in 1952 because its use in routine police checks was regarded as an infringement on citizens' rights. More recently, in the mid-2000s public and political opposition foiled British policymakers' efforts to create a centralized biometric identity database and issue

18 This section draws heavily on Whitley (2018 forthcoming).

ID cards; opponents claimed that the system would be costly, invasive, and prone to misuse.

The challenge for the United Kingdom was to develop a system that would reliably and securely verify residents' identity online, and yet would have flexible registration and authentication requirements and also would limit the ability of the state or any other entity to access personal data and consolidate it across databases. As other privacy-conscious governments develop their own frameworks for providing digital access to transactions and services, the British model offers insights on the use of a federated approach that does not require the existence of a standard national ID, although it could draw on such an ID if one existed. It also illustrates the possible role for private entities in the identity verification process, and the challenges of such a model for broad-based digital identity provision.

Segmented Identity Provision: Separate Roles for the State and Private Entities

In response to continued public concerns about surveillance and the possible abuse of power, the British government's approach to digital identification centers on the segmentation of roles and functions within the ID management process (see figure 6-1). The state maintains the role of providing a "primary" identification by registering births and issuing birth certificates, and it maintains its monopoly on issuing other widely used functional proofs of identity and entitlements such as driver's licenses or passports. These government-issued credentials are the foundation for digital identity verification that can then be conducted by designated private entities. The state also is responsible for defining the standards governing the system: the parameters of the identification and verification process within which the commercial identity providers will operate.

Multiple private companies can then take over the verification role to provide decentralized or "federated" identity assurance for online transactions. The certified identity providers collect evidence across three data categories: information on the citizen, information of a financial nature, and evidence of a living identity. The process uses a potentially wide range of evidence that can encompass more than one category at a time.[19] Evidence can include government-

19 Before choosing their digital identity provider, applicants need to register their name, address, and date of birth. Based on some simple questions about the type of identity documents and information they will be able to provide, they are then directed to a set of identity providers that are most likely to be successful in validating their identity.

FIGURE 6-1   Segmentation of the Identity
Verification Process in GOV.UK Verify

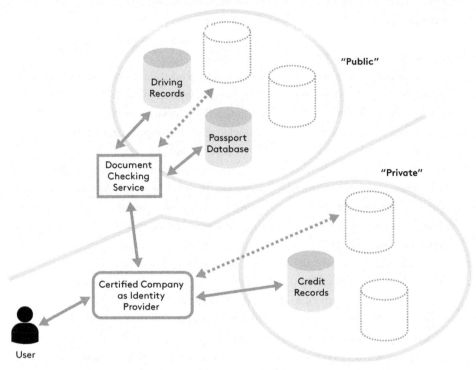

Source: Whitley (2018 forthcoming).

issued identity documents, such as passports and marriage certificates, as well as evidence from commercial sources, such as a bank savings account, property or car insurance, or a mobile phone contract (CESG 2014).[20] Identity providers are also able to draw on other government sources, such as police databases, to check that the claimed identity is not known to be fraudulent. However, only a minimal amount of data is transmitted between the private ID providers (or rather, verifiers) and the state databases. When a private ID provider queries a state registry to check the validity of a document, it receives only a yes-or-no response. No other details of the person being verified are shared.

20 Some examples of how these map into the three categories: *citizen*: passport, police bail sheet; *financial*: bank account; *living*: fixed-line telephone account, mortgage account, National Health Service staff card. A birth certificate is accepted as Level 2 evidence only for the category of citizenship.

Once an applicant's identity has been verified, the end-user can access various government services, such as claiming for redundancy payments, updating vehicle taxes, and filing and signing individual tax assessments. Twelve services were available as of May 2016, and a further 18 were scheduled to be rolled out in the near future, including applying for childcare support and filing for bankruptcy online (Whitley 2018 forthcoming).

The separation between the identity verifier and the service provider has a number of benefits. It enables secure digital access with minimal concentration of information in the hands of either entity. The service organization—say, a government department—has no knowledge of the supporting evidence for identity accessed by the provider. All it knows is that the person has been verified against his or her claimed identity by a certified entity, to the required level of identity assurance. Similarly, the private certified provider does not know which service the applicant is attempting to access. The system is double-blind; there is no central database or unique identity number that could be used to link individual records across databases or to track transactions.

In addition, identity providers are paid according to the number of successfully verified identities. The certification of multiple, competing private sector providers encourages the use of as wide a range of identity checking services as possible. Providers have an incentive to continuously explore documentary evidence and transaction records that can be used as part of the identity verification process, and to suggest innovations to help ensure that as many users as possible can be verified.

To appreciate the prerequisites for the operation of such a federated system, it is important to recognize that, as used in the United Kingdom, this approach builds on, rather than substitutes for, more conventional forms of official identification.[21] Many of the proofs of identity for digital identity verification provided by nonstate sources, such as credit histories or mobile phone subscriptions, do require some form of government-issued ID when first established. For example, official identity documents are needed to open a bank account in Britain, as in other countries. Yet despite its reliance on more traditional forms of identification, the process also adds substantive information (for example, that an identity is active) as evidenced by a transaction record on a long-

21 GOV.UK Verify is increasing the range of supporting documentation to extend the demographic coverage of the system. The process still appears to rely heavily on official identification, confirming its role as a complement to official ID rather than a substitute (Hughes 2015).

established bank account or evidence that the applicant can access and report on the most recent bank or credit card balance. Such "dynamic" proofs of active identity are powerful and accordingly receive additional weight in the formula for assigning identity assurance scores (discussed further below) to the combined evidence during the verification process.

Although GOV.UK Verify's initial rollout was focused on access to government services, it is envisioned that the private sector will also be able to use this state-approved federated digital identity program in the future. To reach that step, the program will have to address several further issues, including the question of how to assign and limit legal liability for errors. As the sole client so far, government can agree to waive or limit its claims. Something similar will no doubt be needed if private identity assurers are to take on the service for private clients.[22] Private sector use might also open up new revenue streams for the certified digital identity providers and, potentially, the government.

Levels of Identity Assurance vs. 'Gold Standard' Digital Identity Management

Another noteworthy element of the GOV.UK Verify program was the adoption of "ID assurance" as a guiding concept in its implementation. In his influential 2008 report on identification, Sir James Crosby (2008) emphasized a critical distinction between "ID management" and "ID assurance." "ID management" was portrayed as a benefit mainly for the holder of the information and the systems (for example, the government), while "ID assurance" focused on bringing benefits to the consumer. The United Kingdom made a conscious effort to follow the second approach. Instead of providing a single, "gold-plated," all-access digital identity—as is the case in Estonia—Verify differentiates between various levels of assurance on the legitimacy of an identity claim, based on the breadth and strength of the evidence provided, the robustness of the validation and verification processes used, and the history of activity associated with the claimed identity (CESG 2014). For countries without any widely held national identifier (and no plans to create one), the most sensible and inclusive model likely will be one that sets levels of assurance for identity verification. The approach could also be used to further reinforce identity assurance even beyond

---

22 The issue is less pressing for government identification, since government agencies and staff enjoy broad immunity, but could become an important question for ID certification performed as a business by private entities.

the level provided by a standard ID credential by including dynamic proofs of active identity.

An important contribution of the Verify program has therefore been to systematize the approach to levels of identity assurance. This tends to be ad hoc for most conventional systems, with assurance levels linked to processes. Is it enough to show a card, or must the card be validated against a database? Is a look at the photo on the card enough to validate the holder, or are additional steps (such as a signature or a fingerprint match to a template embedded in the card) needed? The answer, of course, should depend on the nature of the query. Access to a nuclear facility requires a far higher level of identity assurance than enrollment in an online discussion group. For Verify, the number of data points and the types of evidence needed for online verification depend on the level of assurance required by the service to be accessed.

As set out in table 6-2, the Verify system has four levels of identity assurance. Level 1 is the most basic identity level. Level 2 is stronger; "on the balance of probability" someone is who they claim to be, perhaps to the level normally required for civil proceedings. Level 3 is stronger still—the person is who they say they are "beyond reasonable doubt," to the level that might be offered in criminal proceedings. The program does not yet support level 4 identity assurance, which calls, among other things, for the use of biometrics to prove identity to a very high level of certainty. A number of countries have adopted this four-level identity assurance framework, and an International Organization for Standardization (ISO) standard also has been set for it (ISO/IEC 29115).

The verification process for the identity itself has five elements: the identity actually exists; the evidence of identity is valid (matching against records); the person owns the claimed identity (verification questions); the identity is not known to be fraudulent (checks against records); and the identity is active (recent transaction history) (Hughes 2014). No single proof of identity is needed for verification; instead, the verification process uses a more complex, multifaceted "identity evidence package" that relies on a variety of government-issued documents and registries and a history of (financial) transactions with private companies, including ownership of mobile and financial accounts, bill payments, and credit history.

A Verify-ed identity is considered to be one that could be verified to level 2; this is currently sufficient to access all linked digital government services. This threshold for functionality is also used in the government's performance-based contracts with the certified private identity providers. The government pays the private provider £1.20 each time the provider successfully verifies an identity

TABLE 6-2   Levels of Identity Assurance

LEVEL 1 IDENTITY

At Level 1 there is no requirement for the identity of the applicant to be proven. The applicant has provided an identifier that can be used to confirm an individual as the applicant. The identifier has been checked to ensure that it is in the applicant's possession and/or control.

LEVEL 2 IDENTITY

A Level 2 Identity is a claimed identity with evidence that supports its real-world existence and activity. The steps taken to determine that the identity relates to a real person and that the applicant is owner of that identity might be offered in support of civil proceedings.

LEVEL 3 IDENTITY

A Level 3 Identity is a claimed identity with evidence that supports its real-world existence and activity, and physically identifies the person to whom the identity belongs. The steps taken to determine that the identity relates to a real person and that the applicant is owner of that identity might be offered in support of criminal proceedings.

LEVEL 4 IDENTITY

A Level 4 Identity is a Level 3 Identity that is required to provide further evidence and is subjected to additional and specific processes, including the use of biometrics, to further protect the identity from impersonation or fabrication. This is intended for those persons who may be in a position of trust or situations where compromise could represent a danger to life.

Source: CESG (2014).

at level 2 assurance (Whitley 2018 forthcoming) and the provider receives a second payment for ongoing maintenance once the digital identity account has been active for a year. If the identity assurance process has only reached level 1, the provider receives a much smaller payment for the initial verification—only 5 percent of the level 2 price. For failed verification attempts or where fraud is detected, providers receive no payment.

Standards-based, Continuously Monitored, and Responsive Implementation

Another noteworthy feature of the Verify program has been its standards-based, relatively transparent, and user-feedback-sensitive implementation process. Verify's standards-based approach has a number of elements in common with that of India's Aadhaar program; even though the two programs are different, both have carefully defined technological parameters and have made public performance data regarding (at least some parts of) the ID registration and authentication process.

GOV.UK Verify, like all other government digital services used by the British public, must meet a list of 18 criteria defined by the Digital Service Standard (GOV.UK 2016a). These include basing the service on user needs and continuously monitoring user experience, collecting and reporting performance data, and using open standards and common platforms to ensure flexibility and to avoid getting locked into contracts. Each service, including Verify, goes through a series of phases—Discovery, Alpha, and Beta—and must pass the associated service assessments before becoming widely available for public use (Whitley 2018 forthcoming). The Verify program also complies with nine Identity Assurance Principles developed by the Privacy and Consumer Advisory Group, an independent voluntary body that relies on both expert knowledge and public consultation for its recommendations. These principles emphasize (among others) consent and user control, the need to fully inform residents about the use of their identity, the importance of having a choice in the number of identifiers and identity providers, and the use of minimal data for each transaction (Whitley and Fishenden 2015).

Verify's implementation team is constantly monitoring users' experience with the digital identity verification process and is working to improve the rates of successful identity verification. It regularly publishes performance data along with monthly technical delivery updates that highlight the implementing team's priorities for the upcoming weeks, and changes applied to improve completion rates and the user experience in general.

Exclusion Risks and Other Implementation Challenges

The GOV.UK Verify service went live in May 2016, following almost two years in public beta status. Its progress has been documented online since it was first launched, both in the form of a blog and through a "service dashboard" that lists a number of publicly available performance indicators (Whitley 2018 forth-coming; Hales 2016; GOV.UK 2016b). The data show that by mid-November 2016 a total of 911,000 verified accounts had been created, with more than 50 percent of the digital identities used more than once. The proportion of visits where users have been able to verify their identity online has been fairly steady over the past year, with 70 percent of completed verification attempts re-sulting in the creation of a verified digital identity. User satisfaction, measured through the ease of verification, is on the rise, with about 80 percent of user satisfaction survey participants reporting to be satisfied with the process during September 2016. By August 2017, Verify had been used to access services a total of 3.63 million times.

At the same time, the initial use of the system has highlighted some limita-tions and concerns. Take-up had been slower than projected, though not out of line with the experience of other countries, such as Estonia, whose digital in-novations also took some time to become widely used. Certain groups of people who had limited evidence to draw on and limited technical expertise faced greater difficulties in having their identities verified (Fiveash 2014). Farmers were one such category; as a relatively traditional group, they were often less "connected" and less prone to travel or to have home mortgages. A second set of people that faced difficulties was those in the youngest age group (below age 25); they were less likely to be able to verify their identities because they have a shorter history of documented activity. At the other end of the age spectrum, those older than age 75 were also less likely to be able to complete the process because they were less likely to have a "primary" proof of identity such as a driver's license or a passport. There may also have been an age-related "digital divide," where older people are less able to navigate the system.

Verify itself is not aiming for universal coverage—the program's target is to reach 90 percent of the United Kingdom's adult population. Based on survey data that measure ownership of 20 items of identity evidence as well as technol-ogy use, Verify currently estimates that 79 percent of the United Kingdom's adult population should be able to verify their identities digitally using the certified identity providers (Higson and Dale 2016).[23] Somewhat worryingly, those with low or no income were found to be less likely to be able to access government services digitally because they have lower levels of smartphone and

---

23 This is similar to the percentage of adults with driving licenses or residents holding UK passports; 78 percent and 80 percent respectively (Whitley 2018 forthcoming).

tablet ownership—which are needed to scan an identification document for verification—and also are less likely to have the financial documentation used to verify a history of live activity.

Lessons from GOV.UK Verify

Although the GOV.UK Verify program is still in its early stages, it offers the most advanced blueprint for "federated" digital identity provision, where the government sets standards and a number of private entities verify identities using multiple state-administered registries as well as private sector data sources. This federated architecture can enhance privacy and encourage innovation and effective service delivery through the competitive provision of identity services. It protects users' personal data by ensuring that no entity, including the state itself, has a complete picture of an individual's digital transactions. No single entity or database holds users' information, thereby minimizing the potential damage from and incentives for a data breach.

The flexibility embedded in Verify's verification process reflects both its user-centric approach and the constraints of operating in a country with no widely held national ID credential. The multisource verification process means that no single ID document (such as a passport) is necessary to gain access to the digital services provided. Having several, competing entities as digital identity providers offers users further choice in how their identity is verified. The program's emphasis on user needs and on privacy and personal data safeguards is similarly evident from the standards-based implementation process.

Another of Verify's notable contributions is the development and application of levels of identity assurance, rather than a single, gold-plated identity. Such risk-based identity verification can allow ID programs to be more inclusive: even if users cannot be verified to the highest level of assurance, they are not shut out from all services. It also enables service providers to adjust their own assurance requirements for access based on the type of service offered, the population targeted, and the risk of fraud associated with the given activity. At the same time, Verify offers a caution in this area. Even if, in the end, 90 percent of the population are able to use it successfully, this still leaves 10 percent who are not. Many in this group are likely to be older, poorer, and less connected, and have less evidence of the "citizen," "finance," and "life" categories. In developing countries, the corresponding groups are the most likely to need social protection or other public support. Part of the savings generated by the shift toward digital services facilitated by Verify should be cycled back into improving services for those not able to use the system. This point is not specific to Verify, but is important for all countries implementing digital ID programs.

Finally, Verify confirms that the state still has a critical role, even if the private sector can play a prominent role in authenticating identities. The state provides the foundational identifying data by registering births and issuing passports, driver's licenses, and other ID credentials. It also provides regulatory oversight by certifying the private identity providers and ensuring that the program follows certain standards that maximize its utility, while helping to minimize risks to privacy and the misuse of data. The centrality of the state's role and the need for credible government-issued proofs of identity (even though these are not directly presented to the public service providers) point to the difficulty of envisioning such a federated arrangement as the first stage of an identity management system.

Networks and Crowd-Sourced Digital Identities

Each digitally connected member of society is accumulating a rapidly growing cloud of digital data. Much is held by private companies, including providers of internet services and online social and professional networks that maintain extensive databases of personal information on users and their lifestyles. This information and the corporations that administer them can also play a role in providing digital identification. Members of large online communities such as Facebook (2 billion members) and LinkedIn (500 million members) can now have their identities verified through their connections and activities in the "e-village" to access a limited number of private services.

The role of digital networks in establishing and verifying identities has been modest to date but will likely grow as the volume of digital data grows and the power and precision of identity-related algorithms increase. However, there will still be constraints for the foreseeable future. In many countries, the state is the biggest "consumer" of identification services. A primary use of ID credentials is to be able to access publicly provided services such as education, healthcare, or social transfers, or to travel. Even with authorized private identity verifiers, the core of identity provision is likely to remain anchored in state-managed registries and government-issued ID credentials (as in the case of GOV.UK Verify), because these credentials enable users to access government services. However, private businesses are likely to see increasing value in network-based or "crowd-sourced" identification processes, and these processes could emerge as complements to state-issued identification.

Identification through the e-village bears some parallels to local identification by friends and neighbors before the emergence of centralized registries— based on who you know and who knows you—but extends beyond physical association and into digital communities. There is an important difference: even though a village ID is based on local identification, it may be recognized as official identity if certified by an authorized local worthy or official (chapter 1), whereas e-village identity is not certified in a comparable way. However, as a growing number of activities move online, the quality of information that the e-village can provide is improving. People comment on each other's activities, posts, and pictures. Web-based applications, which have enabled the rise of the "gig economy" by offering car rides or renting out homes or spare rooms, have curated a large number of reviews and references that can provide evidence of existence, residence, and other potentially useful identifying data. Professional networking sites such as LinkedIn allow users to endorse their connections for certain skills and to post longer references on each other's profiles. Data algorithms are improving, and it is not impossible to imagine networked identification being accepted for some official purposes in the future.

These "e-village testimonies" open additional avenues for identity verification by and for private service providers. For example, financial sector entities could use such data to help verify the identities of their clients and even to assess their creditworthiness, much as a local banker might draw on personal knowledge and informal referrals to assess a loan applicant. Although the e-village is more of a feature in richer countries, the digital data cloud is rapidly including a growing number of people in developing regions.

Facebook: Potential and Limitations as an Identity Provider

With more than 2 billion active users worldwide, Facebook has the largest social network database in the world. More than half of its active users live outside of the United States, Canada, and Europe, many of them in developing countries. However, its identity management processes are far from fully rigorous, and it is also not clear whether an inclusive business model that depends on having as many users as possible to maximize network externalities is compatible with rigorous identity screening.

Official Facebook policy allows only the use of one's real identity. Users are required to submit their authentic name and birthday when registering for an account for the first time. Nevertheless, Facebook does not require new users to submit any specific proof of identity when signing up—verification is solely by the email address or the mobile number provided. Government-issued identification is not required; there is also no need to provide a photo of the user. As well as cats, dogs, or other nonpersons, members can use pictures of celebrities as their main identifying photo, provided that the clear intent is not to impersonate another individual. If Facebook suspects that the identity provided at registration is not genuine, or that the user is under age 13 (the minimum age for a Facebook account), it can ask the owner of the account for further confirmation of their identity. Users may then be asked to submit a copy of a photo ID from a range of both government and privately issued ID types (Facebook 2016a). If the user cannot comply or is unwilling to do so, their account may be deleted.

This "light" approach to identity management reflects a social network's need to be inclusive, even as it protects its business model against fake identities created to enable a large number of "likes" to be artificially registered to boost a product, service, or reputation.[24] With such a balance, the number of accounts not uniquely linked to an authentic identity can be relatively high. In 2012 Facebook released data indicating that about 8.7 percent or 83 million of its accounts were duplicates or fakes (Kelly 2012). Duplicates accounted for about 45.8 million accounts; "nonhuman" accounts created for pets, companies, and the like made up about 22.9 million, while about 14.3 million accounts had been set up to distribute spam and for other illicit commercial activities. Although the social networking site has stepped up efforts to eliminate fake sites in the past three years, its 2014 Annual Report put the share of fake accounts between 5.5 percent and 11.2 percent (67.5 million and 138 million). These numbers would need to decrease by orders of magnitude to reach the precision of a modern centralized digital system.

Even if Facebook credentials can be used as sufficient identifiers to access other web applications,[25] such a level of false identities would make it difficult

---

24 Amazon has recently initiated lawsuits against businesses providing positive reviews in exchange for payments and has banned the use of "incentivized" reviews, where the reviewer receives a free product from the seller in exchange for his or her—supposedly honest—review.

25 Through OpenID, many websites and applications rely on third parties like Yahoo! or Google to provide access for users. (Facebook was previously a member of Open ID, but has since moved to Facebook Connect.) OpenID enables users to access multiple applications using the same login credentials, reducing the need to memorize multiple usernames and passwords and saving time spent on setting up new accounts. It also saves time and money for client websites and app developers, who no longer need to provide for their own password management systems. However, the level of assurance provided by such an ID

TABLE 6-3 Some Features of the Cases

Innovative feature	Main expected benefit(s)	Potential risks or limitations	As seen in
Politically (and financially) autonomous ID agency	Efficiency, as a result of having to cover own costs; effectiveness by limiting political interference	Exclusion of remote and poor populations if agency is solely supported by fees	Peru
Performance-based payments for registration	Inclusion, by increasing incentives to enroll	Deduplication essential to prevent multiple registration	Peru, India
Performance-based payments to civil registry	Integration of civil registration data	Also requires investing in capacity of registration offices	Peru
Payment per verification of identity claim	Incentive to perform	If paid by end-user, can increase costs and exclusion	Peru, UK
Identity for all, delinked from status or eligibility	Inclusion: all residents are eligible	Need separate processes, for example, to determine citizenship or eligibility	India
Identification by number and biometric	Lower costs through savings on card issuance and management	Requires connectivity; no credential for offline authentication and if database compromised	India
Standards-based system and rollout	Lower costs, no vendor lock-in	Requires capacity to set and monitor standards	India
Open platform for additional services	Wider use of digital systems and capabilities, efficiency gains	Digital divide between those with and without capacity to use new systems	India
PIN-based match-on-card authentication for digital access to government services	User control of credential; less incentive to hack central database to steal identities	Requires informed users; identity compromised if card and PIN are shared	Estonia

Innovative feature	Main expected benefit(s)	Potential risks or limitations	As seen in
e-Residency	Global identification, portability, business revenues	Limited uptake; potential burden on justice system from disputed digital contracts	Estonia
X-Road	Decentralized data, secure data exchange, user access and oversight	Requires technological capacity to set up and manage secure data exchange layer; universal connectivity needed to ensure inclusive access; legacy systems	Estonia
Multiple companies for federated digital identification to access public services	Privacy, through limited "double-blind" information sharing and no central identification system or number	Requires official identification; could face liability issues or complicated grievance process	UK
Points-based integration of state and private data by authorized entities	Supplements information available from official sources, including with powerful "dynamic" evidence of activity	Requires official identification; exclusion of those who may not have sufficient and varied identifying information	UK
Levels of identity assurance based on needs of particular application	Flexibility rather than uniform "gold standard," inclusion	Requires ability to assess and assign levels of assurance and risks	UK
Identity verification based on digital networks	Inclusion (no "official" state-issued proof of identity is needed); supplement to official identification; growing capability	Not foundational; unclear business case; low assurance potential liability issues; sharing own "networked" profile may infringe on privacy of connections ("friends")	Facebook, other digital networks

for the company to become a trusted, widely accepted provider of digital identity services. Most public and private service providers would require a higher degree of assurance that the claimed identity exists and that the person with the Facebook login information is truly the individual named as the account holder. It is also not clear that the supplementary role of a rigorous provider of digital identity services is compatible with the main social networking function, since tightened identification requirements would alienate many users and cause them to shift allegiance to other social networks. It is also not clear how Facebook (or any comparable network) would handle the liability issues associated with formally providing a high level of identity assurance to third parties. Offering an ID service to those wishing to access multiple services or perform high-value transactions would create additional incentives for users to manufacture fake identities that could be difficult to detect.

Social Networks as a Way of Improving Digital Identity Assurance

Online networks may not provide sufficient levels of assurance to become identity providers on their own, particularly when it comes to identification for government services, but private companies may find them increasingly useful. Airbnb, a website that connects users seeking to rent out their homes with those looking for a place to stay, has introduced a "Verified ID" process that authenticates users through both their online and offline presence. Online identities can be verified via existing Airbnb reviews and LinkedIn, Google, or Facebook profiles (Airbnb 2013). User accounts must have not only a social network presence but also a sufficient number of connections (100 friends on Facebook, for example) to satisfy Airbnb's verification requirements. If users cannot fulfill this requirement, they may upload a video with a personal introduction. Offline identities are normally verified by scanning and submitting an official photo ID. Other companies are exploring similar network-based verification options. In some cases, this may be limited to viewing (future) users' public profiles. Other, more invasive approaches could require prospective clients to "befriend them" to give the company full access to the users' social networks and online activity profiles.[26]

---

process is limited: the client website has some reassurance that the user logging in today is the same one that logged in a week ago, but might not know if the same individual has accessed the service using multiple digital identities.

26 Interviews with Facebook suggest that while this requirement may contravene the spirit of its user policy, there is no clear way to prevent it.

Other private companies have started to use social networks to provide supporting evidence of identity. Fidor, a registered online bank in Germany, allows new customers to complete its initial registration process using Facebook Connect, although customers do need to submit a state-issued ID and proof of address for full account functionality (*Economia* 2013). Lenddo has been providing small loans to individuals in Colombia, Mexico, and the Philippines using their social network data to determine creditworthiness (Groenfeldt 2015). It sells its algorithm, the "Lenddo Score," to financial institutions to allow them to use social networks for credit assessment more broadly. If this is indeed helpful, it could encourage financial inclusion in emerging economies that have limited or nonexistent credit reference facilities.

It is not clear that the companies behind the social networks view such use of their data favorably. Facebook, for example, states in its Platform Policy for developers that site data should not be used to "make decisions about eligibility, including whether to approve or reject an application or how much interest to charge on a loan" (Facebook 2016b). In a recent case, Facebook blocked Admiral Car Insurance from accessing its users' profiles. Admiral planned to offer lower insurance premiums to drivers deemed low risk based on their Facebook profile and activity. However, Facebook did not allow Admiral to view drivers' posts or likes, citing privacy concerns, even where users had given the insurer permission to access such data (Peachey 2016).

An increasing number of businesses are drawing on data derived from the e-village to increase the level of assurance of digital identities, but most service providers will continue to rely on official, state-issued credentials. Online communities can supplement identity-related information—their capabilities are growing, and algorithm-based identification likely will be more widely accepted as experience accumulates—but their role as primary (digital) identity providers will remain limited for the foreseeable future.

Innovative Features of the Cases

Each of the five cases offers distinctive lessons, and technical or institutional innovations that should be of interest to other countries. Table 6-3 provides a selective summary. What has worked in one country's economic, political, and social setting may not work in another, even if both countries share common characteristics. Perhaps the most critical lesson from the cases is that successful identification systems will be those that adapt most closely to the needs of their users—the entities that require that the identities of their clients or customers be verified, and their end-users—those that require a proof of their identity. There will always be trade-offs in terms of the benefits delivered and the risks to the system's effective functioning. The challenge is to find that sweet spot that maximizes the system's value in light of current (and future) priorities and capabilities.

SEVEN

Toward the Future

As is clear from previous chapters, the identification landscape is changing rapidly, particularly in developing countries. The number of ID programs has skyrocketed. Almost all developing countries have, or have committed to, a "foundational" national ID. "Functional" programs to identify people for particular purposes are also multiplying in many countries, though numbers do not necessarily imply quality or effectiveness. Countries are at different stages of the identification revolution: some have already introduced highly advanced digital systems providing full digital identification (e-ID) while others have few identity assets or multiple systems that are not interoperable. Many face common challenges, including the need to strengthen lagging civil registration systems, digitize paper data records, and improve the exchange of information between different databases. In many cases, the systems are not yet being used to their full capability because of inadequate attention to providing an ecosystem for authentication. Legal and institutional frameworks for data privacy and protection are also lagging; only about half of developing countries have data protection laws that broadly conform to fair information practices. Although the number is increasing, many countries lack the capacity to apply legal protections that may be on the books.

Yet the direction is clear, even in countries that have a long way to go to make full digital identification a reality. The trend toward more rigorous identity management is being driven by multiple factors, including security concerns and the demand for more effective public administration. It likely will continue for many years, especially as digital technologies strengthen ID system capabilities at the same time as the spread of mobiles and digital societies and economies creates new demands for secure remote authentication.

Can Digital Identification Be a Good Investment for Development?

What does the identification revolution mean for development? Sustainable Development Goal target 16.9 stresses providing "legal identity for all," but an understanding of this target and the best ways to realize it in today's digital age are still evolving. It is not even obvious how to define "legal identity" from the development perspective. However, it is clear that hundreds of millions of people, mostly among the poorest segments of society, cannot fully participate in political and economic life and realize their full potential because they lack a recognized proof of identity. Based on the most recent UNICEF birth registration figures, some 2 billion individuals, including 650 million children under the age of 16, have not received birth certificates. Recent estimates suggest that over 1.1 billion people would struggle to prove who they are or to validate themselves against a claimed identity.

Considering broader development impact, in addition to being a target in its own right, accurate identification is important—in varying degrees—for at least 8 SDG goals and 19 targets. It can facilitate inclusion and the exercise of rights, strengthen the administration of national programs, and open up opportunities by reducing transaction costs. Far more research—and more rigorous research—needs to be done to understand the use cases and the full impacts, but all three areas have shown evidence of the large potential gains to be had from developing robust ID systems. These gains naturally will tend to be largest in countries where administration is weaker, but whether they materialize at all will depend on how the systems are actually used.

On the other side of the picture, the transition toward more rigorous digital identification raises a number of risks and exacerbates existing ones. They fall into three broad categories: exclusion, particularly of the most vulnerable; misuse, whether for surveillance (beyond the legitimate needs of security and law enforcement) or commercial exploitation; and wasted or ineffective investments. These risks are likely larger in the same group of countries where the potential gains are higher—poorer countries with less effective administration and fewer general legal and institutional protections against abusive use or corrupt procurement.

This balance of benefits and risks indicates the value of the SDGs in setting a compass for investments in identification systems. Together, the 8 SDG goals and 19 targets described in this book cover virtually all of the development-relevant applications of ID systems seen to date—access to finance and economic resources, public payroll management, transfer and subsidy programs, health treatment tracking, gender equality monitoring and enforcement, and tax administration, to name only a few. If ID systems are planned strategically, implemented in a cost-effective manner, and actually used for such applications in an inclusive and responsive manner, then they can be good investments for development and may also provide a fiscal return to governments. If not, they will at best be a waste of resources; at worst, they can impose additional constraints and costs on the population.

Toward a More Strategic Approach
for Development Partners

Creating trusted, effective identity management systems that support development goals and that are operationally and financially sustainable can pose a challenge for even the most well-intentioned and well-resourced countries and their development partners. As the cases considered in this book have shown, there is no single "perfect" and universally applicable system for managing the provision of identity services, but there are a number of common features that ID systems should share if they are to support development and the SDGs. These features can help guide governments, their development partners, and other stakeholders that have an important role to play in ID program design, financing, and monitoring.

It is time to rethink the approach to this area. Development partners have been extensively involved in supporting many different identification-related programs, but they have usually seen these programs as mechanisms to support particular interventions, depending on their particular mandates. (Nevertheless, there are some exceptions to this trend, particularly in Latin America.) Birth registration has long been a focus for UNICEF under the mandate of child protection. Voter registration has been heavily supported by the United Nations Development Programme, as well as other donors. The United Nations High Commissioner for Refugees has focused on the identification of refugees and displaced populations, including for the purpose of delivering assistance. Other development partners, including the Multilateral Development Banks and bilateral donors as well as some nongovernmental organizations, have supported programs in such diverse areas as social protection, financial inclusion, and public health.

This ad hoc approach has had some advantages. It has allowed implementers to experiment with, introduce, and field-test new technologies during a period when the identification industry has been in a state of intense flux. However, it has also contributed to the fragmentation of identity management, often in wasteful ways, reinforcing bureaucratic impulses to defend siloed systems. ID programs often have been implemented using proprietary technology that locks countries into particular vendors, further increasing program cost. Voter registration programs are a prominent example of this problem; their expense—often around $20 per voter per election, a multiple of what it should cost for a well-run foundational system—suggests that without generous continued donor support or a change in the model, elections will not be financially sustainable for some poor countries. Identification has now become a more central focus for development, and the ID industry, though still innovating rapidly, is moving toward a "commodity" industry where many products can compete based on their standards-based performance and price. It is time for a new and more strategic approach.

Development partners are now moving in this direction. The World Bank has launched the Identification for Development Program, a multisector initiative to provide more integrated support to identification systems capable of serving many sectors and purposes. Among other analytical work, it has conducted some 20 integrated country assessments to provide the first systematic analysis of ID systems in developing countries. The other Multilateral Development Banks have also increased their focus on identification and are looking to collaborate more closely with international organizations, agencies, and private sector companies. For example, at the end of 2016 a number of partners, including the World Bank, the UNDP, and the International Organization for Migration, conducted a joint preassessment for a first-ever national and voter identification program for Somalia. Although the participating organizations have different mandates and priorities, they recognized the problems with having many separate initiatives, especially in such a difficult environment.

Another encouraging development is recognition of the importance of South-South learning. Starting in 2015, the ID4Africa movement has been promoting a more strategic approach to identity management in Africa. Its third annual conference in Windhoek in April 2017 brought together over 800 participants, including representatives of 43 African governments as well as donors, international experts and practitioners, and leading firms from the ID industry. Conferences of this type provide an opportunity for countries to learn from each other and, equally important, to share information on further ID program development plans. Mutual learning will become even more important as new systems are rolled out for multiple applications.

Shared Principles for Development-Focused Identification Systems

One essential step is to form a common understanding of how development partners should approach identification. Virtually all of the major players in the area, including the main UN agencies, Multilateral Development Banks, major NGOs and foundations, and some members of the industry, have endorsed a set of common principles (box 7-1), prepared in collaboration with the World Bank and the Center for Global Development. These principles relate to the goals and governance of identification systems, their design and implementation, and their use to support development objectives. They are the start of a shared vision and provide a checklist of areas that should be considered as programs move forward. They will need to be revisited periodically as more evidence accumulates on the use and impact of the systems. Many of the good-practice suggestions that have emerged from the examples and cases considered in this book are closely aligned with those outlined in the principles, and are given as key points in the following sections.

Inclusion: Universal Coverage and Accessibility

Identification systems cannot deliver for development unless they are inclusive. The importance of universal coverage is inherent in the framing of the SDGs to "leave no one behind" and specifically in SDG target 16.9, which calls for "legal identity for *all*." If some groups have no access to identification or confront barriers to the use of the systems, the systems' contribution to other development outcomes, such as ending poverty or achieving gender equality, will also be constrained. Identification will therefore obstruct inclusive development, rather than enable it. In keeping with the principles of ensuring universal coverage and removing barriers to access and usage, the following actions should be considered.

BOX 7-1   Principles on Identification
for Sustainable Development

Inclusion: Universal Coverage and Accessibility
1. Ensuring universal coverage for individuals from birth to death, free from discrimination.
2. Removing barriers to access and usage and disparities in the availability of information and technology.

Design: Robust, Secure, Responsive, and Sustainable
3. Establishing a robust—unique, secure, and accurate—identity.
4. Creating a platform that is interoperable and responsive to the needs of various users.
5. Using open standards and ensuring vendor and technology neutrality.
6. Protecting user privacy and control through system design.
7. Planning for financial and operational sustainability without compromising accessibility.

Governance: Building Trust by Protecting Privacy and User Rights
8. Safeguarding data privacy, security, and user rights through a comprehensive legal and regulatory framework.
9. Establishing clear institutional mandates and accountability.
10. Enforcing legal and trust frameworks through independent oversight and adjudication of grievances.

Source: Principles (2017).

Minimize requirements for enrollment. Strict documentary prerequisites, such as having to produce a birth certificate or to prove that one's parents and grandparents were citizens, can pose insurmountable barriers for many residents, especially from poorer and marginalized communities. Without its "identity first" approach that separates out identification from status and minimizes documentary requirements, India's Aadhaar program would not have been able to enroll over a billion people in five years. Without such a high level of saturation, it would not have been possible to initiate Aadhaar-enabled reforms of subsidy and benefit programs so soon after its introduction and to save resources by doing so.

India is not the only relevant example. Voter registration drives in many countries—for example, the registration of over 23 million voters in under 6 months in Tanzania in 2015—show how quickly "credential-lite" programs can be rolled out to include virtually the entire adult population. In some countries, it may be useful to link such a program to development-related applications, especially if the rollout of the national identification program is constrained by overly restrictive requirements or excessively slowed by other factors.

Consider (and neutralize) the legal provisions and social norms that can exclude vulnerable groups. Such provisions and norms may not pose a "hard" barrier to registration, but they nevertheless can contribute to exclusion. As illustrated by the case of Indonesia, mothers who are not in a legally recognized marriage and their children can face stigmatization when birth certificates are issued without the father's name, and thus mothers may opt not to register their children at all. Gender-based discrimination remains an important source of exclusion risk. Women tend to face greater barriers to passing on their citizenship to their children or spouse. In a number of countries, male relatives must be present for a woman to register. Providing official ID on an equal legal basis to men and women can be a first step, but may not be sufficient. It may be necessary to take active measures; to deploy all-female registration units—as done in Pakistan—and provide added incentives for women's registration, such as Nepal's tax rebate on land registered to women (Daley and others 2013).

Increase development focus on the problem of statelessness. National status is not critical for the vast majority of programs and transactions that are improved by robust identification; indeed, one would want to allow all residents of a country to be identified so as to be able to take advantage of as many opportunities as possible, irrespective of their legal status. It is therefore tempting to ignore the nationality issue, especially as this area has not been a traditional focus for development policies and dialogue. However, the framing of the SDGs has shifted development aspirations closer to a human rights perspective, especially important in this area because of the risk that many people will become stateless as identification is increasingly formalized. States should be expected to ensure that officials implement their own laws and their international commitments. Even if states have sovereignty in the area of citizenship, they should be encouraged to work jointly toward more inclusive policies. Moreover, even where identification is offered to all residents, it is important to

minimize discrimination and access to services and programs based on legal
status. Without a clear understanding on these issues, development partners
could find themselves supporting identification systems that increase the exclusionary barriers that many poor people face. Exclusion on the basis of status
will become more critical as national IDs come to be used to access benefits and
services in place of program-specific ID systems.

**Reduce the barriers posted by biometric exclusion, including dif-
ficulty in using technology.** An important emerging lesson from several
countries is that a considerable number of people will not be able to provide
fingerprints of sufficiently high quality to be authenticated quickly and easily
through this mechanism. They are likely to be older and poorer, farmers or
manual laborers, among the most critical target populations. Iris scanning has
emerged as a more inclusive and accurate technology, and so it can be offered
as one of multiple biometric options to help address this problem. Nevertheless,
no technology is infallible; some people will not be able to use the standard approaches, and so there needs to be provision for people to enroll and be authenticated through other means. People are more comfortable with technology
when human help is readily at hand. Reliable connectivity for online systems
is also a matter of concern. Offline alternatives should be available in the event
that connectivity is unreliable; this will typically be more likely for poor and
remote areas. Part of the savings generated through the use of technology to
support more accurate identification and service delivery should be channeled
toward supporting people who have difficulties navigating the system and who
otherwise could be excluded.

Promote cooperative arrangements and service-based payments.
Stronger collaboration with health ministries could boost birth notification,
since most infants will have been visited by health workers and received vaccinations. Incentive payments to health workers combined with some level of
devolved responsibility for registration could strengthen the supply-side aspect
of registration. Partnerships with NGOs can play a vital role in connecting
government authorities with underserved communities and helping people
to negotiate sometimes complex registration processes. The Female-headed
Household Empowerment Program in Indonesia is one example; it has been
instrumental in supporting civil registration in rural areas by providing paralegal services and helping to convene "one-stop shop" registration fairs in rural
areas. In India, the Aangan Trust has helped over 20,000 children and their
family members to register for an Aadhaar number and access Aadhaar-linked
government benefits.

Prioritize access over cost recovery. Identification is a public good and plays a crucial role in enabling individuals to exercise their rights and participate fully in society and the economy. Fees and charges can help ensure that the system is financially sustainable and responsive to needs, but should not limit access. If average unit enrollment costs are typically around US\$3–\$6, and possibly more for systems requiring sophisticated smartcards, many people in developing countries will not be able to afford an official ID at the full price. Basic ID, as well as the first copy of a birth certificate, should be provided free of charge. High fees for late registration may be intended to encourage prompt action, but are equally likely to deter registration; eliminating fees could improve coverage and make the system more inclusive.

Incentivize the use of the system. Linking registration directly with access to programs such as social transfers, emergency relief support, and voting can encourage broad-based enrollment and continued use. Birth registration in South Africa increased sharply after eligibility for child grants was linked to being able to produce a birth certificate. Similarly, Pakistan stimulated women's enrollment by targeting female members of the household as recipients of social grants through its BISP program. At the same time, the linkage between identification and benefits calls for caution. Registration requirements must not become yet another barrier to access services, particularly for the poor. Anecdotal evidence from Peru suggests that this can happen even when there are exemptions from requirements, if these exemptions are not clearly communicated to local officials and the population. As in India, where poor people could open restricted bank accounts subject to later proof of linkage with an Aadhaar number, carrots are more appealing than sticks.

Look beyond numbers. Although universal coverage and accessibility is vital, from a development perspective registering each person and issuing them with ID credentials is far from the entire challenge. Identification systems should be designed and used in ways that support individual rights and opportunities and strengthen state capacity to achieve development outcomes. Historical experience also confirms that investments in registration and identification systems are more sustainable when they are considered to provide value (Szreter 2006). If a system is not used in ways that move the SDG agenda forward, it is unlikely to be a sound investment from the development perspective, and it is also less likely to be financially and institutionally sustainable.

Design: Robust, Secure, Responsive, and Sustainable

To be considered robust, systems need to ensure that each identity is unique, that any ID credential can be verified, and that any person—and only that person—can be verified against his or her claimed identity. Robustness increases the usefulness of the system to public and private service providers that depend on accurate identification for their effective operation; in turn, reliable and easily accessible systems will be more widely used. This helps to incentivize enrollment and supports the system's operational and financial sustainability. In keeping with the principles of establishing robust identities, creating responsive and interoperable platforms, using and ensuring open standards, protecting user privacy and control, and planning for sustainability, the following points should be considered.

Unify, or at least integrate, civil registration and national identification systems. Many countries with weak civil registration systems have established new identity baselines through mass enrollment (India) or continuous enrollment on adulthood (Kenya). People may need to establish or reestablish their identities, yet this is not always an easy task, especially for mobile populations. Depending on the context, it may require more or less rigorous vetting because the identity baseline was not laid down at birth. Without continuous information from a civil registry, identification systems face a challenge to keep their information updated and must rely on feedback loops from sustained system use (Pakistan). Integrating civil registration and the identity management system can reduce costs through avoiding duplicate systems and facility networks, but even locating them under the same ministry does not guarantee that they will work together or that the practical demands for identification will necessarily strengthen civil registration. However, countries can deploy technology to enable timely data exchange and also, as in Peru, offer performance-based payments to the registries for submitting timely data. Moving to an integrated system increases convenience for people who otherwise need to deal with dual systems (Indonesia).

Lower the age of enrollment. Most countries enroll young adults into their identification programs at ages 15–18, but earlier enrollment can strengthen the link with birth registration and increase confidence in what is now often a weak entry point into identification. Countries increasingly issue identification numbers at birth and link them to the numbers of the newborn's parents. The biometric age frontier is moving closer to birth; India is now registering the biometrics of children as young as age 5 and enrolling newborns into the Aadhaar program, linking their identities to those of their parents. Further advances in technology promise to push the biometric frontier toward even younger children. If successful, these innovations could strengthen the entry point into lifetime identity management and help deliver essential health services and vaccines.

Design and implement identification systems with high-return applications in mind so that, in addition to serving development, they can be sound financial investments for developing countries. Cases suggest a number of high-return applications, including managing public payrolls and pensions, reforming subsidies, and strengthening tax administration. Some of these areas are politically challenging, but countries can reap savings even as they continue to roll out the system. Some of the savings should be recycled, if needed, into financial and resource support for the ID system itself. India's experience shows how ID systems can be leveraged to provide open platforms for a wider range of services.

Establish a well-designed and regulated system of fees and charges as well as performance-based subsidies to keep the system financially sustainable and responsive. Several examples, including systems in Pakistan, Peru, and Rwanda, suggest that a commercial orientation in providing identification services can offer some advantages in sustaining a responsive and high-quality system. But all ID-related service charges need to be subject to independent regulation (Peru). ID agencies are statutory monopolists; without regulation of charges, service fees can be raised to exorbitant levels. Even worse, little may be returned to the government (Democratic Republic of Congo). Moreover, the financing challenge increases as systems move toward full inclusion. Reaching "the last mile" is costly—the unit cost of reaching isolated people will be far higher than enrollment costs in dense urban areas. At the same time, those most difficult to reach will frequently be among the poorest and least included groups.

Performance-based subsidies can fund the provision of identification services to the poor (Peru), or they can be cross-subsidized from payments for providing priority services and authentications for banks and other users (Pakistan, Peru). Subject to controls against multiple registrations, outreach can be encouraged by funding each additional registration on a pay-for-performance basis. India's UIDAI pays registrars for each Aadhaar enrollment, but only once it has been accepted as a new one. Donors have also supported the extension of ID programs by paying for each additional registration (Dominican Republic). To reduce barriers for remote communities, mobile units (used in

Pakistan, Peru, Malaysia, and other countries) can make ID programs more accessible. An increasing number of countries, including Kenya and Tanzania, are also making use of online birth notification and registration via mobiles (Makoye 2015).

Ensure that systems are functional and convenient for both service providers and end-users. In certain areas mobile coverage is absent or spotty systems need to offer both offline and online authentication. People in these areas generally will be poor and more dependent on the services and benefits that identification can unlock. The spread of mobile connectivity raises questions about the value of costly smartcards; countries might not want to go all the way of the Aadhaar in dispensing with cards altogether, but less expensive options with QR or barcodes could provide people with a recognized credential under their control and serve for most purposes. Cards that are compliant with standards for International Civil Aviation Organization machine-readable travel documents could be especially helpful for highly mobile populations, and an increasing number of countries are issuing such cards, but they are costly. This is not to say there is a single answer, but all too often, the focus on building the system and boosting enrollment leaves the authentication ecosystem as an afterthought.

Recognize that not every transaction or citizen-state interaction requires "gold-plated" identity authentication. The "federated model" of identity provision, as in Gov.UK Verify, has helped to lay the foundation for an international standard for levels of identity assurance. Using this approach means giving careful consideration to the rigor of identity verification required, and balancing the objectives of inclusion and convenience with those of minimizing fraud and improving administrative efficiency. For example, biometrics may be extremely valuable for deduplicating enrollments and ensuring that identities are unique, but may be less essential at points of service for many routine transactions.

Recognizing that the degree of ID system integration is a social choice, avoid, if possible, the cost and inefficiency of operating multiple systems, especially if each includes the technology needed to ensure unique identities. The vast majority of developing countries appear to have opted for central identity management—one system, one number—but many are grappling with the difficulty of integrating several existing systems, each with its own political constituency and non-interoperable technology. Not all of the 8 identified SDGs and 19 targets require a common identity management system. Some do, such as the use of a common identifier to merge data on incomes, property, banking, and benefits to strengthen tax administration. Others, such as those used to track tuberculosis or HIV/AIDS patients through courses of treatment, can use custom systems.

Even if it is not possible to have an integrated system immediately, the use of common standards makes it easier to integrate identification systems in the future, lowers costs, and prevents vendor lock-in. Countries can now draw on a range of technical standards that cover virtually all aspects of ID systems. Standards are essential to permit competitive procurement, ensure that systems are interoperable, and help avoid proprietary formats and technology. As is the case for investments in roads, dams, and other infrastructure, development partners should require ID systems to conform to accepted standards as part of providing support for the systems. Development partners should also stand ready to offer neutral experts to serve as a resource for governments that need to manage the procurement process but lack the capacity to do so. Considering the small size of many countries, there could be cost and scale advantages in having fewer but stronger ID agencies, but countries are unlikely to relinquish sovereignty in this area. Nevertheless, development partners should support the efforts of economic communities like the Economic Community of West African States or the East African Community to work toward common standards or at least interoperable credentials.

Publish and share more country-level data on the field performance of biometric enrollment and authentication systems. India has been a pioneer in this area; Pakistan, too, is making data available on authentication success rates, but these are more the exception than the rule. Performance data can help provide a baseline for registration, uniqueness, and authentication standards. Developing countries, as well as donors that are funding a new system or the expanded rollout of an established system, need to be confident that it is performing as represented. This may call for an independent assessment, for example to ascertain that it does indeed have the capacity to deduplicate or identify individuals against records in its database. It will be important to understand how the system handles identification errors, makes provision for those unable to provide biometrics of acceptable quality, and provides for data privacy and protection.

Be realistic on the constraints posed by political economy. All things considered, the political economy of the implementing country will be the most important factor shaping the use of the system even where these good practices and principles are applied to its design and deployment. Robust identification might be applauded for enabling poor female-headed-households to access grants and helping to eliminate fraud in such programs, and it may also have a high payoff in more politically challenging areas such as deduplicating public sector payrolls. But, as in Pakistan, its impact may be limited when it comes to strengthening tax administration or other applications that impinge on the discretion and privileges of elites, even if these are high-value applications.

Governance: Building Trust by Protecting Privacy and User Rights

There are advantages to having identification managed by an autonomous public entity. With a clear and limited mandate, such agencies may be more responsive to user needs and may also enjoy higher levels of public trust as a result of greater perceived political independence. Having user and stake-holder representatives—including representatives of banks, social protection agencies, the elections commission, and civil society organizations, as well as, perhaps, the office of a privacy ombudsman—on the board of the identification agency (Pakistan, Peru) can help to ensure that it remains accountable for service. User representation also provides another layer of protection against predatory pricing. Partly commercializing identification services can further sustain independence of the ID agency, but the structure of fees and charges must not jeopardize the system's inclusivity or undermine the public good of identification. In keeping with the principles of safeguarding data and user rights, establishing clear institutional mandates and accountability, and enforcing legal and trust frameworks through independent oversight and adjudication, the following points should be kept in mind.

Prioritize data privacy and security. The legal and regulatory challenge around identification systems is increasing as they become more powerful and more integrated, and as the locus of activity shifts to countries with lower capacity and weaker democratic checks and balances. Although the number of developing countries with data privacy laws that conform to internationally recognized Fair Information Principles is increasing, only about half of the countries have such legislation, including a data controller or some other independent entity, such as an ombudsman, charged with representing the interests of those who use the system and ensuring that grievance processes are in place and effective. Some countries have laws on the books but are less well equipped to enforce them. Many countries will need sustained assistance to strengthen data privacy laws and their capacity to apply them. Data privacy is not always high on the agenda in countries where digital databases are still modest, but this will change. The area will remain an uphill struggle as efforts are made to extend the coverage of data privacy laws to a wider range of lower-income countries, many with weaker checks and balances and more authoritarian regimes.

Design the identification system to be the first line of defense in data privacy, especially in countries with inadequate legal oversight. Data collection should be limited to the essentials. As countries like Rwanda have learned, information that can be used to profile individuals or discriminate against them, such as ethnicity or religion, should not be collected and certainly not disclosed on cards. Such data, as well as identification numbers that reveal personal details or initial community of registration (which often signals ethnic origin), may have had some identification value in the past but are superfluous in modern systems. Authentication protocols should require only the minimal data necessary to ensure appropriate levels of identity assurance and can now be based on recognized international standards.

Card-based systems (or mobile-based systems) may be more costly than those that use only a number, but match-on-card authentication, possibly using personal identification numbers along the lines of Estonia's system, can help to mitigate the risk of identity theft by giving users greater physical control over their credentials. They may also reduce incentives to hack into the central data base as the information cannot be used directly to steal identities. This approach requires a highly computer-literate population, however, and may not be appropriate for all countries.

Limit data-sharing, including between applications, and increase people's control over the use of their personal data. In Estonia, the X-Road data exchange layer permits the information exchange only as needed by each service provider and program, and individuals can check to see which programs and agencies have accessed their records, except for law enforcement and security. Another emerging example is the permission-based architecture of India's e-KYC and Digital Locker, where data can be shared at the request of the person concerned. Any identification applications that incorporate data sharing can be required to be approved by an independent board, as is the case in Pakistan (Malik 2014). Such a case-by-case approach is not a substitute for strong data privacy legislation or sufficient for the long term, but if buttressed by sanctions for policy violations it can help to provide some accountability in the interim. The extension of ID systems to young children raises further issues for user control. For example, the principle of informed consent suggests that young adults should be able to request that their biometrics be erased from voluntary ID systems if they have been taken during childhood.

It can also be helpful to disconnect transactional identification from any underlying national ID number. One approach is Austria's distinctive system of generating a separate identifier cryptographically for each service; this makes it more difficult to track individuals and assemble a profile based on transactions. The "double blind" approach of the federated model (Gov.UK Verify) is another way to limit unnecessary sharing of personal data. Even if most developing countries are not yet fully digital societies, it is necessary to plan for the future.

Sustaining trust requires at least a minimum level of country capacity to understand and oversee the system. Identification systems are unlikely to be trusted if implemented by vendors as "black boxes" with little or no oversight by national authorities. This too is an area where development partners can be helpful.

Implications for Development Partners

These principles, and the cases discussed in this book, have a number of implications for development partners. As for any other sector, investments in identification systems should be subjected to cost-benefit analysis, including both the socioeconomic and financial perspectives. This will ensure a focus on both containing costs and ensuring effective use of the system to reduce leakage and corruption and improve the delivery of services.

Ensure that investments follow internationally agreed technical standards and develop costing benchmarks to help inform procurement. This guidance matches current practice in other development areas such as power or roads. At present, there is no neutral standards-checking body to help ensure the quality and effectiveness of identification investments and compare them with emerging best practice. Larger developing countries with strong capacity may not need the assistance of such a body, but it would be a helpful resource for smaller ones. It could be a useful follow-up to the principles, involving the international financial institutions, UN agencies, and industry experts.

Remember the importance of safeguards. One initial step to broaden understanding of the complex barriers to full inclusion—including financial, social, and technological exclusion as well as problems related to national status—would be to carry out "exclusion assessments" of countries' laws and practices and their use of identification systems. In particularly intractable cases, where investments in an ID system appear likely to entrench discrimination against particular groups, development partners should decline to offer support.

Undertake a privacy impact assessment as part of any major identification investment. Assessments may not pinpoint every risk, but they can help countries and partners focus on the technical elements of the ID system as well as its governance and the legal regime for data protection.

Partners need to be prepared to offer sustained advisory and financial support to help strengthen the framework for data privacy and protection. In addition to advice, assistance, and model legislation, development partners can convene discussions with stakeholders to raise consciousness of the issues involved; not surprisingly, this is still limited in many countries that are at early stages of the digital transition. Funding should be up front, offering capacity support, if needed, for a number of years. One example of such support could be enforcement capacity through an independent privacy advocate or ombudsman that would have the authority and resources to respond to breaches and violations of agreed business rules on sharing data, and with the power to seek redress and penalties, including (and especially) against public officials. Partners should also encourage strong grievance-redressal mechanisms with periodic reporting.

Help other service agencies adapt to the requirements of a common system. Agencies have a natural tendency to defend their own mandates and systems, not least as a means of preserving control over technology procurement, and may resist the use of a common identification system on the grounds that this involves transitional costs even if it is likely to improve service and save resources in the longer run. Development partners can help by coordinating support to coalitions of users and helping to finance the costs of transitioning to a common ID system.

Support the monitoring of applications to help ensure that the new systems are accountable for results and that people do not face undue difficulties in the transition. Far more work is needed in this area as the frontier moves from creating identification systems to using them to help deliver programs and services more inclusively and effectively.

Areas for Further Research

As is apparent from the still-limited information discussed in this book, there is a large agenda for fact-finding and research in the area of identification for development. One priority is to understand more about ID architecture, governance, and functioning across the developing world. More countries need to be systematically surveyed, as there is still a great deal to learn about how systems actually operate and how their effectiveness can be improved. As well as organizational structure and technology, more needs to be known about the views of people—the end-users of the systems. What factors encourage or discourage parents from registering the births of their children? In what ways are systems thought to be useful or inconvenient? Do people in developing countries have concerns about sharing data, including biometrics, with the system? Surveys of this type are rare, and usually are conducted in the context of market research for the use of new approaches in rich countries.

An urgent priority is to understand more about the use and impact of digital identification technology and systems in areas related to the SDGs. India is a laboratory—there are many different Aadhaar-enabled approaches to reforming subsidy and transfer systems, whether for energy, fertilizer, food rations, pensions, or scholarships, as well as the more sophisticated services associated with the "India Stack"—but new approaches are being implemented in other countries as well. Are the new ID systems really delivering as promised? Do they reduce costs and improve the efficiency of service delivery? Do they improve the experience of users, or do they raise new exclusionary barriers? Is there any wider gender impact, for example from having women designated as heads of households for benefit programs (Pakistan, Rajasthan) or as bank correspondents for cashing out benefits? Few rigorous studies have been made of the impact of digital IDs, often associated with digital payments, on the inclusiveness, efficiency, and costs of public services and programs. This is a potentially rich research agenda considering the rollout of new applications.

There is also room for more empirical research on the impact of identification technology in elections. Although there is warranted skepticism in this area, some countries might soon be able to switch away from one-off voter registration and toward the use of a permanent national system. This would both reduce cost and harness the momentum of voter registration to strengthen identity management assets.

More could also be done to build up knowledge on legal frameworks. Although there are useful summary data on the cross-country spread of data privacy legislation, there is less detailed information on their details and on countries' capacity to implement data protection laws. This topic extends beyond identification and is set to become more important with the spread of digital communications and big data, including in developing countries.

Finally, even though there has been useful work to assemble relevant technical standards, there is not yet a good compilation of standard costs for providing identification services. This may not be easy to create; costs depend on many factors, and technology is still moving forward rapidly. It may not be possible to develop standard costs for ID systems in the same way as for roads where the technology is mature;[1] nevertheless, comparative information on typical costs of ID systems and their individual components would be immensely useful to countries and their development partners as they plan for future systems.

1 See, for example, AfDB (2014). A first picture of the comparative roots of ID systems is in process (World Bank 2018b)

References

Abraham, R., E. S. Bennett, N. Sen, and N. B. Shah. 2017. *State of Aadhaar Report 2016–17*. Delhi: IDinsight. http://stateofaadhaar.in/wp-content/uploads/State-of-Aadhaar-Full-Report-2016-17-IDinsight.pdf.

Accenture. 2015. *How Can Border Management Solutions Better Meet Citizens' Expectations? Report on the Accenture Citizen Survey on Border Management and Biometrics 2014*. www.accenture.com/au-en/insight-border-management-solutions-better-meet-citizens.aspx.

ACHPR (African Commission on Human and Peoples Rights). 2015. "The Nubian Community in Kenya vs The Republic of Kenya." Communication 317/2006, African Commission on Human and Peoples Rights. www.achpr.org/files/sessions/17theo/comunications/317.06/communication_317.06_eng.pdf.

AfDB (African Development Bank). 2014. *Study on Road Infrastructure Costs: Analysis of Unit Costs and Cost Overruns of Road Infrastructure Projects in Africa*. African Development Bank Group Market Study Series. Freetown, Sierra Leone: AfDB. www.afdb.org/fileadmin/uploads/afdb/Documents/Publications/Study_on_Road_Infrastructure_Costs-_Analysis_of_Unit_Costs_and_Cost_Overruns_of_Road_Infrastructure_Projects_in_Africa.pdf.

Africa Check. 2014. "Factsheet: Nigeria's Population Figures." Africa Check. https://africacheck.org/factsheets/factsheet-nigerias-population-figures/.

Agarwal, S. 2017. "Supreme Court's Verdict Does Not Spell End of Aadhaar: UIDAI's Ajay Bhushan Pandey." *Economic Times*, August 26. http://economictimes.indiatimes.com/news/politics-and-nation/supreme-courts-verdict-does-not-spell-end-of-aadhaar-uidais-ajay-bhushan-pandey/articleshow/60229104.cms.

Airbnb. 2013. "Introducing Airbnb Verified ID." Airbnb blog, April 30. http://blog
.airbnb.com/introducing-airbnb-verified-id/.

Aiyer, S. 2017. *Aadhaar: A Biometric History of India's 12-Digit Revolution*. India:
Westland Books.

Akpan, N. 2014. "Baby's Necklace Could End Up Being a Lifesaver." Goats and
Soda blog, December 5. National Public Radio. www.npr.org/sections/goats
andsoda/2014/12/05/366405541/babys-necklace-could-end-up-being-a-life-saver.

Anderson, C. L., P. Biscaye, S. Coney, E. Ho, B. Hutchinson, M. Neidhardt, and T.
Reynolds. 2015. *Review of National Identity Programs*. ITU-T Focus Group Digital
Financial Services, Technical Report. www.itu.int/en/ITU-T/focusgroups/dfs/
Documents/09_2016/Review%20of%20National%20Identity%20Programs.pdf.

Apland, K., B. K. Blitz, C. Hamilton, M. Lagaay, R. Lakshman, and E. Yarrow.
2014. *Birth Registration and Children's Rights: A Complex Story*. Woking, UK: Plan
International. www.planusa.org/docs/birth-registration-rights-2014.pdf.

Arendt, H. 1951. *The Origins of Totalitarianism*. New York: Harcourt, Brace & Co.

Arm, M. 2014. "SK: 12+ Years of e-ID in Estonia." Presentation at the IdentityNorth
2014 Conference, Toronto, Canada. www.identitynorth.ca/wp-content/uploads
/2014/06/e-estonia_052014_2-f.pdf.

Atick, J. J. 2014. *Digital Identity: The Essential Guide*. ID4Africa Identity Forum.
www.id4africa.com/prev/img/Digital_Identity_The_Essential_Guide.pdf.

———. 2016. *The Identity Ecosystem of Rwanda*. ID4Africa Case Study. www.id4africa.
com/prev/img/ID4Africa2016_The_Identity_Ecosystem_of_Rwanda_eBook
let.pdf.

Aung, M. T., and K. Mar. 2015. "Myanmar Officials Issue Green Cards to Muslims in
Rakhine State." Radio Free Asia, June 15. www.rfa.org/english/news/myanmar/
officials-issue-green-cards-to-muslims-in-rakhine-state-06152015145915.html.

Barnwal, P. 2016. "Curbing Leakage in Public Programs with Direct Benefit
Transfers: Evidence from India's Fuel Subsidies and Black Markets." Working
Paper. Washington, DC: World Bank. http://pubdocs.worldbank.org/en/8263
41466181741330/Barnwal-DBT-India.pdf.

BBC. 2016. "Lynette White Murder: Timeline of Events." BBC, June 14. www.bbc.
com/news/uk-wales-15983755.

Bhatnagar, N., A. Sinha, N. Samdaria, A. Gupta, S. Batra, M. Bhardwaj, and W.
Thies. 2012. "Biometric Monitoring as a Persuasive Technology: Ensuring Patients
Visit Health Centers in India's Slums. Persuasive Technology." Design for Health
and Safety—7th International Conference, Linköping, Sweden, June 6–8.

BISP (Benazir Income Support Programme). 2016. "National Socio Economic Registry for the Social Protection Sector in Pakistan—Data Sharing Protocol." BSIP
– Safety Net. http://bisp.gov.pk/wp-content/uploads/2016/10/SharingForm.pdf.

Blake, J. N. 2014. "Haiti, the Dominican Republic, and Race-based Statelessness in
the Americas." *Georgetown Journal of Law and Modern Critical Race Perspectives*
6 (2): 139–80.

Bossuroy, T., C. Delavallade, and V. Pons. 2016. "Can Health Workers Automate Their

Way to Better Monitoring—Experimental Evidence from Tuberculosis Control in India." Draft working paper. http://mit-neudc.scripts.mit.edu/2016/wp-content/uploads/2016/03/paper_65.pdf.

Boston Consulting Group (BCG). 2014. "Digital Government: Turning the Rhetoric into Reality." BCG Perspectives. www.bcgperspectives.com/content/articles/public_sector_center_consumer_customer_insight_digital_government_turning_rhetoric_into_reality/.

Bradley, P. M. 2017. "The Invisibles: The Cruel Catch-22 of Being Poor with No ID." *Washington Post*, June 15. www.washingtonpost.com/lifestyle/magazine/what-happens-to-people-who-cant-prove-who-they-are/2017/06/14/fc0aaca2-4215-11e7-adba-394ee67a7582_story.html.

Breckenridge, K. 2005. "The Biometric State: The Promise and Peril of Digital Government in the New South Africa." *Journal of Southern African Studies* 31 (2): 267–82.

———. 2010. "The World's First Biometric Money: Ghana e-Zwich and the Contemporary Influence of South African Biometrics." *Africa: The Journal of the International African Institute* 80 (4): 642–62.

Breckenridge, K., and S. Szreter, eds. 2012. *Registration and Recognition: Documenting the Person in World History. Proceedings of the British Academy 182.* Oxford: Oxford University Press.

Browning, K., and N. Orlans. 2014. *Biometric Aging: Effects of Aging on Iris Recognition.* Washington, DC: MITRE Corporation. www.mitre.org/sites/default/files/publications/13-3472-biometric-aging-iris-recognition.pdf.

Bruni, L. M. 2016. "Reforming the Social Assistance System." In *Making It Happen: Selected Case Studies of Institutional Reforms in South Africa*, edited by A. Alam, R. Mokate, and K.A. Plangemann (Washington, DC: World Bank), 119–34.

Buvinic, M., and M. O'Donnell. 2016. "Identification and Gender Equality: A Two-Way Street." CGD blog, January 4. www.cgdev.org/blog/identification-gender-equality-two-way-street.

Campbell, B. 2010. "Financial Opportunity." *Profit Magazine*, September 20. www.oracle.com/us/corporate/profit/archives/092010-oppint-176389.html.

Cangiano, M., A. Gelb, and R. Goowin-Groen. 2017. "Digitization of Government Payments as a Key Tool of Modern Public Financial Management." In *Digital Revolutions in Public Finance*, edited by S. Gupta, M. Keen, A. Shah, and G. Verdier. Washington, DC: International Monetary Fund (IMF).

Carter Center. 2012. "Voter Identification Requirements and Public International Law: An Examination of Africa and Latin America." Atlanta: Carter Center.

Cellan-Jones, R. 2015. "Office Puts Chips under Staff's Skin." BBC, January 29. www.bbc.com/news/technology-31042477.

CENI (Commission Electorale Nationale Indépendante). 2015. *Rapport general du scrutin du 25 avril 2015.* www.ceni-tg.org/?p=4453.

CESG (Communications-Electronics Security Group). 2014. *Identity Proofing and Verification of an Individual.* Good Practice Guide 45. London: National Technical

Authority for Information Assurance (UK). www.gov.uk/government/uploads/ system/uploads/attachment_data/file/370033/GPG_45_identity_proofing_v2_3 _July_2014.pdf.

CGD (Center for Global Development). 2015. *Unintended Consequences of Anti–Money Laundering Policies for Poor Countries.* CGD Working Group Report. Washington, DC: CGD. www.cgdev.org/sites/default/files/CGD-WG-Report-Unintended-Consequences-AML-Policies-2015.pdf.

———. 2016. *Financial Regulations for Improving Financial Inclusion.* Center for Global Development Brief. Task Force on Regulatory Standards for Financial Inclusion. Washington, DC: CGD. www.cgdev.org/sites/default/files/financial-access-task-force-brief_0.pdf.

CIS (Center of Internet and Society). 2017. "Information Security Practices of Aadhaar (or lack thereof)." Center of Internet and Society, India. https://cis-india. org/internet-governance/information-security-practices-of-aadhaar-or-lack-thereof/view.

CIS Kenya. 2015. "What Is Credit Information Sharing (CIS)?" CIS Kenya. www. ciskenya.co.ke/cis.

Clavell, G. G., and P. Ouziel. 2014. "Spain's *Documento Nacional de Identidad*: An e-ID for the Twenty-First Century with a Controversial Past." In *Histories of Surveillance in Europe and Beyond*, edited by K. Boersma, R. van Brakel, C. Fonio, and P. Wagenaar (London: Routledge), 135–49.

Clemens, M. A. 2011. "Economics and Emigration: Trillion-Dollar Bills on the Sidewalk?" *Journal of Economic Perspectives* 25 (3): 83–106.

Clemens, M. A., and L. Pritchett. 2008. "Income per Natural: Measuring Development for People, Rather Than Places." *Population and Development Review* 34 (3): 395–434.

Clements, B., D. Coady, S. Fabrizio, S. Gupta, T. Alleyne, and C. Sdralevich, eds. 2013. *Energy Subsidy Reform: Lessons and Implications.* Washington, DC: IMF.

Corbacho, A., S. Brito, and R. Osorio. 2012. *Birth Registration and the Impact on Educational Attainment.* IDB Working Paper Series IDP-WP-345. Washington, DC: Inter-American Development Bank. www.iadb.org/en/research-and-data/ publication-details,3169.html?pub_id=IDB-WP-345.

———. 2013. *Does Birth Under-registration Reduce Childhood Immunization? Evidence from the Dominican Republic.* IDB Working Paper Series IDP-WP-448. Washington, DC: Inter-American Development Bank. https://publications. iadb.org/bitstream/handle/11319/4660/IFD%20WP%20Does%20Birth%20Un der-registration%20Reduce%20Childhood%20Immunization.pdf?sequence =1.

Crosby, J. 2008. *Challenges and Opportunities in Identity Assurance.* London: HM Treasury. www.statewatch.org/news/2008/mar/uk-nat-identity-crosby-report.pdf.

Crunden, E. A. 2016. "U.S. Moves to Lift Sanctions on Myanmar, Despite Ongoing Genocide of Rohingya." ThinkProgress, September 15. https://thinkprogress. org/us-myanmar-rohingya-898dbc242c0e#.2h6oehy9k.

Currion, P. 2015. "Eyes Wide Shut: The Challenge of Humanitarian Biometrics." IRIN News, August 26. www.irinnews.org/opinion/2015/08/26/eyes-wide-shut-challenge-humanitarian-biometrics.

Dahan, M., and A. Gelb. 2015. *The Role of Identification in the Post-2015 Development Agenda.* Center for Global Development Essay. Washington, DC: CGD. www.cgdev.org/publication/role-identification-post-2015-development-agenda.

Dahan, M., and L. Hanmer. 2015. *The Identification for Development (ID4D) Agenda: Its Potential for Empowering Women and Girls.* World Bank Background Paper. Washington, DC: World Bank. https://openknowledge.worldbank.org/bitstream /handle/10986/22795/The0identifica0s000background0paper.pdf?sequence= 1&isAllowed=y.

Daley, E., C. Flower, L. Miggiano, and S. Pallas. 2013. *Women's Land Rights and Gender Justice in Land Governance: Pillars in the Promotion and Protection of Women's Human Rights in Rural Areas.* International Land Coalition Synthesis Paper. New York: Office of the United Nations High Commissioner for Human Rights. www.ohchr.org/Documents/HRBodies/CEDAW/RuralWomen/Interna tionalLandCoalition.pdf.

Debroy, B. 2016. "Of Deaths and Births." *Indian Express, January 21.* http://indian express.com/article/opinion/columns/of-deaths-and-births/#

DELIVER. 2007. *South Africa: Final Country Report.* Arlington, VA: DELIVER, for the U.S. Agency for International Development. http://pdf.usaid.gov/pdf_docs/ PA00KM9H.pdf.

Dener, C., J. A. Watkins, and W. L. Dorotinsky. 2011. *Financial Management In-formation Systems: 25 Years of World Bank Experience on What Works and What Doesn't.* Washington, DC: World Bank.

Department of Homeland Security. 2007. "Regulatory Evaluation Notice of Proposed Rulemaking REAL ID 6 CFR Part 37 RIN: 1601-AA37, Docket Number DHS-2006-0030." Washington, DC: February 28. https://epic.org/privacy/id_cards/ reg_eval_draftregs.pdf.

Deshmukh, V. 2014. "Aadhaar: Once Allotted, You Can Never Cancel It, Reveals RTI." *Moneylife India,* March 27. www.moneylife.in/article/aadhaar-once-allot ted-you-can-never-cancel-it-reveals-rti/36838.html.

DHHS (Department of Health and Human Services). 2000. *Birth Certificate Fraud.* Washington, DC: DHHS Office of the Inspector General. https://oig.hhs.gov/ oei/reports/oei-07-99-00570.pdf.

Dixon, P. 2008. "A Brief Introduction to Fair Information Practices." World Privacy Forum, January 4. www.worldprivacyforum.org/2008/01/report-a-brief-introduc tion-to-fair-information-practices/.

Donger, E., and A. Mehrotra. 2017. "Aadhaar and Child Protection in India: Access for the Poorest Remains Elusive." FXB Center for Health and Human Rights blog, Harvard University. https://fxb.harvard.edu/aadhar-and-child-protection-in-india-access-for-the-poorest-remains-elusive/.

Dreze, J. 2016. "The Aadhaar Coup." *The Hindu,* March 15. www.thehindu.com/

opinion/lead/jean-dreze-on-aadhaar-mass-surveillance-data-collection/arti
cle8352912.ece.

Duff, P., S. Kusumaningrum, and L. Stark. 2016. "Barriers to Birth Registration in
Indonesia." *The Lancet* 4 (4): 234–35.

Dunning, C., A. Gelb, and S. Raghavan. 2014. *Birth Registration, Legal Identity, and
the Post-2015 Agenda*. CGD Policy Paper 046. Washington, DC: CGD. www.
cgdev.org/publication/birth-registration-legal-identity-and-post-2015-agenda.

Economia. 2013. "Fidor: Banking with Friends." *Economia*, July 3. http://economia.
icaew.com/business/july-2013/fidor-banking-with-friends.

Economic Times. 2015. "Government Expenditure on Aadhaar Project Is Rs 5,630
Crore." *Economic Times*, March 13. http://economictimes.indiatimes.com/article
show/46556215.cms?utm_source=contentofinterest&utm_medium=text&utm_
campaign=cppst.

Eng, P. 2017. "Implant Chip, Track People." ABC News, February 25. http://abcnews.
go.com/Technology/story?id=98077&page=1/.

Ensor, L. 2014. "Re-registration of Social Grant Recipients Saves R2bn." *Business Day*,
February 5. http://lrc.org.za/lrcarchive/lrc-in-the-news/3025-re-registration-of-
social-grant-recipients-saves-r2bn.

e-Estonia. 2014. "Become an Estonian e-Resident." Leaflet. https://e-estonia.com/
wp-content/uploads/2014/09/eResident_leaflet.pdf.

———. 2015. "i-Voting." e-Estonia.com. https://e-estonia.com/component/i-voting/.

———. 2016a. "X-Road." e-Estonia.com. https://e-estonia.com/component/x-road/.

———. 2016b. "Facts." e-Estonia.com. https://e-estonia.com/facts/.

Facebook. 2016a. "What Types of ID Does Facebook Accept?" Facebook. www.
facebook.com/help/159096464162185.

———. 2016b. "Facebook Platform Policy." Facebook for Developers. https://
developers.facebook.com/policy/.

FATF (Financial Action Task Force). 2012. *International Standards on Combating
Money Laundering and the Financing of Terrorism Proliferation* (October 2016).
Paris: FATF/OECD.

Fiveash, K. 2014. "Pitchforks at Dawn! UK Gov's Verify ID Service FAILS to Verify
ID." *The Register*, November 2. www.theregister.co.uk/2014/11/02/gov_uk_verify
_id_assurance_experian_defra_test_failure/.

Freedom House. 2016. *Chad Country Report*. Washington, DC: Freedom House.
https://freedomhouse.org/report/freedom-world/2016/chad.

Fussell, J. 2001. "Group Classification on National ID Cards as a Factor in Genocide
and Ethnic Cleansing." Presentation to the Seminar Series of the Yale University
Genocide Studies Program, November 15. The Hague: Prevent Genocide International. www.preventgenocide.org/prevent/removing-facilitating-factors/IDcards/.

FWLD (Forum for Women, Law, and Development). 2014. *Acquisition of Citizenship
Certificate in Nepal*. FWLD Publication 169. Kathmandu: FWLD. http://fwld.
org/wp-content/uploads/2016/06/Acquisition-of-Citizenship-Certificate-in-
Nepal-Understanding-Trends-Barriers-and-Impacts.pdf.

Garenne, M., M. A. Collinson, W. K. Chodziwadziwa, F. X. Gomez-Olive, K. Kahn, and S. Tollman. 2016. "Completeness of Birth and Death Registration in a Rural Area of South Africa: The Agincourt Health and Demographic Surveillance, 1992–2014." *Global Health Action* 9. doi: 10.3402/gha.v9.32795.

Gaskins, K. 2011. "Debunking Misinformation on Photo ID." Brennan Center for Justice, June 9. www.brennancenter.org/blog/debunking-misinformation-photo-id.

Gelb, A. 2011. "Covering the 7 Billionth Child: Can We Learn from Indian Health Insurance?" CGD blog, November 7. www.cgdev.org/blog/covering-7-billionth-child-can-we-learn-indian-health-insurance.

———. 2015. "Labor Pains: Birth and Civil Registration in Indonesia." CGD blog, March 23. www.cgdev.org/blog/labor-pains-birth-and-civil-registration-indonesia.

———. 2016. *Balancing Financial Integrity with Financial Inclusion: The Risk-Based Approach to "Know Your Customer."* CGD Policy Paper 074. Washington, DC: CGD. www.cgdev.org/publication/balancing-financial-integrity-financial-inclusion-risk-based-approach.

Gelb, A., and J. Clark. 2013a. *Identification for Development: The Biometrics Revolution.* CGD Working Paper 315. Washington, DC: CGD. www.cgdev.org/publication/identification-development-biometrics-revolution-working-paper-315.

———. 2013b. *Performance Lessons from India's Universal Identification Program.* CGD Policy Paper 020. Washington, DC: CGD. www.cgdev.org/sites/default/files/biometric-performance-lessons-India.pdf.

Gelb, A., and C. Decker. 2011. *Cash at Your Fingertips: Biometric Technology for Transfers in Developing and Resource-Rich Countries.* CGD Working Paper 253. Washington, DC: CGD. www.cgdev.org/publication/cash-your-fingertips-biometric-technology-transfers-developing-and-resource-rich.

Gelb, A., and A. Diofasi. 2016a. *Biometric Elections in Poor Countries: Wasteful or a Worthwhile Investment?* CGD Working Paper 435. Washington, DC: CGD. www.cgdev.org/publication/biometric-elections-poor-countries-wasteful-or-worthwhile-investment.

———. 2016b. *Using Identification for Development: Some Guiding Principles.* CGD Note. Washington, DC: www.cgdev.org/publication/using-identification-development-some-guiding-principles.

———. 2016c. "What Determines Purchasing-Power-Parity Exchange Rates?" *Revue d'economie du développement.* No. 2, June.

Gelb, A., and B. Manby. 2016. "Has Development Converged with Human Rights? Implications for the Legal Identity SDG." CGD blog, November 3. www.cgdev.org/blog/has-development-converged-human-rights-implications-legal-identity-sdg.

Gelb, A., A. Mukherjee, and A. Diofasi. 2016. "Iris Recognition: Better than Fingerprints and Falling in Price." CGD blog, August 1. www.cgdev.org/blog/iris-recognition-better-than-fingerprints-and-falling-price.

Gellman, R. 2013. *Privacy and Biometric ID Systems: An Approach Using Fair Information Practices for Developing Countries.* CGD Policy Paper 028. Washington, DC: CGD. www.cgdev.org/sites/default/files/privacy-and-biometric-ID-systems_0.pdf.

Giné, X., J. Goldberg, and D. Yang. 2012. "Credit Market Consequences of Improved Personal Identification: Field Experimental Evidence from Malawi." *American Economic Review* 102 (6): 2923–54.

Giri, A., A. Aadil, R. Malhotra, R. Rautela, V. P. Sharma, and S. Roy. 2017. "Assessment of AeFDS (Aadhaar enabled Fertilizer Distribution System) Pilot." Lucknow: Microsave. www.microsave.net/resource/assessment_of_aefds_aadhaar_enabled_fertilizer_distribution_system_pilot.

Government of India. 2016. "Total Savings from the Elimination of Fake/Duplicate/Ghost Connection as a Result of Implementation of DBT for the Two Last Years Estimated at More Than Rs. 21,000 Crore." Ministry of Petroleum & Natural Gas press release, July 20. http://pib.nic.in/newsite/PrintRelease.aspx?relid=147384.

GOV.UK. 2012. *Digital Efficiency Report.* London: GOV.UK. www.gov.uk/government/publications/digital-efficiency-report/digital-efficiency-report.

———. 2016a. "Digital Service Standard." GOV.UK. www.gov.uk/service-manual/service-standard.

———. 2016b. "Service Dashboard. GOV.UK Verify." GOV.UK. www.gov.uk/performance/govuk-verify.

Greenleaf, G. 2013. *Global Data Privacy Laws 2013: 99 Countries and Counting.* UNSW Law Research Paper 2013-58. University of New South Wales. https://papers.ssrn.com/sol3/papers.cfm?abstract_id=2305882.

———. 2015. *Global Data Privacy Laws 2015: 109 Countries, With European Laws Now a Minority.* UNSW Law Research Paper 2015-21. University of New South Wales. https://papers.ssrn.com/sol3/papers.cfm?abstract_id=2603529##.

Groenfeldt, T. 2015. "Lenddo Creates Credit Scores Using Social Media." *Forbes*, January 29. www.forbes.com/sites/tomgroenfeldt/2015/01/29/lenddo-creates-credit-scores-using-social-media/.

GSMA. 2016. *Mandatory Registration of Prepaid SIM Cards.* London: GSMA. www.gsma.com/publicpolicy/wp-content/uploads/2016/04/GSMA2016_Report_MandatoryRegistrationOfPrepaidSIMCards.pdf.

Guillaume, D., R. Zytek, and M. R. Farzin. 2011. *Iran – The Chronicles of Subsidy Reform.* IMF Working Paper. Washington, DC: IMF. www.greenfiscalpolicy.org/wp-content/uploads/2013/08/Iran-The-Chronicles-of-the-Subsidy-Reform1.pdf.

Gupta, M. D. 2016. "Govt Hospitals to Soon Start Aadhaar-linked Birth Registration of Newborns." *Hindustan Times*, May 13. www.hindustantimes.com/india/govt-hospitals-to-soon-start-aadhaar-linked-birth-registration-of-newborns/story-uGAqHm0LDJcj3Yfu7KVfQM.html.

Hales, R. 2016. "A Lesson from GOV.UK Verify: Blog Your Way towards Live." GOV.UK Verify blog, July 14. https://identityassurance.blog.gov.uk/2016/07/14/a-lesson-from-gov-uk-verify-blog-your-way-towards-live/.

Handa, S., L. Natali, D. Seidenfeld, G. Tembo, and B. Davis. 2016. *Can Unconditional Cash Transfers Lead to Sustainable Poverty Reduction? Evidence from Two Government-led Programmes in Zambia.* Innocenti Working Paper 2016-21. New York: UNICEF Office of Research. www.unicef-irc.org/publications/pdf/IWP_2016_21.pdf.

Hanmer, L., and M. Dahan. 2015. "Identification for Development: Its Potential for Empowering Women and Girls." World Bank Voices blog, November 9. http://blogs.worldbank.org/voices/identification-development-its-potential-empowering-women-and-girls.

Hanmer, L., and M. Elefante. 2016. *The Role of Identification in Ending Child Marriage: Identification for Development (ID4D).* Washington, DC: World Bank. http://documents.worldbank.org/curated/en/130281472492551732/pdf/107932-WP-P156810-OUO-9-Child-Marriage.pdf.

Harbitz, M., and J. C. B. Molina, J. C. B. 2010. *Civil Registration and Identification Glossary.* Washington, DC: Inter-American Development Bank.

Harper, J. 2012. "Britain's Visa Rules for South Africans 'Unfair.'" *Telegraph*, October 15. www.telegraph.co.uk/expat/expatnews/9604350/Britains-visa-rules-for-South-Africans-unfair.html.

Haushofer, J., and J. Shapiro. 2013. *Household Response to Income Changes: Evidence from an Unconditional Cash Transfer Program in Kenya.* IPA Working Paper. New York: International Poverty Action. www.poverty-action.org/publication/household-response-income-changes-evidence-unconditional-cash-transfer-program-kenya.

Herlihy, P. 2013. "Government as a Data Model: What I Learned in Estonia." Government Digital Service blog (UK), October 31. https://gds.blog.gov.uk/2013/10/31/government-as-a-data-model-what-i-learned-in-estonia/.

Hicklin, A., B. Ulery, and C. Watson. 2016. "A Brief Introduction to Biometric Fusion." Mitretek Systems and National Institute of Standards and Technology, June 16.

HID Global. 2015. *The West African Examinations Council Mobile Student ID System.* Case Study. Austin: HID Global. www.hidglobal.com/doclib/files/resource_files/hid-botosoft-waec-cs-en.pdf.

Higson, R., and K. Dale. 2016. "Improving GOV.UK Verify's demographic coverage—an update." GOV.UK Verify blog, August 19. https://identityassurance.blog.gov.uk/2016/08/19/improving-gov-uk-verifys-demographic-coverage-an-update/.

Hopkins, A. and J. Hughes. 2014. "Biometrics in a Humanitarian Context." UNHCR. Presentation at the Connect:ID Conference, Washington, DC, March 17–19. www.connectidexpo.com/creo_files/expo2014-slides/1700_Hopkins_Hughes.pdf.

Hosein, G., and C. Nyst. 2013. *Aiding Surveillance: An Exploration of How Development and Humanitarian Aid Initiatives Are Enabling Surveillance in Developing Countries.* London: Privacy International. www.privacyinternational.org/sites/default/files/Aiding%20Surveillance.pdf.

Hughes, J. 2014. "How Does a Certified Company Establish That It's Really You?" Gov.UK Verify blog, November 21. https://identityassurance.blog.gov.uk/2014/11/21/how-does-a-certified-company-establish-that-its-really-you/.

———. 2015. "Making GOV.UK Verify Available to More People." GOV.UK Verify blog, October 20. https://identityassurance.blog.gov.uk/2015/10/20/making-gov-uk-verify-available-to-more-people/.

Hunter, W. 2017. "Haitian Descendants in the Dominican Republic and Retroactive Citizenship Denial: The Possibilities and Limits of International Advocacy Regarding Different Categories of Statelessness." Presented at the Johannesburg Colloquium on the Future of Legal Identity, Johannesburg, February 15–16.

ICAO (International Civil Aviation Organization). 2015. "Machine Readable Travel Documents." Doc. 9303. Montreal: ICAO. www.icao.int/publications/Documents/9303_p3_cons_en.pdf.

ID.ee. 2016. "Statistics." ID.ee. www.id.ee/?lang=en.

IDEA (International Institute for Democracy and Electoral Assistance). 2015. "Voter Turnout Database" [updated August 2015]. IDEA. www.idea.int/vt/viewdata.cfm.

Indian Express. 2014. "Stop Aadhaar Data Use to Probe Crime: UIDAI to SC." Indian Express, March 19. http://indianexpress.com/article/cities/delhi/stop-aadhaar-data-use-to-probe-crime-uidai-to-sc-2/.

Inter-American Development Bank. 2004. Unlocking Credit: The Quest for Deep and Stable Bank Lending. Washington, DC: Inter-American Development Bank. https://publications.iadb.org/handle/11319/416.

IRIN News. 2014. "An Ambitious Plan to End Statelessness." IRIN News, November 7. www.irinnews.org/analysis/2014/11/07/ambitious-plan-end-statelessness.

ITU (International Telecommunication Union). 2016. "ICT Facts and Figures 2016." ITU. www.itu.int/en/ITU-D/Statistics/Documents/facts/ICTFactsFigures2016.pdf.

Iyengar, R. 2017. "Is the Government Correct in Forcing Students to Get Aadhaar Card for Mid-Day Meals?" Indian Express, March 6. http://indianexpress.com/article/opinion/web-edits/making-aadhaar-mandatory-for-mid-day-meals-is-proof-of-govt-arm-twisting-tactics-4555494/.

Jain, A. K. 2017. "Fingerprints: Giving Child an Identity." Presentation at ID4Africa Conference, Windhoek, Namibia, April 28.

Jain, A. K., K. Cao, and S. S. Arora. 2014. "Recognizing Infants and Toddlers Using Fingerprints: Increasing the Vaccination Coverage." Proceedings of the International Joint Conference on Biometrics (IJCB), 29 Sept–2 Oct.

Jain, A. K., S. S. Arora, L. Best-Rowden, and K. Cao. 2015. "Biometrics for Child Vaccination and Welfare: Persistence of Fingerprint Recognition for Infants and Toddlers." MSU Technical Report, MSU-CSE-15-7, 2015.

J-PAL. 2011. "Fingerprinting to Reduce Risky Borrowing." J-Pal Briefcase. www.povertyactionlab.org/sites/default/files/publications/Fingerprinting%20to%20Reduce%20Risky%20Borrowing%2C%20July%202011.pdf.

Kelly, H. 2012. "83 Million Facebook Accounts Are Fakes and Dupes." CNN,

August 3. www.cnn.com/2012/08/02/tech/social-media/facebook-fake-accounts/index.html.

Kulkarni, D. 2015. "Aadhaar Authority Develops Android App for Easier Registration of Infants." DNA India, September 21. www.dnaindia.com/india/report-aadhaar-authority-develops-android-app-for-easier-registration-of-infants-2126997.

Kumar, L., M. Sadana, and M. Sharma. 2015. "Are the $2 Billion Annual Savings Arising from PAHAL Real?" MicroSave blog, October. http://blog.microsave.net/are-the-2-billion-annual-savings-arising-from-pahal-real/.

Kwambai, K. D., and M. Wandera. 2013. "Effects of Credit Information Sharing on Nonperforming Loans: The Case of Kenya." *European Scientific Journal* 9 (13): 168–93.

La Batu, S. 2017. "Indonesia's House Speaker Allegedly Involved in e-KTP Mega Corruption Scandal." *Jakarta Post*, March 9. www.thejakartapost.com/news/2017/03/09/indonesias-house-speaker-allegedly-involved-in-e-ktp-mega-corruption-scandal.html.

La Cour d'Appel de Lomé. 2015. "Pièces à fournir pour l'obtention du certificat de nationalité togolaise." La Cour d'Appel de Lomé. http://lacourdappeldelome.com/pieces-a-fournir-pour-l-obtention-du-certificat-de-nationalite-togolaise/.

Lamtey, G. 2016. "Tanzania: NEC Data to Be Used to Issue National IDs." AllAfrica.com, March 29. http://allafrica.com/stories/201603290811.html.

Leite, P., T. George, C. Sun, T. Jones, and K. Lindert. 2017. "Social Registries for Social Assistance and Beyond: A Guidance Note and Assessment Tool." Social Protection and Labor Discussion Paper 1704. Washington, DC: World Bank.

Le Parisien. 2011. "Plus de 10% des passeports biometriques seraient des faux." *Le Parisien*, December 19. www.leparisien.fr/faits-divers/plus-de-10-des-passeports-biometriques-seraient-des-faux-19-12-2011-1775325.php.

Lewis, D. 2017. "Congo's Pricey Passport Scheme Sends Millions of Dollars Offshore." Reuters Investigates, April 13. www.reuters.com/investigates/special-report/congo-passports/.

Lindskov Jacobsen, K. 2015. *The Politics of Humanitarian Technology: Good Intentions, Unintended Consequences and Insecurity.* New York: Routledge.

Linus, P. 2016. "Tanzania Promises To Issue National ID Cards in Handwritten Signature Format." 24Tanzania.com, March 5. https://24tanzania.com/tanzania-promises-to-issue-national-id-cards-in-handwritten-signature-format/.

Lustig, N. 2017. *Fiscal Policy, Income Distribution, and Poverty Reduction in Low- and Middle-Income Countries.* CGD Working Paper. Washington, DC: CGD. www.cgdev.org/publication/fiscal-policy-income-redistribution-and-poverty-reduction-low-and-middle-income.

Mahdavi, P. 2016. "Stateless and for Sale in the Gulf." *Foreign Affairs*, June 30. www.foreignaffairs.com/articles/kuwait/2016-06-30/stateless-and-sale-gulf.

Makoye, K. 2015. "Tanzania Rolls Out Birth Registrations by Mobile Phone." Reuters UK, October 13. http://uk.reuters.com/article/uk-tanzania-goals-birth-registration-idUKKCN0S71XC20151013.

Malik, T. 2014. *Technology in the Service of Development: The NADRA Story.* Center for Global Development Essay. Washington, DC: CGD. www.cgdev.org/publication/ft/technology-service-development-nadra-story.

Maltoni, D., D. Maio, A. K. Jain, and S. Prabhakar. 2009. *Handbook of Fingerprint Recognition*. New York: Springer.

Manby, N. 2016. *Citizenship Law in Africa*. New York: Open Society Foundations.

Margai, J. S. 2016. "SLPP Calls on Donors to Stop Supporting Civil Registration Authority." *Concord Times* (Freetown), October 13. http://slconcordtimes.com/slpp-calls-on-donors-to-stop-supporting-civil-registration-authority/.

Mede, N. F. 2016. "Nigeria's Experience with Identity Systems for Civil Service Reform." Presented at the ID4Africa Annual Meeting, Rwanda, May 25. www.id4africa.com/prev/img/Mede_ID4Africa_Rwanda_May2016.pdf.

Ministry of Electronics and Information Technology [Govt. of India]. 2016. "A Technology Framework for Electronic Consent." Draft for Public Review. Delhi: Ministry of Electronics and Information Technology. http://meity.gov.in/sites/upload_files/dit/files/Consent-Tech-Framework.pdf.

———. 2017. "Personal Data of Individuals Held by UIDAI Is Fully Safe and Secure." Ministry of Electronics and Information Technology Press Information Bureau press release, March 5. http://pib.nic.in/newsite/PrintRelease.aspx?relid=158849.

Mishra, P. N. 2014. "Can't Share Aadhar Information with Government Agencies, Supreme Court Tells UIDAI." DNA India, March 25. www.dnaindia.com/india/report-can-t-share-aadhar-information-with-government-agencies-supreme-court-tells-uidai-1971925.

Morlin-Yron, S. 2016. "New Technology Could Help 230 Million 'Ghost' Children." CNN, December 1. www.cnn.com/2016/12/01/africa/birth-registration-system-burkina-faso/.

Mott MacDonald. 2016. "Assessment of Biometric based Payment System: Spot Checks and Beneficiary Feedback, National Cash Transfer Programme–Pakistan." United Kingdom Department for International Development, October.

Mukherjee, A., A. Gelb, and A. Diofasi. 2016. "Aadhaar-Based Cash Transfers: Promising Reform, but More Data Needed." CGD blog, August 29. www.cgdev.org/blog/aadhaar-based-cash-transfers-promising-reform-more-data-needed.

Muralidharan, K., P. Niehaus, and S. Sukhtankar. 2016. "Building State Capacity: Evidence from Biometric Smartcards in India." *American Economic Review* 106 (10): 2895–2929.

National Institute of Public Finance and Policy. 2012. "A Cost-Benefit Analysis of Aadhaar." National Institute of Public Finance and Policy. New Delhi, November 9. http://macrofinance.nipfp.org.in/FILES/uid_cba_paper.pdf

Ngetich, J., and W. Ayaga. 2016. "IEBC Officials on Spot over 2013 Poll." *Standard Digital*, March 23. www.standardmedia.co.ke/article/2000195798/iebc-officials-on-spot-over-2013-poll.

Niasse, M. 2012. *Gender Equality: It's Smart and It's Right*. Oxfam Online Discussion Essay. https://ica.coop/sites/default/files/publication-files/gender-equality-smart-right-niasse-dec2012-689053021.pdf.

Nilekani, N. 2009. *Imagining India: The Idea of a New Nation*. New York: Penguin Press.

New York Times. 2015. "Stateless in the Dominican Republic." *New York Times*, July 11. www.nytimes.com/2015/07/12/opinion/stateless-in-the-dominican-republic. html?_r=1.

Nse, A-U. 2014. "Nigeria: FG Uncovers 60,000 Ghost Workers." AllAfrica.com, October 22. http://allafrica.com/stories/201410220230.html.

The Observer. 2016. "Uganda: Don't Impose Unnecessary Fees on National IDs." AllAfrica.com, January 15. http://allafrica.com/stories/201601150723.html.

O'Donnell, M. 2016. "Why Registration and ID Are Gender Equality Issues." CGD blog, July 11. www.cgdev.org/blog/why-registration-and-id-are-gender-equality-issues.

OECD (Organization for Economic Cooperation and Development). 2013. "OECD Guidelines on the Protection of Privacy and Transborder Flows of Personal Data." OECD. www.oecd.org/sti/ieconomy/oecdguidelinesontheprotectionofpriv acyandtransborderflowsofpersonaldata.htm.

Office of the Auditor General. 2014. "Special Audit on Procurement of Electronic Voting Devices for the 2013 General Election by the Independent Elections and Boundaries Commission." Office of the Auditor General, Kenya, June 6. www. oagkenya.go.ke/index.php/reports/doc_download/148-iebc-special-audit-report-on-procurement-of-evds.

Ohlheiser, A. 2015. "How a Teenager's Viral Campaign to Prove Her Citizenship Is Inspiring a New Texas Bill." *Washington Post*, March 12. www.washingtonpost. com/news/post-nation/wp/2015/03/12/how-a-teenagers-viral-campaign-to-prove-her-citizenship-is-inspiring-a-new-texas-bill/?utm_term=.53c669801969.

Open Society Institute. 2010. *Dominicans of Haitian Descent and the Compromised Right to Nationality*. Presented to the Inter-American Commission on Human Rights on the Occasion of its 140th Session, August 5. www.opensocietyfoundations.org/sites/ default/files/Dominican-Republic-Nationality-Report-ENG-20110805.pdf.

Operation ASHA. 2015. "eCompliance Biometric Tracking System." Operation ASHA. www.opasha.org/our-work/ecompliance-innovation-and-health/ecompli ance-biometric-tracking-system/.

Oppenheim, B. 2015. "Legal Identity and Immunization in Vulnerable Populations: Evidence from Kibera." Presentation, NYU Center on International Cooperation / Metabiota.

Opportunity International. 2011. "Opportunity International Launches 'Banking on Women' Campaign." Press release, March 8. http://opportunity.org/news/press-releases/opportunity-international-launches-banking-on-women-campaign.

———. 2014. *Annual Report*. New York: Opportunity International. http://oppor tunity.org/annual-report/2014.

Palacios, R., J. Das, and C. Sun, eds. 2011. *India's Health Insurance Scheme for the Poor: Evidence from the Early Experience of the Rashtriya Swasthya Bima Yojana*. New Delhi: Centre for Policy Research.

Pasricha, N. 2011. "G2P Payment for Flood Victims in Pakistan." Consultative Group to Assist the Poor blog, March 24. www.cgap.org/blog/g2p-payments-flood-victims-pakistan.

Patil, S., and V. Desai. 2014. "Unique Identification Disaster? SC Holds UID Not Mandatory, No Biometric Data to Be Shared without Consent." LiveLaw.in, April 12. www.nishithdesai.com/fileadmin/user_upload/pdfs/Research%20Articles/Unique_Identification_Disaster_SC_holds_UID_not_mandatory.pdf.

Peachey, K. 2016. "Facebook Blocks Admiral's Car Insurance Discount Plan." BBC, November 2. www.bbc.com/news/business-37847647.

Pedak, M. 2013. "eID: Estonian Experience." Zoetermeer, Netherlands: Nederlandse Vereniging voor Burgerzaken. https://nvvb.nl/media/cms_page_media/758/13%20Mari%20Pedak%20eID%20Estonian%20experience.pdf.

Pew Research Center. 2016. "Smartphone Ownership and Internet Usage Continues to Climb in Emerging Economies." Pew Global, February 22. www.pewglobal.org/2016/02/22/smartphone-ownership-and-internet-usage-continues-to-climb-in-emerging-economies/

Pisa, M., and M. Juden. 2017. *Blockchain and Economic Development: Hype vs. Reality.* CGD Policy Paper 107. Washington, DC: CGD. www.cgdev.org/publication/blockchain-and-economic-development-hype-vs-reality.

Postimees. 1996. "Imre Perli peak ise selgitusi andma." November 15. www.postimees.ee/2491909.

Principles. 2017. Principles on Identification for Sustainable Development: Towards the Digital Age. Facilitated by World Bank Group and Center for Global Development. Washington, DC (http://documents.worldbank.org/curated/en/21358 1486378184357/pdf/112614-REVISED-PUBLIC-web-final-ID4D-Identifica tionPrinciples.pdf).

Radcliffe, D. 2016. *Digital Payments as a Platform for Improving State Capacity.* CGD Background Paper. Washington, DC: CGD. www.cgdev.org/sites/default/files/digital-payments-platform-state-capacity.pdf.

Rader, A. 2016. "Politiques de la reconnaissance et de l'origine contrôlée: la construction du Somaliland à travers ses cartes d'électeurs." *Politique africaine* 4 (144): 51–71.

RENIEC (Registro Nacional de Identificación y Estado Civil). 2016. "Usos del DNIe." RENIEC. http://portales.reniec.gob.pe/web/dni/uso.

Republic of Estonia Information System Authority. 2017. "Possible Security Vulnerability Detected in the Estonian ID-card Chip." September 5. www.ria.ee/en/possible-security-vulnerability-detected-in-the-estonian-id-card-chip.html.

Reuben, W., and F. Carbonari. 2017. *Identification as a National Priority: The Unique Case of Peru's ID System.* CGD Working Paper 454. Washington, DC: CGD. www.cgdev.org/publication/identification-national-priority-unique-case-peru.

Reyna, C. 2014. "Civil Registration and Identification System in Peru: Key Features." Presented at the World Bank South-South Social Protection and Learning Forum, Rio de Janeiro, March 17. http://studylib.net/doc/10977370/building-robust-identification-systems.

Rizzatti, L. 2016. "Digital Data Storage Is Undergoing Mind-Boggling Growth." EE Times blog, September 14. www.eetimes.com/author.asp?section_id=36&doc_id=1330462.

Roosna, S., ed. 2016. *e-Estonia: e-Governance in Practice.* e-Governance Academy Report. Tallinn: e Governance Academy. http://ega.ee/wp-content/uploads/2016/06/e-Estonia-e-Governance-in-Practice.pdf.

Rössler, T. 2007. "The Austrian Citizen Card." Presented at the 4th Electronic Signature Congress (JSe), Barcelona, October 29–30. www.a-sit.at/pdfs/TRoessler_The%20Austrian%20Citizen%20Card.pdf.

Rosenberg, E. 2017. "Family DNA Searches Seen as Crime-Solving Tool, and Intrusion on Rights." *New York Times*, January 27. www.nytimes.com/2017/01/27/nyregion/familial-dna-searching-karina-vetrano.html?_r=0.

RSBY (Rashtriya Swasthya Bima Yojna). 2016. "RSBY Home Page." www.rsby.gov.in/index.aspx.

Rutkin, A. 2016. "We Now Have the Tech to Fingerprint Babies – But Should We?" *New Scientist*, June 15. www.newscientist.com/article/mg23030782-200-we-now-have-the-tech-to-fingerprint-babies-but-should-we/.

Sarkar, S. 2011. *The Unique Identity (UID) Project and the New 'Bureaucratic Moment' in India.* Queen Elizabeth House Working Paper 194, October. Oxford: Queen Elizabeth House. www.qeh.ox.ac.uk/publications/unique-identity-uid-project-and-new-bureaucratic-moment-india.

Scroll.in. 2015. "An Official Andhra Survey Shows Why Modi Government Should Stop Pushing Aadhaar So Doggedly." Scroll.in, October 15. https://scroll.in/article/760530/an-official-andhra-survey-shows-why-modi-government-should-stop-pushing-aadhaar-so-doggedly.

Secure Identity Alliance. 2014. *eServices in Estonia: A Success Story.* Secure Identity Alliance Visit Report. www.secureidentityalliance.org/index.php/resources/preview?path=14-06-02-SIA-Estonia%2BVisit%2BReport.pdf.

Seringhaus, M. R. 2009. *"Forensic DNA Profiles: Database Expansion, Familial Search, and a Radical Solution.* Association for the Advancement of Artificial Intelligence. www.aaai.org/ocs/index.php/SSS/SSS10/paper/viewFile/1187/1503.

Sharma, S. K. 2016. "India LPG Experience PAHAL." Presentation at the 2016 ID4Africa conference, Kigali, May 25.

Singh, M. 2017. "No One Can Build Aadhaar's Users' Profile: UIDAI Chief." *Times of India*, May 7 (https://timesofindia.com/india/no-one-can-build-aadhaar-users-profile-uidai-chief/articleshow/58556043.cms).

Snidal, S. J., G. Barnard, E. Atuhairwe, and Y. Ben Amor. 2015. "Use of eCompliance, an Innovative Biometric System for Monitoring of Tuberculosis Treatment in Rural Uganda." *American Journal of Tropical Medicine and Hygiene* 92 (6): 1271–79.

Soares, S., R. G. Osorio, F. V. Soares, M. Medeiros, and E. Zepeda. 2009. "Conditional Cash Transfers in Brazil, Chile, and Mexico: Impacts upon Inequality." *Estudios Economicos*, Special Issue: 207–24.

Solli, J., L. Galindo, A. Rizzi, E. Rhyne, and N. van de Walle. 2015. "What Happens to Microfinance Clients Who Default?" Washington, DC: Smart Campaign. www.smartcampaign.org/tools-a-resources/1030.

Srivas, A. 2016. "Twenty Crore Bank Accounts Opened: Where Does Jan Dhan Yojana Go from Here? An Explainer." *The Wire*, May 3. https://thewire.in/33272/twenty-crore-bank-accounts-opened-where-does-jan-dhan-yojana-go-from-here-an-explainer/.

Statistics South Africa. 2015. *Recorded Live Births 2014.* Statistical Release P0305. Pretoria: Statistics South Africa. www.statssa.gov.za/publications/P0305/P0305 2014.pdf.

Storisteanu, D. M. L., T. L. Norman, A. Grigore, and A. B. Labrique. 2016. "Can Biometrics Beat the Developing World's Challenges?" *Biometric Technology Today* 11: 5–9.

Sumner, C. 2015. *Indonesia's Missing Millions: Erasing Discrimination in Birth Certification in Indonesia.* CGD Policy Paper 064. Washington, DC: CGD. www.cgdev.org/publication/indonesias-missing-millions-erasing-discrimination-birth-certification-indonesia.

Szreter, S. 2006. "The Right of Registration: Development, Identity Registration, and Social Security—A Historical Perspective." *World Development* 35 (1): 67–86.

Tonurist, P, V. Lember, and R. Kattel. 2016. *Joint Data Platforms as X Factor for Efficiency Gains in the Public Sector.* Working Papers in Technology Governance and Economic Dynamics 70. http://technologygovernance.eu/files/main//2016082501020202.pdf.

UIDAI (Unique Identification Authority of India). 2012a. *The Role of Biometric Technology in Aadhaar Enrollment.* New Delhi: UIDAI. https://uidai.gov.in/images/FrontPageUpdates/role_of_biometric_technology_in_aadhaar_jan21_2012.pdf.

———. 2012b. *The Role of Biometric Technology in Aadhaar Authentication: Authentication Accuracy Report.* New Delhi: UIDAI. https://uidai.gov.in/images/role_of_biometric_technology_in_aadhaar_authentication_020412.pdf

———. 2012c. *The Role of Biometric Technology in Aadhaar Authentication: IRIS Authentication Accuracy, POC Report.* New Delhi: UIDAI. https://uidai.gov.in/images/authentication/iris_poc_report_14092012.pdf.

UNDP (United Nations Development Programme). 2015a. "Innovative Payment Technology for Ebola Response Workers Launched." UNDP Sierra Leone press release, January 28. www.sl.undp.org/content/sierraleone/en/home/presscenter/press releases/2015/01/28/building-transparent-payment-systems-through-deployment-of-innovative-payments-technology-for-ebola-response-workers-.html.

———. 2015b. *Payments Programme for Ebola Response Workers: Cash at the Front Lines of a Health Crisis.* Issue brief. www.undp.org/content/dam/undp/library/hivaids/English/Payments-Programme-Ebola-Response-Workers.pdf.

UNHCR (United Nations High Commissioner for Refugees). 2014a. *Background Note on Gender Equality, Nationality Laws and Statelessness 2014.* New York: UNHCR. www.unhcr.org/4f5886306.html.

————. 2014b. *Ending Statelessness within 10 Years.* New York: UNHCR. www. unhcr.org/en-us/546217229.pdf.

————. 2015a. "Citizenship and Statelessness in Myanmar." UNHCR Briefing for the World Bank, September 3.

————. 2015b. "Biometric Identity Management System." UNHCR Division of Programme Support and Management Key Initiatives Series. www.unhcr. org/550c304c9.pdf.

————. 2016. "Persons of Concern." UNHCR Population Statistics. New York: UNHCR. http://popstats.unhcr.org/en/persons_of_concern.

UNICEF. 2002. *Birth Registration: Right from the Start.* UNICEF Innocenti Research Centre. www.unicef-irc.org/publications/pdf/digest9e.pdf.

————. 2013. *Every Child's Birth Right: Inequities and Trends in Birth Registration.* New York: UNICEF.

————. 2014. "Birth Registration Dataset" (updated November 2014). *UNICEF Global Databases.* New York: UNICEF. http://data.unicef.org/child-protection/birth-registration.html.

United Nations (UN). 2015. "Sustainable Development Goals. Goal 16: Promote just, peaceful, and inclusive societies." www.un.org/sustainabledevelopment/peace-justice/.

————. 2016. *United Nations E-Government Survey 2016: E-Government in Support of Sustainable Development.* New York: UN.

UNSD (United Nations Statistics Division). 2014. "Coverage of Civil Registration System Dataset" [updated December 2014]. New York: UNSD. http://unstats. un.org/unsd/demographic/CRVS/CR_coverage.htm.

UNSTATS. 1998. *Handbook on Civil Registration and Vital Statistics Systems: Developing Information, Education, and Communication.* New York: UN.

————. 2002. *Handbook on Training in Civil Registration and Vital Statistics Systems.* New York: UN.

Usman, A., C. McDaniel, and S. Schropp. 2016. "Digital Remittances: Enhancing Financial Health for Families around the World." PayPal, Inc. www.pay palobjects.com/digitalassets/c/website/marketing/global/shared/global/media-resources/documents/digital-remittances.pdf.

Vandenabeele, C., and C. V. Lao, eds. 2007. *Legal Identity for Inclusive Development.* Manila: Asian Development Bank. www.adb.org/sites/default/files/publication /29046/legal-identity.pdf.

Vassil, K. 2015. *Estonian e-Government Ecosystem: Foundation, Applications, Outcomes.* World Development Report 2016 Background Paper. Washington, DC: World Bank. http://pubdocs.worldbank.org/en/165711456838073531/WDR16-BP-Estonian-eGov-ecosystem-Vassil.pdf.

Veldre, A. 2016. "Introduction to X-Road." Republic of Estonia Information System Authority. www.ria.ee/en/introduction-to-xroad-part1.html.

VISA. 2010. "Pakistan Flood Victims Receive Government Relief Aid on 'Watan' Visa Cards." Press release, September 9. http://pressreleases.visa.com/phoenix. zhtml?c=215693&p=irol-newsarticlePR&ID=1468949.

Warman, M. 2013. "Say Goodbye to the PIN: Voice Recognition Takes Over at Barclays Wealth." *Telegraph*, May 8. www.telegraph.co.uk/technology/news/100 44493/Say-goodbye-to-the-pin-voice-recognition-takes-over-at-Barclays-Wealth. html.

Wehr, J. 2004. "Malaysia's National 'MyKad' ID Card Succeeding Through Service to Citizens." SecureIDNews. www.secureidnews.com/news-item/malaysias-national-mykad-id-card-succeeding-through-service-to-citizens/.

Whitley, E. 2018 (forthcoming). *GOV.UK Verify: Development, Operation, Governance and Prospects.* CGD Policy Paper. Washington DC: CGD.

Whitley, E., and J. Fishenden. 2015. "GOV.UK Verify: Identity Assurance Principles." GOV.UK Verify blog, September 11. https://identityassurance.blog. gov.uk/2015/09/11/gov-uk-verify-identity-assurance-principles/.

Wilhelm, S. "Breeding Change: Puerto Rico's New Birth Certificate Policy," September 26, 2012 (www.documentsecurityalliance.org/news/09-26-2012_1.html).

The Wire. 2015. "Most Aadhaar Cards Issued to Those Who Already Have IDs." *The Wire*, March 6. http://thewire.in/3108/most-aadhar-cards-issued-to-those-who-already-have-ids/.

World Bank. 2009. *Conditional Cash Transfers: Reducing Present and Future Poverty.* Washington, DC: World Bank. http://siteresources.worldbank.org/INTCCT/Resources/5757608-1234228266004/PRR-CCT_web_noembargo.pdf.

———. 2011. "Wage Bill and Pay Compression." Dataset. Washington, DC: World Bank. http://data.worldbank.org/data-catalog/wage-bill-pay-compression.

———. 2012. "Indonesia: Women Headed Household Empowerment Program (PEKKA)." Washington, DC: World Bank. www.worldbank.org/en/results/2012/04/19/indonesia-women-headed-household-empowerment-program-pekka.

———. 2015. *The State of Social Safety Nets 2015.* Washington, DC: World Bank. http://documents.worldbank.org/curated/en/415491467994645020/pdf/97882-PUB-REVISED-Box393232B-PUBLIC-DOCDATE-6-29-2015-DOI-10-1596978-1-4648-0543-1-EPI-1464805431.pdf.

———. 2016a. *Identification for Development (ID4D): Identification Systems Analysis, Country Assessment—Kenya.* Washington, DC: World Bank. http://documents. worldbank.org/curated/en/575001469771718036/pdf/107277-WP-P156810-PUBLIC.pdf.

———. 2016b. *Identification for Development – Strategic Framework.* Washington, DC: World Bank. http://pubdocs.worldbank.org/en/179901454620206363/Jan-2016-ID4D-Strategic-Roadmap.pdf.

———. 2017a. "Identification for Development Global Dataset." Updated June 1. Washington, DC: World Bank. http://data.worldbank.org/data-catalog/id4d-dataset.

———. 2017b. *The State of Identification Systems in Africa: A Synthesis of Country Assessments.* Washington, DC: World Bank. http://documents.worldbank.org/curated/en/156111493234231522/pdf/114628-WP-68p-TheStateofIdentificationSystemsinAfricaASynthesisofIDDAssessments-PUBLIC.pdf

————. 2017c. *The State of Identification in Africa: Country Briefs*. Washington, DC: World Bank. http://pubdocs.worldbank.org/en/940071497322166382/ID4D-coun try-profiles-report-final.pdf.

————. 2018a forthcoming. "Snapshot of Technical Standards for Digital ID Systems." Washington, DC: World Bank.

————. 2018b forthcoming. "Understanding the Cost Drivers of ID Systems." Washington, DC: World Bank.

World Bank and Vietnam Academy of Social Sciences. 2016. *Vietnam's Household Registration System*. Hanoi: Hong Duc Publishing House.

World Bank/WHO (World Health Organization). 2014. *Global Civil Registration and Vital Statistics Scaling up Investment Plan 2015–2024*. Washington, DC: World Bank.

World Health Organization (WHO) 2016. "Immunization Coverage." Factsheet. Washington, DC: WHO. www.who.int/mediacentre/factsheets/fs378/en/.

Yadav, A. 2016. "Chhattisgarh's Way of Dealing with Aadhaar: When Fingerprints Fail, Take Photos." Scroll.in, December 21. https://scroll.in/article/822764/ chhattisgarhs-way-of-dealing-with-aadhaar-when-fingerprints-fail-take-photos.

Yeboah, O. A. 2016. "E-Zwich Helps Flush Out 35,000 Ghost Names From Payroll . . . Saves Gov't GH146m." *Business & Financial Times*, April 21. //thebfton line.com/business/ict/18576/e-zwich-helps-flush-out-35000-ghost-names-from-payroll-saves-govt-gh146m.html.

Zelazny, F. 2012. *The Evolution of India's UID Program: Lessons Learned and Implications for Other Developing Countries*. CGD Policy Paper 008. Washington, DC: CGD.

Zetter, K. 2012. "Reverse-Engineered Irises Look So Real, They Fool Eyes-Scanners." *Wired*, July 25. www.wired.com/2012/07/reverse-engineering-iris-scans/.

Zorz, Z. 2017. "Security Flaw Affects 750,000 Estonian ID Cards." HelpNetSecurity, September 6. www.helpnetsecurity.com/2017/09/06/estonian-id-cards-security-flaw/.

Index

Aadhaar Program. *See* India, Aadhaar Program

Abraham, R., 171

Accenture, 101

Accountability: in elections, 88; governance and, 210; for performance, 102; privacy and, 139–40, 189, 211; of public institutions, 28, 60

Affidavits as identification, 12

Afghanistan: gender, ID registration and, 128; voter registration in, 55

Africa: birth registration in, 44; death registration in, 52–53; ID4Africa movement in, 29, 200–01; identification system in, 25, 29, 51–52; statelessness in, 131. *See also specific countries*

African Charter on the Rights and Welfare of the Child (1990), 133

African Union, 131, 141

Agency, 68. *See also* Financial control, gender and

Airbnb, 194

Alcohol consumption, identification for, 25

Angola, privacy in, 136–37

Arendt, Hannah, 38

Argentina, tax collection in, 87

Asia: birth registration in, 49–50; household registration systems in, 11; identification systems in, 26. *See also specific countries*

Asian Development Bank, 39–40

Atick, J. J., 51, 142

Austria: privacy protections in, 140; transactional identification in, 211–12

Authentication of identification, 21, 98–99

Autonomous agencies for identification systems: advantages of, 118, 210; cost comparisons for, 143; institutional framework for, 157–59, 162; necessity for, 110, 113–14; trust of, 33, 92

Bangladesh: gender, ID ownership and, 53; national identification rates in, 53; voter registration in, 123

Banking industry: access to, 7, 63–64; biometric identification systems and, 64, 69; credit access and, 65–66; gender and, 68; identity management of, 15, 18, 63; remittance flows and cross-country payments, 67. *See also* Know-Your-Consumer (KYC) regulations

Barriers to identification systems: birth registration access, 46–49, 127–29, 203; cost, 20, 48, 57, 116, 127, 131, 158; technology, 128–29, 132, 150, 187, 204

in, 2, 197; purpose of, 17–18, 171–72; reverse engineering of, 33, 92–93, 122–24; in United Kingdom, 154
Future of identification, 34, 197–215; bridging identification gaps, 58; design, 206–10; development, investment for, 198–99; development partners and, 199–201, 212–13; governance, 210–12; inclusion, 201–05; research needs, 213–15; shared principles for, 201–13

Garenne, M., 53
Gelb, A., 29, 41–42, 44, 59, 129
Gender: birth registration and, 46, 127–28; child marriage, 74–75; equality and, 68–69; exclusion risk and, 125, 127–28, 131–32, 203; financial control and, 68–69, 79, 128, 209–10, 214; identification gap and, 50, 53, 58, 62; nationality laws, discrimination and, 130; property rights and, 63; registration and, 101, 115, 128, 132, 204
Germany: biometric use in, 101; ID assurance in, 195
Ghana: biometrics use in, 150; public payroll management in, 85–86, 146; voter registration in, 55–56
Ghost consumers, 77
Ghost workers, 7, 85–86, 146, 150–51
Giné, X., 65
Global health emergencies, 73–74, 85–86
Global identification systems, 24
Goldberg, J., 65
Governance of identification systems, 116, 118, 157–58, 210–12
GOV.UK Verify program, 34, 179–89; data sharing in, 212; features summary of, 155; ID assurance and, 15, 183–85; identity providers, government authorization of, 15; lessons from, 188–89; privacy protections in, 140; segmented identity provisions, 180–83, 181; standards-based implementation of, 186
Grants, 77–80
Greece, voter registration in, 55
Greenleaf, G., 136–37
Green taxes, 81
Grievance processes, 103, 134, 210, 213
Guerre, Martin, 6

Guidelines on the Protection of Privacy and Transborder Flows of Personal Data (OECD), 136

Haitian people in Dominican Republic, 126, 129–30
Healthcare: biometrics use in identification for, 40; diseases, management of, 48, 70–74, 85–86, 209; identification requirements for, 160–61; tracking patients for, 62; vaccinations, 48, 70–71, 74, 109
Hidden biometrics, 99–100
High-income countries (HICs): birth registration in, 54–55; digital identification systems in, 21–22; identification systems, increase in, 16–17; privacy laws and, 136–37; voter registration in, 54–56
Household registration systems, 50, 121, 132, 204
Human trafficking, 74

ICAO (International Civil Aviation Organization), 24, 208
ID4Africa movement, 29, 200–01
Identification: challenges and risks in, 23–29; changes in, 9–23; development and, 5–8; history of, 9; management systems overview, 16–20; political limits of, 150–51; principles for development of, 30–31, 201–13; transformative technologies for, 20–23. See also Future of identification; specific types
Identification for Development (ID4D) Program, 16–17, 44, 93, 200
Identification gap, 32, 35–58; Aadhaar program and, 105; birth registration, 43–51; bridging, 8, 58; citizenship and, 42–43; legal identity, interpretation of, 3–4, 38–43; national identity programs, 51–54; official identification forms, 54–58; poverty and, 6, 35–36; regional differences in, 35–36; voter registration, 54–58. See also Statelessness
Identification systems, 32–33, 91–124; Aadhaar program, 1–2, 103–05; attitudes on, 100–01; benefits of, 146–47; biometrics overview, 93–103; challenges and risks in, 23–29; children and,

About the Authors

Alan Gelb is a senior fellow and director of studies at the Center for Global Development, where he specializes in the development applications of biometric ID technology, aid and development outcomes, and the special development challenges of Africa and resource-rich countries. He was previously director of development policy at the World Bank and chief economist for the World Bank's Africa Region.

Anna Diofasi Metz is a consultant with the World Bank's Identification for Development (ID4D) initiative and a former policy analyst at the Center for Global Development. Her recent research includes the use of biometric ID technology in elections and financing for global public goods.

Center for Global Development

The Center for Global Development works to reduce global poverty and inequality through rigorous research and active engagement with the policy community to make the world a more prosperous, just, and safe place for us all.

The policies and practices of the rich and the powerful—in rich nations, as well as in the emerging powers, international institutions, and global corporations—have significant impacts on the world's poor people. We aim to improve these policies and practices through research and policy engagement to expand opportunities, reduce inequalities, and improve lives everywhere. By pairing research with action, CGD goes beyond contributing to knowledge about development. We conceive of and encourage discussion about practical policy innovations in areas such as trade, aid, health, education, climate change, labor mobility, private investment, access to finance, and global governance to foster shared prosperity in an increasingly interdependent world.

As a nimble, independent, nonpartisan, and nonprofit think tank, we leverage modest resources to combine world-class scholarly research with policy analysis and innovative outreach and communications to turn ideas into action.